Malta Spitfire Pilot

The future? What?
16/5/42.

Self portrait.

Malta Spitfire Pilot

A Personal Account of Ten Weeks of War,
April–June 1942

Denis Barnham

Foreword by Diana Barnham
Introduction by James Holland

FRONTLINE BOOKS

Malta Spitfire Pilot: A Personal Account of Ten Weeks of War, April–June 1942

This edition published in 2011 by Frontline Books,
an imprint of Pen & Sword Books Limited,
47 Church Street, Barnsley, S. Yorkshire, S70 2AS
www.frontline-books.com

Copyright © Denis Barnham, 1956
Introduction copyright © James Holland, 2011
Foreword copyright © Diana Barnham, 2011
The edition © Pen & Sword Books Limited, 2011

The right of Denis Barnham to be identified as Author of this
Work has been asserted by him in accordance with the Copyright,
Designs and Patents Act 1988.

ISBN 978-1-84832-560-9

PUBLISHING HISTORY
This memoir was first published in 1956 by William Kimber & Co. Ltd.
(London) under the title *One Man's Window*. This edition includes a new
introduction by James Holland, a new foreword by Diana Barnham, the
author's wife, and a new plate section with previously unpublished
photographs provided graciously by the family.

A CIP data record for this title is available from the British Library

For more information on our books, please visit
www.frontline-books.com, email info@frontline-books.com
or write to us at the above address.

Printed in Great Britain by CPI Antony Rowe

CONTENTS

ILLUSTRATIONS

FOREWORD

Malta Spitfire Pilot is about the air war in Malta and my husband Denis's part in it. More than sixty years have elapsed since he wrote about his ten weeks on the island during the critical months of April, May and June in 1942. When this book was first published in 1956, every adult reader had strong memories of the war, and could relate to the events. Precious few of today's readers share this direct experience. Yet, and to my astonishment, interest in the war years is still very much alive and the period has not yet been consigned to ancient history.

My own memories of 1942 are still vivid; and of all the events of that extraordinary year, none was more important and agonising to me than those weeks when the Battle for Malta was raging. All of us in England was aware of the significance of what was happening there, though I must confess that I was much more worried about my husband than the implications of Malta succumbing. If the island had fallen, no doubt we would still have won the war, but it would have taken longer, and the loss of life would have been higher. After the war, Denis often thanked God that the Germans and the Italians hadn't realised how close they were to victory. There were days when they could have landed on Malta virtually unopposed. At those times, hardly any of our airplanes were still flying and stocks of food, ammunition and water were virtually exhausted. It was a close-run thing.

Ancient history or not, this is a personal record of a crucial period. Much of the text has been taken straight from the diary that Denis kept during the battle, written within hours of the events he describes; and Denis made the deliberate decision, when he set out to write this book, not to 'water down' his emotions. In consequence, the text is embarrassingly personal at times. He was a meticulous artist and he wrote as he painted: bold ideas and sweeping thoughts followed by carefully crafted 'infill' to bind it all together. I spent many evenings in the period 1949–51 acting as an audience of one as Denis developed the text out loud. He wrote in longhand and my job was to correct his terrible spelling and to type draft after draft from his handwritten manuscripts. The book was both a labour of love and a personal catharsis.

Denis had three great loves in his life: aviation, painting and (a bad third) me. The first two passions started early in life. His mother told me that as a child he was known as Buzz Buzz for his habit of pretending to be an airplane. By the age of 10, (at Holyrood School in Bognor), he was filling scrapbooks with photos and beautifully drawn sketches of airplanes. At his next school (Repton) he walked off with all the art prizes, and spent his spare time making model aircraft. It surprised no one when he pestered his parents, who ran a prosperous market gardening business at Hampton in Middlesex, into giving him a studio at home where he could paint pictures … and flying lessons. He learnt to fly at the age of 16 at Hanworth near Feltham, in a C30 Autogiro as he persuaded his mother that this was safer than a fixed-wing aircraft! He received his official licence to fly 'all types of land rota-planes' in January 1937, a few days after his seventeenth birthday. Five months later he gained admission to the prestigious Royal Academy School of Painting in London, and seemed set for a career as an artist. Then the war intervened, and in September 1939 he left the RA Schools to join the RAF Volunteer Reserve.

1940 saw Denis in Rhodesia, first at the Elementary Flying Training School at Belvedere flying Tiger Moths; then on to Cranbourne to fly Harvards. Then back to England. He left Rhodesia at the end of December, and celebrated his twenty-first birthday (on 3 January 1941) at Cape Town in South Africa, on top of Table Mountain. His UK destination was 57 OTU at RAF Hawarden near Chester, where he learnt to fly Spitfires. From there in April, Denis was posted to Lincolnshire, to 65 Squadron at RAF Kirton-in-Lindsey. Kirton at that time was a joint Army–RAF camp, and a cosmopolitan place. Troops and pilots were there from all over the world, including a significant number of Australians and Americans who had come to join squadrons of their countrymen that were being formed at the camp.

It was at Kirton that Denis and I met on June 28 1941 at a dance at the officers' mess. I was accompanying my father, a professional soldier since before the Great War, who was based at Kirton where he commanded 39 Anti-Aircraft Brigade. At the time, I had just come out of the ATS (the Auxiliary Territorial Service, the forerunner of today's Women's Royal Army Corps) and was working nearby for the Rural Food Control Office in Brigg. For his part, Denis was flying Spitfires most days over the English Channel and northern France.

We had a whirlwind romance. Denis proposed to me the day after we met. I told him not to be silly. He persisted. I relented, and we were married six months later in January 1942 by the Bishop of Lincoln at St. Andrew's Redbourne, a charming little church, alas now de-sanctified. We saw a lot of each other during our engagement, even though Denis had been posted to 609 Squadron at Biggin Hill a few days after we met. He was now flying what are described in his log-book as 'offensive sweeps' but frequently, he would borrow a Spitfire and come up to Kirton to see me.

Denis stayed with 609 Squadron until the end of 1941, when he was posted to 154 Squadron at Fowlmere near Duxford and where, after we were married, we were billeted in the local vicarage. His involvement with 154 lasted for only three months as in March, Denis's old squadron leader at 609, John Bisdee, was transferred to 601 Squadron, and he pulled strings for Denis to join him as one of his flight commanders. And so on about March 23 we moved back to Lincolnshire, to Digby where 601 was based; but not for long as within a month, the squadron was in Malta.

Denis was a good choice as a flight commander. He was a fine pilot and a 'team man' with a very paternal attitude towards the men for whom he was responsible in the air; preferring to bring them back safely from contact with the enemy, rather than abandon anyone in order to add to his personal score of air victories. This score grew quickly as the Battle for Malta intensified. Our losses were awful, but so were those of the enemy, of whom Denis shot down a fair number. When not flying, Denis found solace in painting the rugged beauty of the island. At the same time he was impressed by the dignity of the Maltese people. If possible, he vowed to return after the war.

As I mentioned earlier, Denis's great passions in life were flying and painting – not writing. He didn't keep a diary before 1942, and he didn't keep one afterwards. It was only when he received orders to prepare for an overseas posting in April (he thought he was going to the Middle East) that he bought himself a substantial 'page a day' diary, which he kept assiduously for the next seven months until October 1942. The words that he wrote form the basis of this book.

The Denis I fell in love with was full of enthusiasm, charm and joie de vivre. He was also extremely good looking and pin-up photos of him in his pilot's uniform appeared in various wartime magazines. But I didn't enjoy this reflected glory for long as our early married life, prior to his departure to Malta, lasted a mere two months. The husband who returned to me later in the year was a shadow of his former self. He was thin, ill and distraught; physically intact but wounded in spirit. It took a long time for him to fully recover.

Denis's 'post Malta' career was tame in comparison to the previous drama. On his return to England, he spent 18 months with Training Command as a flying instructor, before being posted to the Air Ministry's Public Relations Branch in March 1944 as an official war artist. Thereafter he alternated between operational flying and painting pictures (some of which can be seen today at the RAF museum at Hendon and at the Imperial War Museum). According to his log book, he last flew a Spitfire in December 1944. At the end of the month he was hospitalised with a duodenal ulcer, and this caused him to be invalided out of the service in the following April.

After he left the RAF, Denis never flew again, but he kept in close touch with many of the pilots he served with. He also numbered amongst his friends such personalities as Air Chief Marshal Sir Arthur Tedder, Chief of the Air Staff in the post-war RAF, and Sir Barnes Wallis, designer of the Wellington and the Bouncing Bomb. We knew them and their families well.

Denis never boasted about his war record, but he took pride in his achievements and his record of six confirmed air victories and one 'probable'. I remember him telling me that this score would have been higher if he had been a better shot. (He blamed the lack of training). At home we did not talk about the war much; but nonetheless, a thing that continually rankled was that the DFC for which he had been recommended on Malta never materialised.

Like so many other ex-servicemen, Denis found it hard to settle down to civilian life. He tried to make a living as an artist, but preferred painting his favourite subjects rather than the commissions that came his way. This may have been therapeutic but it didn't pay the bills; and the need to support his young family led him to take up a teaching post at the Epsom School of Art in 1949. At about the same time he began to write this book, and shortly afterwards he was offered the headship of the Art Department at Epsom College.

The artistic environment at Epsom College in the 1950s was not glamorous. To paraphrase a charming letter from an old boy (Barry Davies) that appeared in the school magazine in 2009:'Art was a minor subject like fencing and carpentry. It did not conform easily to gaining academic or sporting achievements. But Denis Barnham was a remarkable person. A modest and intensely sympathetic man. Inevitably he and his subject were heavily overshadowed by the high profile masters of the teaching staff: the housemasters, heads of department, the rugby and cricket coaches and the extroverts. In contrast Denis, perhaps more in the spirit of Epsom today, had a wider view of what education was about, and applauded any talent with enthusiasm. He was concerned with things like the meaning of life, self-expression and human interaction. He was a family man and not a regular in the staff common room. In retrospect, and maybe as a result of his war experience, he seems to have been a more rounded and worldly wise character than some of his contemporaries.'

Another old boy (David Anderson) writes about Denis as being 'an inspirational and fascinating figure … humanity writ large in an otherwise rather arid landscape.' David goes on to recall a memorable throwaway line from Denis, when he was lecturing about mediaeval architecture. He was talking about the magnificent cathedral at Reims in France, and casually told the class about a time in 1941 when he was flying with his squadron on a sweep over the town, and got into trouble for breaking away from the formation to fly down and get a close look at the cathedral's flying buttresses. The class was most impressed.

And so Denis settled down to life at Epsom, teaching, painting pictures and tending his garden. He was a good husband, but not a particularly easy man to live with. It may have been delayed stress, or simply his artistic temperament, but he tended to be on a tremendous high or deep in the Slough of Despond. Together with my two boys, Oliver and Michael, we learned how to respond to Denis's moods and appreciated that a) we needed to treat him gently at all times, and that b) Art Came First. We were lectured at mealtimes on art appreciation; and on holidays, when father was not painting, we visited galleries, stately homes and ancient monuments all over Europe. (Oliver and Mike referred to these jaunts as the ABC tours - as in Another Bloody Cathedral). I remonstrated that he should 'do more' with the children. This didn't happen often but, when it did, Denis was stimulating company, and life was fun.

Though we lived in England, Malta provided a second, spiritual, home. Throughout his life, Denis retained a special place in his heart for the island. He took me back soon after the war to visit old haunts and to explore the places he had never seen before. Over the years, we returned regularly, and accumulated many Maltese friends.

Sadly in the mid 1960s Denis underwent a slow change of personality. He became distant and volatile and started to drink too much. At the same time, the pictures he painted changed from representational to abstract, and took on a 'caged' look. We could not understand what was happening until his doctor diagnosed a pituitary tumour on the brain. This was successfully removed in 1971, and Denis returned to his old self; but the operation sapped his vitality and he had to retire from Epsom College. Following this upheaval, we moved to the village of Gussage-all-Saints in Dorset, where Denis painted prolifically until his death in 1981.

I have been on my own now for about thirty years, and Denis is constantly on my mind – as is Malta. My last visit was in 2009, two months before my 90th birthday, when I returned to deliver Denis's old wartime flying clothing to the Malta Heritage Trust for one of the museums on the island.

I am proud of my man. In his short life of sixty-one years he fought for his country, wrote this book, had a successful career as a painter and teacher, was a good husband and fathered two very satisfactory children. I miss him.

Diana Barnham
Lymington, Hampshire

INTRODUCTION

When Denis Barnham touched down on Malta on 20 April 1942, he was entering the mad, surreal world of an island under intense siege. Just sixty miles from Sicily, Malta lay at the heart of the Mediterranean. A strategically important staging post with deep natural harbours, it also offered a wonderful base from which to attack Axis shipping heading to North Africa, where vicious fighting raged. So much of the war was about logistics and supplies, and as both Allies and Axis forces were keenly aware, the side that could bring most tanks, guns, aircraft and bullets to bear would inevitably win the day. Thus, the Allies were determined that Malta should not fall, while the Axis were equally set on pounding this thorn in their side to such an extent that it would sink back into the sea.

Denis was the pilot of one of forty-six Spitfires that were being flown in that day, the first large number of the RAF's premier fighter to reach Malta. The islanders and the tiny garrison of soldiers, airmen and submariners had been valiantly holding out for almost two years, first against the Italians and then the combined Axis forces. Since the German arrival in January 1941, the intensity of the attacks had risen noticeably, yet that had been nothing compared to the horrendous pummelling the Luftwaffe had been giving them for the past seven weeks. Already the tonnage of bombs dropped had exceeded that suffered by London during the Blitz, and Malta was a tiny place – no larger than the Isle of Wight. The island had become the most bombed place on Earth.

Now, far from stopping Axis supplies to North Africa, it was the Axis that was stopping supplies to Malta. Convoys were sent, from Britain and from Alexandria, but most were harried almost all the way by enemy U-boats, torpedo boats, and by air. Those few that did make it into harbour where often then blitzed the moment unloading began. A convoy in February had completely failed. Another set off in March, and two ships managed to reach Grand Harbour. A third, having been hit in the engine room, got tantalisingly close to the island's southern shore, before being hit again and then sinking. Of the two survivors only a fraction of their precious cargoes had been unloaded before they were attacked again. One sank, the other had to be scuttled; the plumes of dark smoke billowing above the capital, Valletta, could be seen across the entire island.

Thus by the time Denis arrived four weeks later, the island, for so long struggling to survive with very little, was now beginning to starve. All normal levels of existence had gone. There was almost no food, no fuel, no wood, and rubble everywhere. During the Battle of Britain, pilots had been given plenty to eat and drink, and there had been pubs and well-stocked messes to go to when the day's fighting was over. On Malta there was nothing – except, in the case of the fighter pilots, the small matter of fighting daily in the most intense and protracted air battle since the summer of 1940. As one pilot noted, fighting on Malta made the Battle of Britain look like child's play.

In April 1942, Denis was a dark-haired strikingly good-looking twenty-two year-old, only very recently married and embarking on his first overseas posting. Brought up in Feltham, Middlesex, he was the son of a long line of farmers. With no brothers, but two older sisters, he was expected one day to take over the family farm. But Denis's first love was painting. At an early age he had demonstrated a precocious talent as an artist, and for his seventeenth birthday his mother had given him a present of a studio, a room above the garages at home that had once been a chauffeur's quarters. There he had hidden himself away to paint whenever he could. At seventeen, he had won a scholarship to the Royal Academy School of Art, and began to think he might even be able to make a career as an artist.

Such plans were abruptly halted with the outbreak of war. Joining the fight had caused a certain degree of soul-searching. Both he and a friend at the Royal Academy had joined the Peace Pledge Union, but, on the other hand, he strongly believed Hitler was evil and should be stopped. With some misgivings, he joined the RAF, as soon as war was declared. If painting was his first love, flying was his second. He had learnt to fly at sixteen, and well before war broke had already gained his civil pilot's licence and joined the RAF Volunteer Reserves. This helped him enormously when he was sent off to Rhodesia for training, although he was naturally talented sportsman and pilot and gained his wings with the highest of marks. From their he was posted to fly fighters, but the moral conundrum of having to kill remained unsolved, and was still causing him some anxiety two and a half years later as he headed for the ferocious combat zone of Malta.

And Denis was also, quite understandably, afraid. Outwardly, he was a confident and calm individual, but this masked his true fears and emotions and a tendency towards introspection, which he confided with brutal honesty to his diary. It is this openness combined with a startling immediacy, so effortlessly transported from the pages of his diary into the book he subsequently wrote that sets *Malta Spitfire Pilot* apart from so many other wartime memoirs. There is no false modesty, no gung-ho bravado. Rather, it reflects how he felt at the time and depicts, quite brilliantly, the utter mayhem and madness of those days. The reader is instantly transported to that hot, dusty place; somehow, the sounds and smells of aero engines and bombs seem to ring in the ear as his words are read. Moreover, Denis was a superb observer, and not only is the young pilot he then was a very real and living person, but so too are many of his colleagues. Malta attracted mavericks – its isolation and stretched resources meant that not only was military discipline somewhat relaxed, but that individuals were necessarily given the kinds of opportunities and chances to shine that may not have been forthcoming in more strict times or circumstances. But Malta also tended to exaggerate eccentricities too. The lack of food, the repeated bouts of debilitating dysentery – known as 'Malta Dog' – the shortage of sleep, the strain of incessant combat and of being repeatedly bombed, all took their toll. No wonder people went a bit mad on Malta.

His description of his arrival at the battered airfield of Luqa is quite superb. Already that day, Denis had flown off an American aircraft carrier, an experience he had never once practised before, and had then flown for four hours across the dark, deep blue Mediterranean, and found the pinprick of an island before his fuel ran out. He landed just after a raid and was shocked by the columns of smoke rising over the island, the vast number of craters and piles of rubble. His stunned innocence, contrasting with the battle-hardened insouciance of the men already long stationed on the island, is brilliantly portrayed.

His first combat sortie over the island took place the following morning. Already, many of the Spitfires they had brought in had been destroyed and so it was just Denis, and his squadron CO and friend, John Bisdee, who volunteered to join the Luqa station commander, Squadron Leader 'Jumbo' Gracie, into the air. Just three Spitfires was all that could be managed to meet ten times as many enemy raiders.

'Sir,' Denis asked Gracie, 'what are the best tactics to use?'

'You'll learn,' Gracie replied, glaring at him, 'but don't go chasing the bastards all the way to Sicily.'

'If we are separated from you,' Denis persisted, 'with formations of 109s around, what's the best technique then?'

'If you're by yourself,' Gracie replies, 'weave around at nought feet all over the island, or better still do steep turns in the middle of Takali aerodrome, inside the ring of Bofors guns...But don't take any notice of their fighters, it's the big boys we've got to kill.'

Needless to say, Denis survived this first encounter with the enemy but only just, nearly colliding with Gracie on take-off, and soon finding himself swirling and turning for all his life in a terrifying, dizzying mêlée in which his plane was badly hit in the engine. Crash-landing, he managed to jump out unscathed and run for it as several 109s swooped over from behind. When he finally made it back to Luqa, he discovered John Bisdee was missing, and that Gracie had already reported both of them as being killed. 'So you're alive are you?' Gracie said on seeing him. It turned out Bisdee was too, but wounded, and so Denis became acting CO of the squadron, one day after his arrival on the island.

For all the ferocity of the siege, there is no doubt that the British had made life harder for themselves and the Maltese civilian population. Too many simple mistakes had been made. Not enough effort had been made to unload supplies quickly enough when precious boats did reach port, for example, while it had taken too long to send Spitfires to the island. Not until March 1942 had the first Spitfire Mk Vs reach Malta, the only aircraft with the speed, rate of climb, and firepower to be able to take on the latest Messerschmitt 109s. And even with the arrival of these machines, no thought had been given to having them quickly made airborne again for action over Malta. Most of the batch of new Spitfires that Denis had helped fly in were destroyed on the ground before they had been refuelled, rearmed and made ready for combat.

The lessons of this particular disaster were learned, however, and when the next batch arrived a few weeks later, each Spitfire was quickly led to a pre-designated blast-pen, hastily rearmed and refuelled and a fresh pilot put into the cockpit. Some planes were airborne again in just a few minutes and this time they were able to meet the enemy raiders on a far more equal footing. On 10 May, sixty-five Axis aircraft were shot down or damaged to the defenders' four. It marked an extraordinary turn-around, and thereafter, the balance of the air battle began to slowly but surely turn in favour of the RAF.

Conditions on the island, however, remained brutal. 'I have never been to a place before or since,' wrote one American RAF pilot, 'that had such a visible atmosphere of doom, violence and toughness about it.' A normal tour of operational duty was six months, but on Malta it was recognized that three was about as much as a pilot could cope with. Denis survived even less. In the middle of June, 601 Squadron were posted to North Africa but Denis, having flown more than most from the squadron over Malta, and suffering from repeated bouts of Malta Dog, was told he was going to be heading home to England – back to his wife and away from the island that in two long months had very nearly tipped him over the edge.

I first came across his book some years ago while perusing through the secondhand stalls at an air show at Duxford. I was captivated by the sketches – both of places and people – that he included in the book and particularly by the self-portrait included opposite the title page. It depicts a serious, clearly exhausted man, with dark hollow rings around his eyes. Underneath was written, 'The Future? What? 16/5/42.' At that time, Denis had barely been on the island four weeks. I then read it, almost in a single sitting, absorbed by his deeply moving and often thrillingly exciting account, and at the end felt as though I had as good an understanding of those astonishing, crazy times as it would ever be possible to have.

James Holland

PART ONE

BACKGROUND

CHAPTER I

THE GIRDERED CAVERN

"WILL Flight Lieutenant Barnham report to the R.T.O. immediately—Flight Lieutenant Barnham report to the R.T.O.
immediately."

They're calling my name over the Station Tannoy, and my train,
which has just pulled in four hours late, hasn't even coasted to the end
of the platform. I'm running, trotting, half-staggering as fast as I can
go towards the distant exit gate at Glasgow Central Station. My bulky
parachute bag is banging and lurching against my knees; inside, all the
precious equipment which may soon be in use, my parachute, my
emergency dinghy, in case I bale out into the sea, my yellow Mae West
life-saving jacket, my flying-helmet, goggles and steel helmet make the
bag heavy.

I'm just approaching the engine, but I still have a long way to go.
This great swollen cylinder of steel is oily and hot, it's relaxing with a
gush of steam, while the driver, in dirty blue overalls, stands with
indolent satisfaction on the footplate. To my mind the engine hasn't
even exerted itself: it not only stopped three times along the length of
Preston station when I was saying goodbye to my wife, but it has stopped
repeatedly since then. The three hours' margin which I allowed myself
to get from Glasgow to Abbotsinch aerodrome has been used up and
overrun.

The end of the platform at last.

"Where's the R.T.O.'s office?"

"Over the far side, chum."

Why was the train late? There was no air raid—goods trains had
priority, I suppose—but my mission's vital too. Yes, there's the office:
R.T.O. in bold letters.

"You're Tannoying for me?"

"You're Barnham? You were expected hours ago. Come on then—
as quick as you can—down these stairs."

I'm bundled into the back of a dark blue Austin Ten with all my kit.
Glasgow streets, tall black buildings, tram lines and impatient halts at red
traffic lights. Suburbs, with buildings thinning out a bit.

What's my Squadron Commander going to say to me? Orders came
through so suddenly that there was no time for official embarkation

13

leave—on his own initiative the C.O. gave us all forty-eight hours; a precious gift, for Diana and I have only been married a few weeks. He particularly asked us not to let him down—and that's just what I've done.

So this must be the aerodrome: low-lying grass, wide and flat, supporting two ancient black hangars under a heavy grey sky. No aeroplanes of any kind, just a few huts.

The C.O., broad and tall, with the blue and white diagonal stripes of the D.F.C. that he won in the Battle of Britain looking brilliant and clean under his R.A.F. wings—particularly brilliant against the blue-grey of his large but well-filled uniform—how ashamed he makes me feel. It's no good making excuses to him. Everything he says is quite true, and I nod my head in silence. That a brand new Flight Commander should have let the Squadron down—he need not rub it in.

All the pilots are now streaming past us, taking their seats in the bus. They are very discreet—I think they guess that I'm in trouble. I am so bewildered by the crazy rush from the station that they all stream past in a blur of R.A.F. blue. Now, beyond the C.O., I notice the Rhodesian shoulder flashes on the "Dreaded Hugh's" uniform as he hurries along with Ken, his wide English friend. Ken is the oldest man in the Squadron. I notice the large American eagle flashes on the handsome Tilley's jacket and I notice his Clark Gable moustache. "Pancho", from the Argentine, must have passed us already; and Pip from "B" Flight, and probably slender Cyril with his unusual South African Air Force wings—but there's "Baby Face", the other South African pilot: his smart khaki uniform is very conspicuous. Last of all come Max and Scotty, one tall figure, one very short, in their dark blue of the Royal Australian Air Force, together as usual. I smile to myself as I watch these two buddies walking closely side by side, for they share a kind of conspiracy, a mutual reaction to everything.

We have taken our places. The other pilots are laughing together. I have a window seat; the C.O. is just in front of me; I'm still in disgrace. In silence I look out at the landscape that slides past: I watch it hungrily, for it may be my last chance. Cobbled streets, more tram lines, drab yellow and soot-red walls, corrugated-iron roofs stained and rusty, slate roofs chipped and damp, neglected fields and a few trees whose Springtime has been delayed by breathing smoke. All too soon great cranes and masts finger the skyline as we turn off the main road. Before us is a gigantic ship, an aircraft carrier; it towers up above us like the side of a flat grey mountain, its complex of turrets and radar masts receding towards the clouds. The bus squeaks to a standstill: climbing out and staggering with our luggage, we pick our way over the rusty railway lines, past three grimy trucks, and over cinders from which a few blackened weeds struggle gallantly to life. Just a brief impression of the ship's carefully painted sides as we file up the gangway.

We are sailing almost at once, so, finding a hole through which I can look back at the derelict landscape, I watch the ropes that bind us to the shore being cast off one by one. As the last rope, the last link with home, splashes into the sea, trails in the water, and finally hangs limp and vertical from the overhanging catwalk, seven labourers with their hands rumpling their trouser pockets stare down into the increasing space between us and the dock.

Deep in the ship the engines are now throbbing and shuddering. The shores of the Clyde slide by more and more rapidly. Next comes the open sea, darkly overcast. As we plough our way into it not only does a screen of destroyers take up protective stations around us but a battleship moves into position. It's good to see such an imposing array because last month, March 1942, had the worst shipping losses of the war: over eighty merchant ships, totalling almost five hundred thousand tons, were sunk by enemy submarines. As it grows darker I watch the battleship *Renown* on our starboard bow dip slowly into the black waves; she rises majestically up again; the reflected light from the churned water races along her camouflaged sides and a plume of white streams out behind her.

It was with a mounting sense of adventure that I followed two of my American hosts through a labyrinth of corridors into the ship. I know the corridors fairly well now, having been several days on board, but in that first impression I quickly lost my sense of direction. Twisting and turning we passed through the openings of watertight doors and ascended clanging ladders. We were in artificial light all the time: predominantly orange, but sometimes blue. These lights played over the uniforms of the two American officers, changing the immaculate Naval Air Arm green into unusual hues. At first the two officers looked like twins, for they both had long legs, tightly pinched waists, broad square shoulders and their hair was so short that it bristled from their skulls, but, as they walked in front of me, I soon became aware of their differences: the first one went solidly on, always presenting a rounded back view, while the second was all angles, all arms and legs, contorting himself against the corridor wall, continually turning to speak with me.

He talked and asked questions all the time. He talked in the wardroom, where I learnt that ships of the American Navy are "dry" ships, serving soft drinks, mostly Coca-Cola, where we each had an excellent cup of coffee served by a negro barman and where I first heard the characteristic Tannoy message "The smoking lamp is out throughout the ship, gasoline system in operation", that I have heard repeatedly since. After coffee the Americans led me down the corridors past the hum of dynamos, through the hangar deck filled with aircraft and smelling of dope, into other creaking passages where cigar smoke lingered outside half-opened doors. They told me that our carrier is the U.S.S. *Wasp*—or as they

rolled their tongues so delightfully around it—the "Wa-aasp", the first
ship of the U.S. Navy to be sent into action in "The European Thee-at-er
of Operations".

"What's the Messerschmitt 109 like to fight against?" they asked me.

"It's very fast," I replied. "It's generally been higher than us when
we've encountered it. In combat, of course, the Spitfire can turn much
better—that's the best advantage to have."

"And this new pursuit ship of theirs, the F.W.190, how does she
compare?"

So I told them.

"And how many sorties have you done?" they asked.

I was listening to their soft round accent—the questionable innuendo
in their voices took me by surprise. I thought the enquiry blunt.

"A few convoy patrols," I replied, "and about sixty-four trips over
France."

"And how many Germans have you destroyed?"

The question was embarrassing because I've only shot down one enemy
plane. I've always felt ashamed that I've not done better—indeed I still
dream of the combats in which I've bungled wonderful opportunities,
manœuvred the wrong way due to some false alarm or other, or simply
missed through bad shooting.

We had by then stopped outside my cabin door. I wondered if I
should tell them the whole story of my F.W. 190, or not? I had been
chased in a state of terror all the way across the Channel by three of these
formidable machines. They were so very much faster than my Spitfire
that I couldn't get away from them. Close to the cliffs at Folkestone I
made one last desperate turn. The Spitfire was very much more
manœuvrable than they were and as I turned inside them, I took careful
aim at the leader before giving him all that I'd got with cannon and
machine-guns: to my astonishment the second plane fell into the sea with
a great splash!

"I've destroyed one, a F.W.190," I replied, hoping that I would be
able to go in and unpack—but they lingered.

"Why is it," they asked me, "that with all those sorties you don't wear
any medals?"

That was almost too much. I had to explain that thousands of R.A.F.
pilots had very much more experience than I had, and that very few of
them had been given decorations. I added that if there really were going
to be campaign medals for this war, then the British would only make
up their minds about it years afterwards. I looked at the many coloured
ribbons that the Americans sported on their green jackets, learning that
one was for prowess at shooting and another for being on the western sea-
board of America when certain parts of it were shelled by a Japanese
submarine; I wanted to say the C.O.'s D.F.C. really is a medal—but I

didn't dare. After all the Americans, who have only been at war a few months, will soon have their equivalent.

"Well," they said, "here's your cabin, your kit's been put in there; we live three doors up; we've got a library, and, if you like music, we've got lots of recads, Bach, Mozart, Beethoven, Schubert—make yourself at home, any time. Here, have a cigar."

I have seen the Americans since and I like them more and more, but when they left me that first evening I stood outside my cabin door, staring at it. I think I was afraid of finding a dormitory packed with people. I was remembering my last trip abroad: it was early in 1940, in a liner converted to a troopship sailing to Capetown—I was on my way to Rhodesia for my flying training. Together with a lot of ground-crew airmen, we were herded into a small gymnasium, but so great was the overcrowding, with all of us interlocked on the floor in the tropical heat, that no one could sleep. The airmen were in high spirits—their songs were shouted into my ears—I hadn't been long in the Air Force—I was new to the sexual barbarity of military songs—in my inexperience I found the three weeks' voyage a taste of hell.

Opening the door I found my cabin on this aircraft carrier was a small, quiet room for two people. On the opposite side of the cabin, smoothing the creases from the tropical uniform that he'd just unpacked, stood the "Dreaded Hugh". He's the other Flight Commander; he has a ginger moustache, rather sparse in its texture, filling his upper lip, straight sandy hair brushed back over his head, while his face and thick-set neck are salmon pink in colour—odd for a Rhodesian. We call him the "Dreaded Hugh" because he prefixes the word "dreaded" to all our names. I am the "Dreaded Denis", and his close friend is the "Dreaded Ken". Although he had made himself thoroughly at home, he had made no claim on either of the two bunks that fitted into an alcove on the right-hand wall. I guessed he would be playing cards or dice with Ken for most of the voyage, and I didn't want his great feet in my face in the early hours of the morning, so I took the top bunk; soon after this Hugh seized a pack of cards and was gone.

I had a good long look around me. I realised at once that with such a comfortable home I would spend a lot of my time here, and that's just what I've done. It's as good as having a cabin to myself, for I only see Hugh in the morning. I watch him from my bunk. He staggers in a sleepy condition up and down the tilting floor, shaves, dresses, then disappears for another twenty-four hours.

It's pleasantly warm in here—in fact I can control the cabin to any heat by re-setting the thermostat. I can also make it deliciously fresh by lifting a small eyelid vent and letting cool air rush in. There are two deep, friendly armchairs on the carpeted floor, and two metal writing-desks, each with its own shaded reading-lamp. Across the end wall a celadon green curtain is drawn, but behind it the side of the ship leans outwards, no doubt to support the flight deck above. There's a port-hole there, but at the moment there's a steel blackout panel fitted across it, out of sight, of course, behind the curtain.

I have written long letters to all my family and many of my friends. I have read a little, while at times, as now for instance, I look about me: I find such a luxurious cabin a strangely incongruous thing in war. A U-boat may have its sights upon us, and a torpedo may be approaching— now—at this very moment. Apprehensively I wait for the bang. There would be a rush of water. I would grab the life-jacket that hangs on the back of the closed door and race for life to the rendezvous point on the flight deck above. But suppose the door was buckled in the explosion— jammed tight? I would be trapped: but there is no bang; there's a long creak every few moments, there's the beat of engines and there's a rhythm of movement in the way our carrier rides the waves.

All around us, thousands of yards out across the dark water, the destroyers and the battleship must be forging ahead in their allotted stations. Thousands of men must be alert. Look-out men must be straining their eyes watching the water, while deep inside the ships men on duty behind complicated asdic instruments must be listening and watching for the blip that would betray a submarine's imminent attack. We are taking reinforcement aircraft to the besieged island of Malta and it is vital that we get through.

This is the blackest moment of the war so far—we have had strategic withdrawal after withdrawal, then a new wave of reverses started last December when the Japanese hit the Americans in the back—with the might of America in with us it looked as if the war would be quickly over—but no: Germany, Italy and Japan appear to have consorted to- gether. Japan, cutting the world in half longitudinally, has swept south- wards across the Pacific Islands and will undoubtedly invade Australia next; simultaneously she has struck westwards towards India. In her invasion of Malaya our great battleships, the *Prince of Wales* and *Repulse*, were quickly sunk; Singapore fell next and now two attacks are converg- ing on India itself: one Japanese army is sweeping through Burma in the north, while in the south we have just learned that a Japanese fleet, with troopships, is attacking Ceylon. At this same moment the Germans and Italians are making an all-out offensive south-eastwards across the Mediterranean towards the Middle East—no doubt they expect to join up with the Japanese forces in India. Although the Balkans have been overrun, Crete captured by an airborne invasion, and although Rommel is advancing along the North African coast towards Egypt, the island of Malta still stands behind enemy lines, a constant menace to Rommel's supply routes. Malta is vital and the enemy realise that they must not only neutralise the island but capture it. Malta is cut off from effective

Allied succour by almost a thousand miles of sea from Gibraltar on one hand and by another thousand miles of water from Cairo on the other. She is brooded upon by the underside of Italy and Sicily, a bare sixty miles away. The Germans have assembled a bombing fleet of five hundred planes on the Sicilian airfields; for months they have been hammering and hammering at the tiny island. The island's R.A.F. bomber force has been wiped out. The dwindling number of fighter planes are battling against odds of forty or fifty to one. Will we be in time before the German invasion? Will the fifty Spitfires we are taking be enough?

A few minutes ago I was in the hangar deck looking at our cargo of Spitfires. The hangar is a vast girdered cavern stretching away into the distance like the inside of a whale; in it our fighters are lashed into position, parasites to Leviathan. It is impossible to cross the deck without ducking under wings and tails, all tucked into one another. The Spitfires' wheels are steadied by wooden blocks, their wing tips lashed to the deck by ropes and cables, but more Spitfires are suspended from the roof girders, slung there by canvas loops—they sway gently as our carrier rolls. Staring at these planes I could not help wondering how many of them and, indeed, how many of our pilots will be left in a week's time.

In order to get into the Mediterranean without being seen by enemy agents on the shores of Spain or North Africa, our fleet is going to pass through the Straits of Gibraltar in the dead of night. Once inside, the Navy, who have precious few heavy ships left, dare not take us very far— we will have to take off and fly about seven hundred miles to our destination. I hope we are taken far enough: of the last formation that left a carrier in this way, only four reached the island—nine others ran out of petrol: the machines were lost and the pilots drowned.

Even the take-off will be an ordeal—in order to avoid a similar disaster we will be carrying an extra ninety gallons of fuel in larger long-range tanks attached under the belly of each plane: but a new problem arises— weight. We have each been limited to ten pounds of personal luggage in order to keep our machines as light as possible—but the planes themselves, with an extra powerful armament of four cannons and four machine-guns, are unusually heavy. Is the deck going to be long enough for us to take off and climb into the air? It looked awfully short when we came aboard and none of us have ever taken off from an aircraft carrier before.

Thus we face the octopus future that draws us steadily towards it. As a fighter pilot I know I have little chance of coming out of such a battle alive, so it is with sorrow that I look back on what I have done with my life so far and on what I hoped I might achieve.

CHAPTER 2

OPERATIONAL TOUR

THE last time I was in an aircraft carrier I was eight years old, for my mother had taken me to a Navy Week at Portsmouth. It was the scale of the aircraft carrier that assaulted my child's eye, with its flight deck so horizontally flat and its vertical surfaces, its superstructure and masts rising up into the sky like Jack's Beanstalk—I was excited by the secret caverns to explore in such a ship, but, alas, many of them were forbidden to the public. I am still that child on just such a carrier now—I am rather disappointed that the burly American seamen call me "Buddy" instead of "Sir", although I am able to explore. But I am astonished to find myself here, just twenty-two years old, a married man, an Officer in charge of a Flight of twelve Spitfires and their pilots, on a carrier that is steaming into action in WAR—I expected to be an artist, a painter.

On my seventeenth birthday my mother gave me a present of a studio; once a chauffeur's quarters above the garages at home; in it I painted pictures, listened to music and read avidly. I had begun that hunt for truth that so many other adolescents must have begun just before the war. In my case it was particularly my love of music and paintings that nourished my inward life; furthermore, as I became aware of the beauty and structure in the music of Bach and Beethoven, and in the paintings of della Francesca and Blake, I linked them with what I was reading about the universe. In paintings I knew it was quite impossible to be aware of the design of a picture if my eyes were too near the canvas—thus I felt that man was too much implicated with the universe to be aware of its order; but I sensed an inner significance and perhaps an intuitive part of my nature was being stirred. As I continued to read and think about things, there was, from time to time, deep inside me a great flash of brilliant inward light. It was a kind of love, a kind of inner recognition of the Truth, thus I began to feel my way towards religion. At seventeen and eighteen I had my first pictures in the Royal Academy, but in 1939 I started a picture which was going to be my most ambitious work so far: I wanted to say something about my new awareness and its problems. The main theme of the picture was Christ calling one of his disciples from a family of fishermen busily mending their nets. Christ was walking along a narrow path symbolising eternal life, but he did not stop walking

as he called. The disciple, who had rushed forward from the family and
fallen on one knee before the Master, was twisting round in a kneeling
attitude as if imploring the Master to stop. He wanted to have time to
decide what to do. There was, of course, no time, and in this brief
moment of decision the disciple was caught between the beckoning hand
of Christ and the outstretched hand of his father, between his spiritual
destiny on one hand and his earthly duties and obligations on the
other.

I had hardly started this painting when the war began. All the life I
had known hitherto stopped abruptly. I knew next to nothing about
politics and international affairs. Hitler claimed Lebensraum for himself
and the German people, but whether his claim was just or unjust I had
no means of telling; we had given a guarantee to the Polish Nation,
Hitler walked in despite that guarantee, our ultimatum had expired and
the sirens in London were already wailing. Like thousands of others
I had to face this situation and make a decision about the war. I found
myself pulled in two directions.

In my adolescent search I had thrashed out certain principles and I felt
that, as a human right, all individuals should have their chance in the
adventure of living, a chance of unfolding their lives and developing
their talents so long as they never wreaked their wills upon, and therefore
never jeopardised, the chances of their fellow men. Yet here were Hitler
and his Nazis stamping about with terrible ruthlessness, destroying the
hopes and chances of millions. I felt it ought to be stopped. On the other
hand—"Thou shalt not kill." This dilemma baffled me; but the whole
new atmosphere of war was baffling.

I thought we English were tolerant yet many people I met in September
'39 were pouring scorn on the Conscientious Objectors who, facing the
pressure of public opinion with great courage, had come to another
decision over the problem of killing. I was angry with the scorn levelled
at such men—I still am. There seemed to be a violent upsurge of blind
and emotional Nationalism. I have always lamented Nationalism—I
have always felt that it provokes division rather than unity amongst the
peoples of the world. In 1938 I had been shocked to find an acquaintance
focusing his idealism solely on his country. He was German—but I
found many Englishmen doing very much the same.

In such an atmosphere, trying to decide whether to fight or not to
fight, I felt like the disciple in my painting—hoping that time would
stop so that I could sort out my dilemma. I could not solve the moral
problem of killing—it still worries me. On the other hand I knew I was
afraid to fight and I wanted to face my fear squarely; I also felt that here
was a wonderful opportunity to fly, and that, I am ashamed to say, must
have influenced me. Perhaps I was swept along in the stream, doing
what was expected of me, nevertheless, although I signed the papers and

took the Oath, I made the mental reservation to follow my own conscience.

Having joined up I found myself experiencing a common emotion with all those who listened to stories about 1914 as they grew up—a sense of excited resolution that we too could cope with this monstrous reversal of life. Now, however, sitting here in this quiet cabin with the pulse of the engines under my feet, I'm already looking back on two and a half years of war and I'm beginning to see it for what it is. I know very well that all over the world cities are being bombed, people are being split into small fragments of flesh and bone, they are being drowned in cellars or burned alive; columns of refugees are being machine-gunned, children are being thrown into ditches and women raped. Indeed, imagining these things I am immediately apprehensive for the safety of my wife and I wonder if there's an air raid going on at home. Such horrors are in the nature of war and have to be faced, but there are other, more insidious things.

When war began our Authorities stated that we would uphold Christianity and the Truth, but it seems to me that most Christian principles have been discarded. Serenity, love and tentative reflection as to what is the Good, the True and the Beautiful thing to do are impatiently dismissed as irrelevant to the war effort. Anger, Hate and Ruthlessness are blessed by silence or openly encouraged as "qualities" in the fighting man. I am told that such things are expedient. I have even met a man, a clergyman in peacetime who will no doubt return to his parish when it is all over, who openly avows that he has shelved his Christianity for the "duration". To be a good fighter pilot a common saying is that "You should feed, fight and f . . ." We are encouraged to live like animals so that the pressure of sex does not interfere with our efficiency as fighting machines.

And what has happened to the ideal of Truth? I think the very nature of war has twisted it. Propaganda tells us as much of the Truth as is considered good for us, good for us in so far as we are instruments of war, and not individuals with a spiritual destiny. Our information about the Russians is a typical example of such distortion. When they were on the German's side we were told they were treacherous, cunning brutes; we were shown photographs in the newspapers of the Russian leaders and Rippentrop, the German Foreign Minister, smiling together over their pacts and treaties, but last year, when the Germans stabbed their old ally in the back, the beastly Russians became the gallant Russians in a twinkling of an eye. Now we are asked to help the courageous Russians by parcels and contributions of all kinds. I am denying neither their gallantry nor our obligation to help them, but I am aghast at our Propaganda, our so-called Voice of Truth, which gives whatever part of the truth suits the war effort and suppresses everything else. I am told it is expedient. But what are the true facts about the Russian people? We may never find out. Even the personnel of the R.A.F. Wing, who went to Russia with their Hurricane fighter planes and who have recently returned, are under strict orders not to talk about what they heard, saw or experienced there.

Propaganda is designed to provoke us to action; but such selected information is having the reverse effect on me: it's undermining what belief in action I have got. I ask myself where do I stand and how do I orientate myself to a world gone mad. I still hold the same ideals as I held at the beginning of the war while my dilemma about everything has increased.

What of the future? There is only one consolation—I still love flying. I know that of the fifty Spitfires in the hangar deck, one Spitfire will bear me skywards next Monday morning, high above the blue Mediterranean.

I loved flying as a child and my nickname at my prep. school was "Buzz-Buzz". I was continually zooming my model aircraft over the school desks and delighting in side slips and manœuvres of forced landings in between the ink pots. It was the very limitations of manœuvre that appealed to me—that if the aeroplane flew too slowly it would drop and spin and fall out of control: in a forced landing, therefore, the plane had to be continually descending in a glide to keep up the speed. In flying real aeroplanes the same things appeal to me now—few joys can compare with gliding in to land.

My love of flying ran like a continuous thread through my 'teens. If I was painting and I heard the hum of an aircraft, especially if it was late in the evening, I would lay down my brushes and, rushing to the window, look out towards the aerodrome. I would look down the whole length of the kitchen garden, over the rows of vegetables, over the shapes of the fruit trees to where, beyond the distant tennis court, the branches of three oak trees wriggled their way up into the luminous sky. I could watch the planes gliding downwards from the sunlit cirrus clouds.

What wonderful skies I saw from that window, skies that often stimulated paintings. I remember a great edifice of cumulus standing quite alone in the evening light—it was flushed pink—the foreground garden was dark below it; I was seventeen and I was in love for the first time—I felt all the anguish of that experience, for the girl lived far away:

> Thunder clouds, poised, floating on still air,
> And yet within, what currents stir in painful bliss
> The memory of her loveliness.

But there was on the other hand a more macabre indulgence with the space of the sky and aeroplanes. I don't know why I used to play such a terrible game; it was probably a relic from my earlier childhood; of being given toy soldiers and playing with them; of becoming bored and planting fireworks in the ground to make the game more realistic. I used to make a model glider of carefully folded paper and I would fill the body and wings with gunpowder. Standing at the top of my studio steps, I would strike a match, light the fuselage, and send the model soaring out over the cabbages—what delight as it exploded into flame!

I now know the difference between such childish games, such indulgent thrills, even the armchair excitements of the cinema, and the reality of flying in war. The difference is fear.

There are many kinds of fear, and it is said that the primeval fear of an eerie unknown, encountered in dreams and at other moments of intense solitude, is the worst of them all. Fear in action is not of this kind; it is essentially the simple fear of what may happen. It is the same kind of fear as may obsess the simplest actions in life. It is possible to experience it when walking downstairs if imagination feeds into the mind pictures of gouged eyes and broken bones as a result of falling to the bottom. This, of course, is fear of an accident, and if one were afraid of accidents instead of having the normal, healthy respect of their causes, one should never fly at all. In flying the possibility of accidents is balanced by a confident pride in one's skill in handling even emergency situations—it adds a certain zest to flying, and accounts for the fact that fear is not a companion of one's training period but only comes with the more deliberate hazard of facing the enemy. It is no accident that the enemy have one objective in mind: your destruction. The fact that your body may be burnt or broken or mangled is more than real—you know it's going to happen within the next hour—this is particularly vivid before the moment of take-off. Once in the air this dread anticipation is quickly forgotten. The act of flying drives it away, but in combat it is revived in a far more dreadful form. At certain moments it becomes a sudden explosive terror. Curling blue tracers of enemy bullets, a few feet away, are racing towards you. You see them photographed in detail. They appear to stand still. Time is stopped, but fear, that detonator of panic, holds you in a paralysis of horror. If you're not hit, the terror is quickly forgotten in the urgency of combat that goes on. But perilous moments can be strung together. When you are coned at low level by anti-aircraft shells, squirted up towards you like hoses of red-hot meteorites, you know that each flaming blob is searching for you; even while you throw your aircraft about in a frenzy of escape, each full moment is prolonged to the next, and what may take only a minute or less is slowed down to an hour of agony.

The fact that you are deliberately inviting circumstances such as these on every flight you make, adds to the long-drawn-out fear of waiting to fly. It is not only mutilation of one's body but periods of emotional torture that have to be faced. This has to be continually undergone. After days and weeks and months of its continual pressure fear assumes a separate entity. It stands unbidden by any thought or imaginings as an invisible presence, an uninvited guest behind your shoulder, an extra weight to carry, an enemy to be grappled with and overcome by repeated acts of deliberate will. It affects different pilots in different ways, but sooner or later all pilots need a rest from its pressure. As a pilot gains experience in combat flying so the graph of his efficiency rises steadily, but when the cumulative strain tells severely upon him, such a graph drops steeply away. I'm told that he doesn't care any more, he becomes foolhardy, takes unnecessary risks; he cracks, as they say, but not having experienced such a state, I have no clear idea what happens. Surely, however, different temperaments must produce different reactions to the strain: perhaps the over-imaginative pilots might crack up quickly, while others may be unaffected and get steadily more efficient. Some directive has to be laid down, and at present in Fighter Command a tour is two hundred hours spent in actual flights against the enemy; after this the pilot is sent for a rest as an instructor. I have done a hundred and forty "op" hours, so officially I am in full bloom. Part of me is therefore intensely interested in what lies ahead, but I have never had to face such odds as I will have to face in Malta.

Will Malta be anything like the "sweeps", "rhubarbs", and other sorties we made over Northern France last year? Fear will undoubtedly be my close companion again. I remember the day last year, when, after living closely with fear, I saw it and understood it for the first time. It was on a day when I returned from leave. On leave, I had been sure of having a tomorrow to live in; I could lie in bed late or get up early just as I wished; I could make plans for the days ahead with the certainty that I would be there to carry them out. Even when I got off the bus at the end of my leave and walked up from the main road to the entrance of Gravesend aerodrome, I had no real apprehension about the immediate future and I had no fear. It was when I entered the dispersal hut that I found it waiting for me.

The Squadron had already done two sweeps over France and was about to go out on a third. I assumed at once that I would be flying on the operation, and that was the moment that fear came back. I was enveloped by it as if I had never been away at all. I was adjusting myself to it when I learned that, as all the places had been allocated, I would not be needed. What a relief it was. Fear was gone. Although it had gone I began to feel acutely uncomfortable: all the pilots were gay, incredibly gay, and I remember thinking how childish it was to throw all the cushions about. I suddenly realised that I was cut off from them. Each one of them had deep within him that dreaded anticipation of the coming flight. Fear was amongst them—not that it could be detected from anything they did, for all was gaiety—yet I could feel its intense presence. Then I saw it, like transparent smoke wrapped round the flesh of each one of them quite separately.

One pilot standing alone was choked with fear. Despite Bob's shock of hair curving upwards over his forehead like a fountain, he was very good looking; indeed, arriving at night clubs in London, I had often noticed how women's eyes used to follow him as we crossed through the semi-darkness to our table. Bob stood quite alone in the corner of the dispersal hut with fear playing over the features of his proud face like small flames on a gas-fire.

I went over towards him for he was an experienced pilot and I had never seen him like this before. He wanted to talk about it so I let him explain. He told me he was "jinxed". He explained that on his last three trips he had been in trouble; on the first, the evening before, they had mixed it with a lot of 109s: some cannon shells had struck along the side of his cockpit and his perspex canopy had been blown off. On his next, the first that morning, his wheels wouldn't retract properly so he'd had to return. On the last trip he'd got as far as mid-Channel when his engine developed an oil leak; the temperature had risen so alarmingly that he'd broken away from the Squadron and returned to the aerodrome yet again. Small things mostly, I didn't think these were much to worry about. There he stood, about to go up for the fourth time and I'll never forget his face. He certainly didn't seem in a fit state to fly and I offered to take his place. He wouldn't hear of it. "I'll break this hoodoo," he said. But I thought that the shrug of his shoulders as he tried to laugh it off was far from convincing.

Thus the Squadron set out. An hour and a half later most of the Spitfires returned again. Another trip was laid on for the early evening and I was allotted my position in the formation. I took my place in the briefing hut where all the narrow benches were bending under the weight of pilots. Fear had returned to me. I could feel the inner tension of my muscles braced against it. I was surprised to find myself happy to accept this burden; facing its pressure was so very much better than standing around in separated safety. Fear is the passport to comradeship. But not, alas, with Bob. Less than two hours previously his Spitfire had been seen falling in flames near Le Touquet, and no one baled out.

The huge engines of our aircraft carrier throb and shudder—I can feel the cabin floor vibrating. I can hear the swish of water passing swiftly below the port-hole. That afternoon I had no time to wonder if Bob knew he was going to his death, or to ask myself if the strain of repeated trips might have sapped his reserves, cracked his resistance, over-intensified his imagination, and rendered him vulnerable. I was too busy with the technicalities of my trade.

I watched the Intelligence Officer step up on to the platform at the far end of the room, and point to a map that covered the end wall. He explained the course we were to fly and he pointed out the red string which stretched from the rendezvous point with the bombers we were to cover, southwards over the English Channel, across the French coast and down into enemy territory towards the target. France was thickly punctuated by small round plaques of different colours. The officer explained:

"These are heavy anti-aircraft gun positions; these are light flak positions; these are Luftwaffe fighter units, these new ones have just been moved in from the Russian front—they seem prepared to play ball with us today, so you can expect to have some fun, particularly here and here. . . ."

His voice droned on, he cracked his little jokes, for he was not going. He explained the importance of the target, how the route had been chosen to give us the tactical advantage of the sun, and other details. One trained part of me listened and absorbed the information because it might determine a decision later, while a second part of me continued my fight with fear.

As the Intelligence Officer stepped down, our Squadron Commander took his place. He gave us an accurate time check and told us that we would start our engines in twelve minutes' time.

My Spitfire was only a few hundred yards from the hut, so, as the other pilots were taken by lorry to their aeroplanes parked in more remote places, I set out alone towards mine. There was no hurry so I deliberately checked my rapid pace. I passed the patches of oil-clogged grass where the Spitfires were run up in the mornings, and I could see my shapely grey Spitfire ahead of me. I delighted in the rhythm of my step, in the easy flexing of muscles and in the silent articulation of joints. I had mastered the fear. I was resigned to whatever events the next hour might bring, I knew my body might be pulped and blackened by fire in a heap of molten aluminium in a French field like Bob's, or become flotsam on the sea bed, but I did not want to die. Walking slowly towards the wing tip, I looked at the lush spreading leaves of summer trees on the far side of the aerodrome and at the smoothness of the rounded hillside as it dropped down towards the wide silver Thames in the distance. That smooth round hillside; I thought of the shape of women and what subtle loveliness is theirs. I was intensely aware of the warm sun, the blue sky, the tufted grass so springy to walk upon, and even the beauty of my coffin Spitfire.

The parachute was waiting for me on the eliptical wing tip, with one strap of its harness already fastened, hanging down in a loop. As I passed I slipped my left arm through it and the heavy 'chute, with the seat type dinghy attached to it, slid off the wing and swung awkwardly and painfully against the back of my knees. I clamped the rest of the harness tightly around me, and then, in a doubled-up attitude like a crab in its shell, I trudged towards the fuselage.

Two grinning mechanics, in oil-spattered blue uniforms, were waiting, their voices cheery and encouraging as they mothered me into the cockpit. I fastened myself into the seat by the straps: not too tight—I had to allow for my expansion as the aircraft climbed upwards and out from under the daily weight of air that encloses us at sea level; yet tight enough —I didn't want to fall about the cockpit when flinging my aircraft upside-down.

Next the oxygen tube, for had I no oxygen my machine would come crashing down from high altitude. The tube had to be secured against flapping into my eyes while I was fighting, yet loose enough to enable me to swivel my head to see if I was being attacked from behind. It led into a mask that covered the lower half of my face, a mask that also contained my radio-microphone. A helmet covered the rest of my head with radio earphones protruding each side of it. Thus, to outward appearances, I shed my humanity and became part of the machine.

As I checked the array of instruments, almost ninety dials and levers, I glanced repeatedly through the thick windscreen towards a cluster of Spitfires in the distance. Suddenly two puffs of blue smoke lingered for an instant above the long fuselage of one of them. The C.O. had started his engine. Peering round the long nose of my own aircraft lest anyone was in the way, I reached down and pressed the starter buttons: the huge black propeller blades ahead of me jerked twice like the arms of a marionette. Then all violent mechanical life and noise; the indicating needles on the dials crept unto the allotted positions showing me the health of my Rolls Royce engine; the consciousness that I had of my own body, bottled in perspex, gradually extended to include the short eliptical wings outstretched each side of me and the cigar-shaped fuselage tapering behind me to the tail. The power of the Spitfire was my power, its graceful shape was my shape. I was a bird. Yet the bird could sting: five thousand eight hundred bullets and shells each minute were my responsibility.

As a heavy bird is often ungainly on the ground so must I have appeared to the watchers on the control tower as I waddled past; yet inside the machine, trundling over the bumpy grass, I watched the wing tip dip and jerk against the line of distant trees. I was blind with that long flat nose tipped up in front of my eyes; yet, as I swung it to the left and to the right, I could see the other machines of our Squadron lurching up the field: we were about to position ourselves for the Squadron take off.

On that particular occasion I remember positioning myself close to the Spitfire flown by Roger, a Belgian pilot, and I remember his helmeted head turning and how he winked at me across the narrow space between our wings. Beyond him I had a fine view of all the machines as they assembled. It was a full complement of Spitfires as usual. We were always up to strength. If we had losses, replacement aircraft were flown in immediately. Our part in the operation—the small fleet of twelve fighter planes was a magnificent sight: their propellers churning, their grey and green fuselages emblazoned with red and blue roundels, cannons pointing forward from their wings and the late afternoon sunlight glittering on their perspex cockpit canopies.

The "sweep" was much the same as all the sweeps, yet in this carrier in which I am forced to live for a few more days before we fly off and head eastwards towards Malta, it occurs to me that the other services have nothing to compare with going into action as we know it in the R.A.F. We leap into a new element, totally different from our normal life on earth.

On that afternoon fear receded because, near the zenith of the sky, I was enjoying looking back at the remote world. From thirty thousand feet I peered down through my bubble perspex at the retreating patchwork of English fields, at the Channel, and at the slowly approaching French coast. The view was like a child's atlas, beautifully drawn and tinted, in lavender grey for the sea and lavender green for the land. I peered upwards at the inverted blue saucer of sky: immediately over my head it was violet but near the horizon a pale blue-green, very faint and tender.

How slowly the French coast approached; our formation appeared to hang motionless. I was no longer aware of the engine roar, for it had become a background upon which other sensations were experienced. I could hear the air hissing past the side of the cockpit; I was aware of my inhalation of oxygen and my breathing out against the hollow amplification of my microphone; I was aware too of the sensitive balance of flight expressing itself in the gentle pressure of my finger-tips on the control column.

Through the frosty air to my right, I could see the two other sections of our squadron: from each leader, as if attached to him by a long wire, trailed his three supporting Spitfires. Still further away, but quite motionless against the horizon, rode other squadrons, tight bunches of aircraft in the distance like clouds of gnats. There were still more below us, closer to the chariot of nine bombers which we, two or three hundred Spitfires, had to protect.

I was flying on the end of our section of four, and my flight was dominated by the gigantic presence of Roger's Spitfire. Its underside was huge, brooding upon me, reflecting the silver light from below. It hung almost motionless, swaying gently from side to side and occasionally undulating. I noticed that there was a leak of oil from somewhere under his engine, and fascinated, I watched the black stream creep back towards me along the bottom of his fuselage. Slowly it blackened the clean metal plates, the fierce stream of air beating at it and piling it up in black wavelets like an incoming tide. I watched it glisten among the rivet heads with tiny twinkling highlights, and finally it reached the very end of his tail. There it disintegrated into millions of infinitesimal particles which were being left in the sky behind us.

With a thrill of fear I noticed that we had almost reached the enemy coast. I knew that behind me was a yawning chasm of emptiness and I turned my head to look at it: the pale turquoise-and-grey space was beautiful—but I knew that very soon squat, black angular fighters would arch down from above. We would soon have to keep a sharp look-out by "weaving"—our section would stay one behind the other in a long line of aircraft, but, since it was impossible for any of us to see into the blind spot immediately behind our own tails, we would twist and turn independently, with each pilot craning his head round to search that dangerous vulnerable space. In turning fiercely from side to side there would be an overwhelming sensation of weight. My neck would be compressed. I would have to fight the pressure as I twisted my body to look round over my shoulder. It would go on for an hour or longer. It would get steadily worse as more and more 109s would gather above us. The search behind my tailplane would have to be more and more thorough, for my life would depend on my vigilance. I knew from experience that our leaders would start flying faster, that it would be difficult to keep up with them. If they started to turn, I knew I would have to cut the corners to stay in formation. In doing so I would not be able to weave or guard myself from attack. Our leaders would yell at us, as if we were some extra incumbrance that they carried into action— "Keep up, keep in position, don't straggle." They realised that most of the casualties were amongst the men on the end of the line—they knew that an error of flying might cause a man to lag, and that, as bomber escort, they could not turn back to save him from the enemy.

We were soon over the French coast. We started weaving. I flung my Spitfire to and fro with determination that no enemy fighter would get me. Roger's Spitfire, its huge tilted wings filling the sky, shot out to one side of me, then turned viciously, rushing back across my nose. If I got a little too close to him there would be a collision. I might have to slam my throttle closed to drop back out of his way. By deceleration I might fall back that little bit too far—109s would pounce.

As Roger's Spitfire raced past my nose once more, I noticed, high above him, six Spitfires like pink fingers against the deep violet, travelling fast in the opposite direction. I wondered why they were heading back. My head twisted round in an effort to follow them: straight wings, red noses: they weren't Spits at all—they were the enemy. Voices called out:

"109s above, Beauty Squadron, 109s above and behind."

"Dozens of them."

"No, only four."

Turning over sideways, they lunged down upon us like sharks. . . .

The "sweep" was very much the same as all the sweeps. We proceeded to the target and we turned for home. 109s were constantly above us, waiting their opportunity to strike, yet a great dark area of enemy territory had still to be covered before we reached the pale sea that fringed the horizon. I was continually heaving my Spitfire up on one wing tip; heaving it round one way—then heaving it back again; twisting my head up and round and back over the other side—pushing my head hard up against the refreshingly cool perspex; peering backwards down the side of the fuselage—searching the sky behind my tail. I was tired. I grew excessively hot round the top of my stomach, I seemed to be fermenting like a compost heap under the weight of my clothes and harness. The straps bit into my shoulders, my oxygen mask was clamped tightly across my face, my jaw hurt and I felt sick. I felt so wretched that I remember whispering a prayer: "Shoot me down quickly, let me get down on the ground again"; then, with what terror I noticed more 109s behind me, summoned, as it were, to execute the task.

The 109s banked away from us as we returned across the Channel. What relief—the slow joyous approach of the English coast, and beyond it the familiar towns. Short of fuel, I decided to land at Hawkinge aerodrome, just inland from Folkestone. What relief!—the long, floating, dipping, sighing, irresponsible diving, twisting, spiralling downwards over the white cliffs! It was glorious! With the throttle closed and the engine popping, coughing, choking, then gently murmuring, I made the long, straight, sinking journey inland towards the aerodrome. With a quiet turn along the chosen path of air, round the hangars and over the last of the tree-tops, my Spitfire dropped on to the green turf. . . .

I was soon stretched out on a bank of grass, watching the refuelling. A petrol bowser was parked in front of my Spitfire's motionless propeller, and in the end compartment of the bowser's oval sectioned tank a small engine had been started up;—although there was a shrill ringing in my ears as a result of flying for so long, I could hear the clug-clug-clug-clug-clug of the pumping engine. An airman, sitting astride the nose of my

Spitfire, held the wriggling pipe-line in place: I watched it jump and leap as fuel was spurted along it.

There were already fifty Spitfires drawn up in a flat semi-circle that foreshortened back towards the hangars. Several bowsers were in position replenishing their tanks. The line was being continually lengthened, as, one by one, more fighters dropped down from the long queue that murmured overhead. Each needed almost ninety gallons—thus, about twenty thousand gallons had been consumed on the operation. I reflected that the day before, when on leave, I had argued with men of the local Council, trying to get supplementary petrol coupons for four gallons, so that my mother, far from well, could do her shopping by car. How crazy it all was: during the sweep a few bombs had been dropped and several aircraft from both sides had been shot down. The victims, who should have been enjoying the evening fading from gold to grey, were now dead.

On the grass bank I looked down at a sentinel ant who peered out from the mouth of a lush cavern. As I regarded him, he, and three friends, clambered quickly over my finger-nail then sported together amongst the sun-bleached hairs on the back of my hand. But my Spitfire was soon ready. I decided to fly back to my home base before it grew dark.

The take-off speed increased; easing back the control column—the uppermost branches of the trees flashed past—Romney Marsh slid below me, all dark and quiet, with the sea shining like a flat opalescent shell above my left wing tip. Although the apprehensive fear I had felt earlier in the afternoon had been totally unnecessary, for the sweep had not been particularly dangerous, I felt quietly joyous to be alive; the responsive Spitfire felt the same—I flung it into a steep diving turn towards the north, levelling out just above the tree-tops.

I was enjoying flying as flying should always be, relaxed and smooth and undulating. A lazy evening. Stretching out my legs I tapped the rudder bar with my toes: the tapered fuselage swung into the stream of air, first one side, then the other. Ahead I glimpsed some labourers returning from the fields. My heart went out to them. They disappeared below the wing and reappeared in the open space between the wing and the tail. Two of them waved to me, but before I could wave back some foreshortened tree-tops hid them. A farmhouse down on my left, and carts, and a dog in a funny position—probably barking.

Thus I flew home; the aerodrome when I arrived was drifting remotely below transparent veils of fog. After circling slowly above the white floor, watching two factory chimneys like incongruous lighthouses on the uncharted ocean of steam, my gull-winged Spitfire and I turned gently downwards. Skimming across silver tissues of fog we sank through them into the darkness. Turning steadily as buildings and belts of trees grew larger and darker, descending as some telegraph poles and a fence floated past, then the aerodrome grass widened out each side of the lifted nose. Bang—lurch—bounce—I made a bad landing: two mechanics who had been watching my arrival re-entered the hangar doors. I switched off the engine. Exhausted I just sat there. I had accomplished nothing—I hadn't even fired my guns—it had been a "sweep" very much the same as all the other sweeps.

CHAPTER 3

FINAL BRIEFING

I'M IN my cabin, and our aircraft carrier is pitching forwards and backwards and rolling from side to side. This comfortable little cell of mine leans over and when it ought to stop it goes on further. I'm at my writing-desk—feeling vaguely seasick. Perhaps it's the chocolate I've eaten—three bars of it and I'm just not used to the stuff. Real milk chocolate too, in real silver paper, quite different from the ersatz chocolate in transparent wrappings that we've been getting on the ration at home. I can't bear to look at the creamy-brown lump with its crinkled paper twinkling and sparkling in the cabin lights. I push it away into the shadow of the books piled up in front of me. Not far enough—I push it out of sight behind the books.

Before me I have H. G. Wells' *Outline of History*, a History of Art, an Atlas and the third volume of the history notes I am making. To bring these books, as well as my sketch-books and painting equipment, in addition to my clothes and personal kit, is to break the orders we've been given about the limited weight of luggage. I hope that the heavily laden Spitfire, with all its extra fuel and guns will lift off the flight deck when we set out for Malta in two days' time. But I refused to leave these things behind—surely there'll be some opportunity to draw and study despite the battle we're going into?

But I'm restless—I can't seem to settle to my work now. Perhaps it's being in an aircraft carrier—how I'd hate to be permanently stationed in this electrically lit prison below decks. I've tried to work—perhaps I'm thinking overmuch of the battle that draws minute by minute closer. I've even been along to my American friends' cabin where they played some records to me. Mozart and Beethoven were torture to listen to. At times in the past I've been lifted to ecstasy by such music, but this morning, since it would not have been polite to leave as soon as I arrived, I sat there in their cabin, chained to agony like Prometheus.

What else can I do? Where else can I go? I've been in the hangar deck and in the wardroom. I was in the wardroom last night—I smelt the expensive aroma of cigar smoke in the corridors long before I arrived there. When I finally went in through the swing doors and stood inside the wide, low room, with its white-painted girders stretching across the ceiling, I found it packed tight with people. Although there was a barricade of people linked together in conversation across the bar, the negro barman in his white coat leaned over their heads and handed me an iced Coca-Cola. Holding the tall glass, deliciously cool and moist in my hot hand, I looked around and spotted the Dreaded Hugh, with Ken and two Americans, seated at my favourite table. I couldn't get to them because of the crush, but across the din, I watched the dumb play of their moving lips. They made urgent gestures with their hands, banging them on the table with delight: they were obviously telling stories. Ken's dark eyebrows oscillated up and down as he spoke, his mouth smiled wider and wider, his cheeks were two round lumps and he was shaking with laughter—his eyebrows shot up in the middle with the painful effort to get the rest of his story born. I suppose it all came out for there was a sudden burst of movement: Hugh doubled up across his great arms while the American, with his back towards me, arched backwards like a released spring.

At last I got near enough to realise they were relating the adventures of their last few hours before sailing. I still couldn't see the chair-tipping American's face, but he gestured with the back of his thumb towards his gaunt-faced companion.

"Gus here," he exclaimed. "He was staggering round and round the lamp-post outside her apartment. That lamp-post—he was clasping at it and asking, over and over again, if it's name was Mary."

I thought of my own last evening in England—walking alone with Diana along the darkened shores of Derwentwater, looking out together across the quiet smooth surface of the lake.

I am holding Diana's photograph in front of me but it's no good writing another letter—I'm totally unable to express my feelings any more clearly. This just has to be borne but my heart goes out to all other young men and women who have been wrenched apart by this war.

It's no good sitting down here, imprisoned in this cabin, feeling sorry for myself. There's one place I haven't visited—a vigorous blow of fresh air would do me good: I'll go up on to the flight deck.

The carrier is steaming at full speed, now up into the air, now down into the sea, but this is no deck with a railing to hold on to as the ship rolls, or to lean against as you come down from the sky to meet the sea, for here is the largest sheet of metal you have ever walked upon, wet and slippery with nothing to stop you being shot over the side. I've walked out from the metal island all too confidently—I'm much too close to the prow—it's a balancing feat to stay here and not to slide away. I'd like to get back but I can't move without sliding. Through eyes screwed up against the wind I peer at the end of the square deck curving downwards just a few feet away—the actual brink is out of sight below. The deck's dropping—where there was sky a moment ago, now there are waves. I'm still dropping and I look up at the dark sea stretching away into the distance. A wall of green water is rising above me. The deck's at a crazy angle. My feet are slipping. Oh God, I'm sliding towards the brink.

The deck's coming up again—reprieve—got to get back to the island. She's rolling a bit now—slope's increasing—being pitched outwards—no rails and menacing sea on my left. Can just balance. Managed to turn round—am climbing back to security—no hand or footholds—lines of rivets give more grip to my shoes than the wet metal plates.

Now, with the rising prow lifting me high into the air, I'm looking down the whole length of the great runway towards the stern. I feel much safer; there's such a long way to slide and plenty to grab on to at the end. There's a line of fat little American fighter planes down there: a dozen or more. I can see the taut ropes that lash them into position. Above them a churning wake flattens the wave tops away to the distant horizon. Moving forward down the runway with the force of the wind in my back I'm like a swimmer swept by the tide, but I'm crabbing steadily towards the island and safety. The black oval doorway that leads below looks very small at the base of the towering mountain of metal. The mountain itself slopes back in a series of horizontal platforms. On these platforms there are guns and there are men there!

Men—I'd quite forgotten about men! Wearing coal scuttle helmets, they are slung behind their weapons whose black muzzles are pointing skywards looking up the barrels of their guns, watching the sky, watchful against attack, unaware of my predicament down here. "You might please glance this way in case I need help"—but their heads do not move—the blurred grey clouds seem to spin round above them. Taking my oval doorway with it, the island lifts high into the sky. I'm climbing the fierce slope, carefully picking my way along each line of rivets—the gradient slackens—I'm walking normally—now, pitched straight into the open door, I grasp the metal and hold on tight.

I'm astonished that any one can come up from below and walk out on that perilous slide—if they went overboard the ship would not stop. This is war. The Americans are watching for submarines and enemy aircraft, not for fools like me.

As I climb the ladder back to the interior labyrinth I notice that my forearms and hands are trembling a little. I am reminded that this is not a Navy Week for children.

It's Sunday morning in the Mediterranean. I am standing on a narrow catwalk a few feet below the level of the flight deck. The fierce sun glares down out of the cloudless sky and a gentle breeze blows the smell of hot paintwork into my face. Today the flight deck is horizontal and flat, it has the solid security of a billiard table, it's dry metal plates are a pale yellow grey in the sunlight while a dark violet shadow lies motionless upon it. The shadow is cast by the metal superstructure whose gun platforms, funnel, masts and radar aerials are a dark silhouette, steady against the sky. Our carrier is moving forward across a brilliant blue sea and gay little waves come dancing diagonally from the hazy distance to greet us. The weight of our ship is quite indifferent to their welcome; the catwalk below my feet is of latticed steel and far below I can see the waves being turned aside—their happy porpoise-like flourishes are left behind as the water streams past—our shadow on the water races along with us and our bow wave breaks out of it into dazzling whiteness.

We came through the Straits of Gibraltar during darkness last night. We have left behind the cloud screen which saved us from the searching eyes of enemy reconnaissance aircraft in the Atlantic and our fleet of ships is now fully exposed as it rides deeper into enemy waters. In her usual station on the starboard bow, our battleship *Renown* is dipping and rising very gently, a faint wisp rising straight up above her funnel. Ahead of her is a cruiser and flung out fanwise in front of the fleet are three destroyers. Everyone is alert and if all goes according to plan we'll fly off our Spitfires at dawn tomorrow.

I suppose it's only natural to have a tingle of apprehension. A few minutes ago Squadron Leader Hughes, the R.A.F. engineering officer on board, who has been giving the Spitfires a final check, was up here taking the morning air and he assured me that we should have no mechanical trouble. I hope he is right. We've got to fly nearly seven hundred miles, as far as from London to Venice, and we're over the sea all the way; if any fault develops in the single engine we will have to come down without any hope of rescue. Hughes should know, indeed, he is a man with a reputation, for, on a previous reinforcement trip, he discovered a manufacturing fault in all the long range tanks: he would not let a single aircraft take off. Although the Admiral and the Captains were furious for having come so far in vain, Hughes would not yield; he thus became known as the junior officer who turned back the Fleet. I have just completed a pen drawing of him and I observed him closely: he certainly appears confident this time.

I have done two portraits this morning and the comparison between them was most interesting. Hughes was gay, even mischievous—but although he bears a considerable responsibility he can afford to be gay, for when we have taken off tomorrow the carrier will turn round and bear him home again to England. It is a strange coincidence that he's on board, for I first met him a year ago in Lincolnshire at the identical time and place where I met my wife. He thus represents my own happiness during the past year, he has become a symbol of the past, the last connecting link with home.

The other drawing was of Squadron-Leader Gracie. He is symbolical of the future. Gracie is the only man among us who has been to Malta,

and he looks like it. Our voyage and the fifty Spitfires in the hangar
are in many ways the result of his energies, for he was sent to London
by the Officer Commanding the R.A.F. in Malta to report on the desperate
condition of the island, to stir up trouble, and to bring back reinforcements
at any cost.

When I was drawing him I learned a few more facts about Malta.
I knew that the bomber force lay wrecked on the aerodromes, but I did
not know that in March alone over two thousand tons of bombs had been
hurled down upon the island; this is ten times the tonnage that fell on
Coventry during the Blitz. Not only this, but when Gracie left about
two weeks ago the rate of bombing had been trebled. Malta is now being
bombed at the rate of six thousand tons a month; it is Coventrated every
day, day after day. When he left there were only six serviceable fighters
left, not twelve as I had been told earlier. Now the situation is probably
worse.

"If you're lucky enough to fly," Gracie told me, "then you're generally
outnumbered forty or fifty to one."

The same facts as I knew already, but "lucky enough" indeed! I
stared at the man who had actually done this thing. A sad hunched figure
with the ribbon of the Distinguished Flying Cross. His face did not bear
his usual vigorous and forceful look, his expression betrayed his thoughts
as he looked towards the horizon. I followed his gaze. With the carrier
so steady and peaceful, and the blue sea so wonderful to look upon, it
seemed impossible to realise that beyond the horizon was dust and blood
and destruction. I wondered what the battle would be like, and I am still
wondering. The odds are fantastic. All that I feel is the impossibility
of survival for long.

None of the other pilots has a face like Gracie. They are much younger.
Watching them drinking coffee, reading books, playing dice or cards,
they don't seem to think about what lies ahead. Even when their faces
are relaxed they show no strain or apprehension. Frankly I wonder if
they have any imagination whatsoever—perhaps they are better off
without it. I only hope that I give the same impression of innocent
calmness.

Spiritually I feel dreadfully alone. Last night I went to see the Padre.
The visit was a great disappointment. I was told all the usual stuff
designed to make a fighting man fight. I was told that I should fight the
enemy because of his barbarity. I was told that this was a war to end wars;
that the future would be rosy and glorious, that a single state might soon
develop in which men would be bound together in friendship by modern
communications. I was not satisfied and asked more questions. God was
described to me as an invention of highly evolved man, as a crystallisation
of his more civilised feelings and values, but of God himself, and love,
and the dilemma of love in a world at war, the Padre did not talk.

Sadly I returned to my cabin. If I believed wholeheartily in war how simple and straightforward this life would be. If only the Padre could have helped me resolve the problem of how it is possible to fill the heart with grace yet to spatter the wriggling brains of a fellow human on to a rock at one and the same time. We are often told that God is on our side in war and against the other side—I just can't believe He makes any such choice. God is not in war—God is the still small voice that speaks to the heart. In the holocaust of war it is so difficult to hear Him.

What of tomorrow? I suppose I will have to fly with the same sorrow and solitude as I bear now. I know the details of how we are to get up at 3.45 a.m., breakfast at 4.15, have a final briefing at 4.45 in the wardroom, start our engines at 5.15 and take-off immediately afterwards, and I make one last prayer: I ask for continual realisation that all men, particularly my enemies, are innocent if they are doing their best to lead good lives, and that I may never, whatever the circumstances, hate.

PART TWO

MIDDLE DISTANCE

CHAPTER 4

MALTA BOUND

IT IS 5.15 a.m. on Monday, April the twentieth. Although I'm strapped into my Spitfire, with the bag containing my painting things squeezed under my left arm threatening to jam the throttle lever, I can feel the heaving and shuddering of the ship's engines racing more vigorously than they have ever raced before: our carrier must be moving at full speed so that the Spitfires, whose engines I can already hear roaring from the flight deck above, are able to take off. There goes the first, passing slowly across the space where a panel has been removed in the side of this huge hangar, a tiny aircraft low over the framed strip of dark water, almost invisible in the grey light of dawn. In the black tunnel of girders, stretching into the distance beyond my Spitfire's long nose, pools of electric green light reveal closely packed aircraft with many pilots still climbing in. Mechanics stand by their allotted positions, others are ducking hurriedly under metal wings and tail planes. Somewhere behind me an engine chokes then bursts into life, sending a cloud of blue smoke drifting over my head. More engines start.

Strapped tight I can't look round. Glancing into the mirror above my windscreen I observe that the Spitfire behind me, with the C.O. inside, is being wheeled backwards towards a great lift—a pause—then, with the propeller turning in a transparent arc, the perspective of his plane changes as it disappears bodily, the floor with it, up into the blackness of the girders. Down comes the lift again, and monkey-faced Scotty, one of our Australians, gives me a wide grin from the cockpit as his plane is dragged into it. Down comes the empty floor again, hungry for more machines and their pilots. Up goes Max. I am signalled to start my engine. It bursts into life. The lift with Max in it pauses in the roof, makes one gigantic swallow, then comes down again empty, this time for me.

Mechanics grab my wings. I am pulled backwards towards the lift. Last glimpse of the hangar as the floor heaves beneath me: propellers turning, people running, a red sack has been thrown on to the floor down there. My God! Someone must have walked into a turning propeller. I'm on the deck in white daylight. Clouds: sea: flight deck in front: the superstructure half-way down, right. A white-sweatered American mechanic, much closer, wearing goggles—a red skull cap on his head: a red skull cap: I must watch him. With his legs wide apart, he's bending forward like a rugger player, clenching his hands high in the air: I put on the brakes. His hands begin to rotate rapidly: I open the throttle. The engine is roaring, brakes are slipping; a checkered flag falls: release brakes, throttle wide open, gathering speed, tail up, looking over the nose: deck's very short. Going faster. The overhanging bridge on the superstructure sweeps towards me: pink faces, pink blobs with no features on them—quick, wave goodbye to the Americans! Grab the stick again—end of the deck. Grey waves. Keep her straight—stick back. Out over the sea. Waves nearer. Stick further back—at last she begins to fly. Gaining more speed. I now start climbing. I don't suppose any enemy pilot could see the battleship, just below on my right, as close as this and survive. Changing on to long range tanks I'm circling away to the left, climbing steadily—the engine does not falter—this is fine! With the ships looking like toys I take position well to the left of the C.O. while the other three Spitfires which I have to lead clamber into formation behind me.

As we set course towards the East the sun rises out of the sea, filling the whole of space with light.

We have been flying through turquoise and silver space for four hours with the long Mediterranean unwinding below us. For a time after climbing to ten thousand feet, the russet-coloured mountains of Algiers accompanied us, but finally they retreated into the haze. The sun, mounting higher, has been a blinding light in our eyes. I watched its reflection glistening in the ruffled surface of the sea. With nothing else to look at, I watched the strange patterns blown on the seascape by the wind, but then, about an hour ago, a sheet of white cloud extending below us obliterated the ocean. Because it hid some lumps of rock that should have been our first navigational check we didn't know we were off course. The wind must have blown us a hundred miles from our estimated position, for, as the clouds started to break up, the C.O. discovered that he was about to steer us along the north coast of German-held Sicily. He made a radio call to Malta for a course to steer but it must have been an enemy voice, loud and jeering, that answered. Glancing southwards, in which direction we had been ordered to fly, I saw the clouds draw back like a curtain to reveal an island, a brown conical hill, floating innocently on the blue water: it was Pantelleria, an enemy fighter base. That was a few minutes ago. We have been flying onwards in a south-easterly direction with our fuel levels sinking lower and lower, with a thousand miles of sea between us and Egypt, and I can believe the stories that pilots, flying this route by night, have been lured on to enemy aerodromes so that their transport machines and crews have been captured. The clouds have disappeared, empty sea stretches in all directions, but undoubtedly the most vivid impression made upon me by this flight has been caused by the metal bottle in my dinghy pack upon which

I am sitting. I am obviously developing a whale of a bruise for no matter how I squirm and wriggle in this tiny cockpit I can't get comfortable.

A disturbance of colour on the horizon is growing steadily nearer. From navigational logic it's just where I expected it to be. We are changing formation: each section of four aircraft has now become a tightly packed arrowhead. As the apex of the left hand arrow my outstretched eliptical wings are overlapped by other wings for three profile Spitfires are sliding downwards beside me. Two islands, like two autumn leaves floating on the water, grow larger and larger. The steep cliffs of the smaller and nearer, which must be Gozo with Malta lying beyond it, rush towards us. White walls crinkle a hilltop. The small fields are yellow. Blue water in front of my propeller and, as we cross the channel between the two islands, I can see the waves breaking on the sunlit rocks ahead. Now we are leaping inland over the island of Malta.

"All Balsam aircraft pancake as quickly as you can." That must be the controller. Damn it. I would like to have looked around our new home, for it is beautiful; we are passing over domes and towers, white blocks of houses huddled into villages, baroque churches all yellow and white against the rim of blue sea in the distance; jig-saw patterns of white walls, a few stunted trees, a craggy valley, now an aerodrome sweeps beneath our wings. That would be Takali. I beckon my flanking Spitfires still closer: I want to make the people down there feel proud of their reinforcements. We bounce with the speed of our dive as another aerodrome with runways swings into view. This must be Luqa to which we have been detailed so I give the order:

"Yellow Four—break. Yellow Section—break."

The pale undersides of my Spitfires leap sideways as I search the air for the landing queue. I'm approaching some steep hills clustered thick with buildings that protrude into the sea: it's a harbour and there's a ship down there, low in the water, smoke coming from it. Peering down on top of its fore-shortened black masts I look deep into its splintered hold: tiny flames are dancing in it: it's blackened with fire. Sweeping back in the direction of the aerodrome I glimpse a strange red cloud sloping up the sky: can't stop to wonder what it is because it is difficult to pick out the Spitfires in the landing queue: I can see their shadows flickering up and down over the hills and valleys. I count them as one by one they settle on the runway—my turn next. Reducing speed I slide back the perspex hood, lower the wheels and finally put down the flaps. The tilted runway, rushing forward, seems to engulf me. I level out gently and drop on to the careering dust and stones.

Leaving the glaring sunlight it is into pitch blackness that we feel our way down the steep steps, first to the left then to the right—here the narrow passage slopes straight down into the solid rock for several fumbling paces towards a single electric light bulb. Still sloping the passage zig-zags again, but it is better lit and refreshingly cool and damp. We pass batteries in niches and hear the whine of a transmitter; further down we pass an officer and some airmen working on typewriters; finally we enter a level cavern with grimy airmen seated on benches either side of it: an outpost of England, for in the far corner, next to a door marked "Strictly Private, Authorised Persons Only", there is an airman brewing tea.

I never expected to undergo our first Malta air raid in a place such as this, Station H.Q. referred to by the old hands as "G" shelter; I thought we would be flying, yet here we seat ourselves on vacant benches, experiencing the earthquake underground. Trying to balance my alarm at the unusual noises, I'm watching the pictures of undressed pin up girls glued to the rock above the airmen's heads, for, as the rock quivers, so these girls dance for us. The airmen are staring at me so I stare back at the airmen. Every time the cavern gives a convulsive shudder they grin at our bewilderment.

It was airmen like these who welcomed me at the end of my landing run about an hour ago. One leaped up beside my cockpit, shoved a happy sunburnt face close to my helmeted ear and yelled something. I watched the ginger whiskers round the sides of his chin and the silent movement of his cracked lips, but after being wedded to a roaring engine for hours I couldn't hear what he or the others who gathered round were saying. I took my time in climbing out and gradually the shrill singing in my ears died down.

"You've just missed the nine o'clock raid, sir," said one.

"We had a hundred bombers over here a few minutes ago," added another.

I smiled back at them but I wondered what it would be like to have a hundred bombers overhead when one's own aerodrome is the target. The red cloud leaning up the sky must have been bomb dust—I should have guessed.

The airmen opened up the gun panels in the wings of my Spitfire with a bayonet. I was staring with astonishment at the stuff I had been carrying in my aircraft—spanners, screwdriver, mosquito nets, long cellophane cartons of Camel cigarettes and not many bullets; then a dilapidated bus, filled with the other pilots, drew up to collect me. We set off with a crash of gears accelerating along a narrow roadway between high stone walls. The airman driver braked fiercely. We shot off our seats into a tumble of luggage. As he shrugged his shoulders I saw that the road was blocked by a mountainous heap of rubble. "Don't they even know the way round their own aerodrome?" I asked myself, but, as the bus backed violently in the direction we had come from, I remembered the air raid.

We finally arrived at the officers' mess, the sixth officers' mess, we were told, the other five having been flattened one by one. We gathered on the carpeted floor of the single room, the Dreaded Hugh and Ken talking with the C.O., with Pancho and quiet Cyril standing on the edge of the group; I watched Max and Scotty investigate the rickety furniture, then look out through the glassless windows, but, thirsty after our long flight, we were soon consuming drinks from the angled bar that crossed one corner of the room. We were chatting merrily when the air raid sirens screamed: my heart seemed to rise up inside me. I looked at the older inhabitants, lounging back in their armchairs, but they went on reading their papers. I was glad when a guide led us out from the porch and up the road. On our left, spilled from crevices between tumbled rectangular blocks of heavy stone, were tiny fragments of crushed glass; they glittered in the rubble like jewels. Our guide gestured towards the heap with the palm of his hand uppermost as if throwing something away.

"Doc O'Dowd's Sick Quarters," he explained, "his third sick quarters this week."

I heard the murmur of approaching engines, but the C.O. and the guide continued to lead our party over the pot-holes. The C.O. is a big man, very tall, very broad, I'm six foot and I look up at him; he's the kind of man who holds his head high and only looks down with his eyes; well, there he was glimpsing up at the Messerschmitt 109s which were turning in pairs over the aerodrome. "Oh, the Battle of Brit all over again," he proclaimed.

I wanted to run but I strode along beside him, a Flight Lieutenant apparently in no hurry. My heart was beating wildly as I listened to the other pilots who made taunting remarks about the circling Luftwaffe. At last and with considerable relief I saw we were approaching a shelter. But we passed it. We went on past crumbled buildings: I looked at the heavy stone blocks which had crushed black iron bedsteads into wriggling concertina shapes. I looked at unrecognisable wooden structures which had been wrenched into heaps of splinters. As we walked slowly up the hill, more and more 109s arrived in the sky. Feeling that something was about to happen I put on my tin hat.

"Oh, Denis," laughed the C.O., "you do look a sight in that."

I smiled. I felt most indignant. I kept it on.

As we continued I noticed an airman digging close beside a tiny red flag hammered into the side of the road. I turned to our guide for an explanation.

"He's digging for an unexploded bomb."

Having read of such heroes during the blitzes in England, I stared at this airman by himself just digging—I was secretly pleased when he smiled back at me but at that moment, from the top of a flat-roofed structure like a tall concrete garage ahead of us, a white light shot up and a red flag was

hoisted: "The Take Cover signal," gasped our guide, out of breath, as
we ran. At the side of the concrete structure was a grave of rubble
and the entrance to "G" shelter was at the end of this heap. We entered
the narrow doorway, filed down the steps into the dark, and here we are.

The door at the end of our cavern opens and the aerodrome controller
leans round it.

"Sixty bombers are diving on Takali—why not go up and watch the
fun?"

Back up the steep steps we climb. German planes, which I recognise
as Junkers 88 twin-engined bombers, are streaming down the sky in the
distance. Black bomb bursts gush back from the ground, huge globules
of smoke, heaving and bubbling, some of them rolling off long stalks like
mushrooms. Layers of them brood grotesquely over the network of
white walls, over villages that lie scattered over the scene like dice,
monstrous clouds rising higher and higher. It is quickly over: the
German planes have disappeared behind the curtain of destruction. The
bomb smoke slowly clears, leaving a more flimsy veil of red dust. I can
see many black pin points each with tall streamers of smoke spurting high
into the sky.

"Our new Spitfires burning on the ground," states an experienced
erk at my elbow.

It's our first evening here, quiet and colourful. We have boarded the
same bus as this morning with its sides splintered by bullets and cannon
shells and without glass in its windows; we have looked ahead, down past
the driver's back, into the valley below the aerodrome; we have set off
with the same crash of gears; over the rubble outside bombed sick
quarters and past the officers' mess. I had hoped to follow our route
carefully, and thus learn something of the geography of the island, but
my attention has been distracted by the fellow sitting next to me. This
old hand who is coming along for the ride, has been telling me where
we are going and who we are likely to meet.

We're on our way to Rabat, some town in the island, where the
Officer Commanding the R.A.F. here, Air Vice-Marshal Hugh Pugh
Lloyd is going to talk to us pilots who arrived today from the aircraft
carrier. My neighbour says that we'll like Hugh-Pugh and that we're
bound to meet Woody as well. Woody or Group Captain Woodhall,
is the senior Controller who conducts all the air battles from the Valetta
"Ops Room". I am told he's a "wizard" controller who has psychic
powers about what the enemy "little jobs" (fighters) and "big jobs"
(bombers) are going to do next. Although I'm looking forward to
meeting these senior officers I wish I could have kept track of our route.
I'm hopelessly lost. All I know is that we're somewhere in the valley.

In the front of our cabin our driver is wearing a khaki shirt and a round blue airman's hat tipped back onto the nape of his neck; as an organist sways so sways our driver as he drives, forwards and backwards, and over from side to side. He is steering our bus through a labyrinth amongst Maltese dwellings. The buildings have stone balustrades fringing their flat roofs and wrought iron balconies outside the upstairs windows overhanging the road. We are now squeezing our way through a narrow opening between bomb-spilt stonework stacked up each side of us. We have already passed through several places like this with the sides of the bus being scratched and scraped by the jagged rocks. The pilots behind me have been yelling advice to the driver; he has either taken no notice or looked back over his shoulder with a huge grin: this time the back-seat pilots have given up, for, despite the dust drifting in through the windows, they've started to sing.

What a bewildering day it's been; there was another air raid this afternoon. Before it started Max and I who happened to be in "G" shelter overheard a senior officer complaining that two Spitfires would have to be left on the ground. We looked at each other: after all, we were pilots—so we offered to fly them; we secretly liked the prospect of being the first of our Squadron to fly into action here. We were thus to operate as a pair and detailed to "aerodrome defence"—something to do with protecting the main force of Spitfires as they came in to land: a vital job; for the Spitfires, short of fuel and ammunition, are very vulnerable as they land and a special patrol of 109s inevitably arrives to shoot them down. Since we had no chance of asking questions, being ordered to get out to our machines at once, I assumed we should fly round and round the aerodrome attacking any 109s that came near. A Flight Sergeant called "Chiefy" told us that we would find one Spitfire in North Sigiewi Blast Pen and the other in the pen between E and F. Since we knew nothing of the layout of the aerodrome we persuaded him to make a sketch map on the back of an envelope. In a battered old Hillman car that was loaned to us, thus we set out. We went round the aerodrome three times but we couldn't find those planes. There were hundreds of sandbag or rock constructions called pens, built to protect aircraft, but none of them marked, most of them filled with wreckage, and when we did discover a complete Spitfire we found completely strange pilots in charge. They had never heard of E or F or North Sigiewi Blast Pen. They told us to "F . . . off". "We've waited for these bloody aeroplanes for weeks and weeks," they said, "and it's our Squadron that's going to fly them." Max and I looked at each other: the men of the main force we were going to protect were not being particularly helpful. Then, by sheer chance, we found one of the Spitfires. Leaving Max and feeling an ignorant fool, but nevertheless anxious to avoid any further wasted time, I drove back to "G" shelter to have more advice from Chiefy.

With his hands on his hips he looked at me scornfully, explained the map in greater detail, assured me that there was no other pilot in charge and that the airmen ground crew were waiting for me. I shot round the perimeter track faster than ever. I glimpsed the broken transport plane with its wings drooping in the centre of the aerodrome, raced past many other fascinating wrecks, gave the thumbs up signal to Max as I passed him and crested the dust-blown hilltop beyond which I had been told that I would find my Spitfire.

Safi valley lay ahead of me, a quiet area of sun-scorched grass in a hollow. On my left, beyond a hillside of stunted trees, up which low walls elbowed their way, there was a village, crowned by a domed baroque church, all saffron yellow with violet shadows, against the blue sky: it looked deserted: the buildings just stood there like broken teeth. On my right a craggy landscape rolled away to a distant escarpment of hills, while in the immediate foreground was a deep pit filled to over-flowing with the bones of wrecked aircraft. But there was something about the quiet valley ahead that made me lift my foot from the accelerator. The short dry grass stood motionless, while on the descending track in front of the bonnet, little heaps of powdered dust lay undisturbed; it was as if a figure stood in the middle of the track, raised its head slowly and stared at me. There was, of course, nobody there, the track was quite deserted.

I drove slowly into the valley. From the main track, narrow paths led across the grass to the sides of the valley where lines of sandbag pens resembled sentinel tombs. I stared at the blackened heap in each pen as I passed. In one I recognised the rounded shape of a wheel, wing tips flanked the melted metal in another, in another an oval fuselage had vomited the entrails of a bomber. I crept onwards but there was no one, absolutely no one there. Suddenly, in a pen, tucked into the trees at the bottom of the hillside, I saw my Spitfire. I pulled in towards its lonely shape and stopped; the dust blown up by my car drifted quietly past me. Standing beside the wing tip I shouted for the airmen. No answer. I didn't like shouting in the valley but it had to be done so I called loudly three times. Not even an echo. I waited just in case some airmen had heard me and were on their way back—but there was no movement in the silence. I looked round for the starter trolley which they should have brought—but it was nowhere to be seen. I don't believe they had even been there: there were no footprints in the dust, only my own tracks and the tyre marks stretching out behind my car. Wreckage and empti-ness, not even the whisper of the wind or the sound of a bird.

A sudden roar of planes: a Spitfire taking off turned steeply over-head; it was quickly followed by a second, a third and a fourth. I was watching them climb away towards the south-west in line abreast, battle formation, when the sirens wailed. There was another roar—Max starting up his engine. We were to operate as a pair—it would have been mad for him to go into the air alone without Malta experience: leaping into the car I accelerated wildly over the hill in pursuit of his taxying plane. The car went over on to the wheel rims as I swung round in front of his nose giving the scrub-out signal with my hands. It was a great relief to watch the tornado backwash from his propeller stop abruptly, a relief to greet his familiar figure climbing out; I was suddenly aware of engine noises in the sky: clouds of bombers were approaching. I experienced a vivid mental picture of high explosive bursting all round the Spitfire so hopelessly exposed in the open: we had to push it back to its pen. The two of us heaved desperately but it was too heavy; then I spotted an airman watching us.

"Come on, man, come and push," but he was sleepy, or bewildered or both, "at the double," I yelled, putting an edge of command on my voice.

The three of us strained at the wings. We only had to go a few yards. But the aeroplane would not move.

"Are the brakes off?" I yelled at Max.

As he leaped to the cockpit to check I was aware of six Ju 88s poised in the sky. The brakes were off but a second glimpse upwards revealed ten more 88s. As we pressed our shoulders at the curved metal the anti-aircraft defences opened up, buffers of pressure cushioned our ears and live black spots appeared amongst the oncoming planes. As the barrage spread and smeared I noticed still more bombers while the leading machine with slow inevitability started to slide down towards us. We bent our backs against the wing in one final exasperating effort but the Spitfire remained blocked on one wheel.

From this bus, lurching its way past Maltese buildings in the secure quiet of the evening, it is strange to piece together the events that followed: I could have won a medal or a severe reprimand for being a damned fool, but much more humiliating was the emotion that triggered off my actions.

"Where's the nearest shelter?" I called. The airman raced away over some rocks behind a broken hangar. Within a few seconds he was descending into a vertical black hole into the earth.

"What's this?"

"A well, sir."

"Get in then . . . if you want to." I added as an afterthought.

In an instant the horror of possible entombment had overwhelmed me: the idea of compressed burial deep underground without anyone knowing where we were terrified me. I preferred to take my luck with the high explosive. I even remembered my duty as a Flight Commander not to leave a Spitfire in the open—although I don't know what good I could have done in the few seconds before the bombs struck.

"Come out quickly when you see me coming back," I called to the half swallowed figures as I ran back to the car, "I'll bring more men from 'G' shelter."

The crash of gunfire, the sharp blast of exploding bombs and the reek of smoke are blurred in my memory for, as I plunged the car flat out across the centre of the aerodrome, my attention was riveted upon the race of grass immediately in front of the bonnet and the already familiar building in the distance. About half-way across the totally exposed ground I realised what I was doing. There was a clatter of machine guns just above my head, much louder than the avalanche of bomb clouds that sprang up beside me, tossing the car. I crouched over the steering wheel, swerved to miss some newly-thrown up rocks and watched "G" shelter drawing nearer and nearer. I skidded to a standstill in front of its entrance and leaped down the shelter steps, but "at all times save petrol, it is precious"— some order that someone had given us—hammered in my head and with annoyance I remembered that I'd left the engine of the car running. My muscles ached as I leapt back up the steps to the bombing again. I opened the car door. I turned off the ignition. Holding the ignition keys in my hand I asked myself if there was any danger of anyone stealing the car. I decided that there wasn't, so quite deliberately I put the keys back. "Madman, get into the shelter!" My automaton legs obeyed the strange order inside my head. I found myself half falling, half tumbling, my legs buckling beneath me as I crumpled down the stairs. The blurred rock walls seemed to dance as I burst into the cavern: everyone was sitting motionless, heads turned, mouths open. A thunderclap roar in our ears; white dust burst from the walls; the cavern filled with smoke: we'd been hit.

When it was all over we staggered up into daylight: lumps of rock, large and small, knives of bomb casing, both jagged and curly, and the squashed relics of the Adjutant's bicycle lay scattered around. Max reported that the Spitfire had not been hit after all, but I was in trouble. "You bloody fool, why didn't you put the car in the concrete blast pen?" the old hands cursed at me.

The car had weathered the raid fairly well: admittedly the tyres were in shreds, the side wings all twisted up. The windscreen, opaque like milk and flimsy to touch, had great holes in it where pieces of bomb casing had passed through it, through the front seats, embedding themselves in the seats at the back. I must have looked miserably bewildered for the Dreaded Hugh, playing with the ignition switches, started to laugh.

"Don't worry, old man," he said, "the car still works."

We had a similar raid later, but now our bus is emerging from the Maltese buildings and swinging sharp left on to the first main road we've seen. We accelerate along the main road with new freedom, faster and faster over the tarmac which shines like a mirror and is gorgeously smooth. The air, blustering through the large window frame at the front of the bus, makes my eyes water. My cheeks, damp with streaming tears, are deliciously cool in the wind. Max, just in front of me, is pressing his heavy body hard up against the rattling wooden frame of the bus with his left arm curled through the side window; his right arm is stretched along the back of the seat. Scotty sits next to him, alert and tensioned, his short little figure bolt upright and bouncing.

The rocks plunging past along the side of the road are all blurred but the fields and rock walls in the middle distance moving past more slowly, are relaxing in the reflected light from the sky. It is dusk. Although the landscape is quietly darkening it is still luminous with colour. The pale walls, flushed with pinks and yellows, are violet in the shadowy parts, while the ground, the grass, or whatever crops are passing, are grey: it's an endless succession of exquisitely varied greys; blue-grey, green-grey, brown-grey, one after another, even a yellow-grey at times, only the purple hills ahead of us stand still.

The road is beginning to curve round and sweep upwards towards the nearest hill: our bus begins to labour and lose its momentum. I assume that the small but ancient walled city that is poised high above the road, on the steep brink of the hill, is our destination. Looking to our right the hill slope is more gentle but, about half a mile away, it has been cut by an artificial cliff with five huge caverns carved into it. The ground this side of the caverns is unnaturally flat. I can see some dispersal pens and a Spitfire's propeller sticking up: this must be Takali aerodrome, which we flew over this morning.

Amongst the wreckage there's a most exciting ruin swinging along the side of the road towards us: a very tall bombed house that's simply refused to collapse. Its outside walls have crumbled revealing the inside compartments; these compartments, like the inside of a card house, rise upwards for three stories to be capped by a steep pitched roof with a few slates still on.

"What a subject for a drawing!" I exclaim to the old hand.

"Yes, 'The Mad House'," he answers, "a good symbol of Malta."

I am standing up watching, for, as the ruin passes our bus, it seems to rotate like an exhibit of modern sculpture—but my twisting antics seem to be disturbing everyone. . . .

"Denis, for God's sake sit down," says the C.O.

The bus is struggling up an even steeper gradient between shadowed hundred-foot bastions—already I have to look steeply upwards to see the city. I glimpse the top of a fine baroque church foreshortening towards the pale sky; in the centre of its warm stone tower there is an open arch, a rich orange curve, voluptuously smooth yet crisply hewn like a young girl's lip. Alas but a glimpse, for in bottom gear, we are jerking our way up a very steep hill enclosed by bastion walls—it is a place of echoes, hammering engine echoes—I can hardly hear what my companion is shouting at the side of my ear.

This is Rabat and he's telling me its history. It was called Melita in Roman times. Saint Paul stayed here after he was shipwrecked on the island. I can hardly believe that this is the actual spot about which a companion of Saint Paul wrote: "In the same quarters were possessions of the chief man of the island, whose name was Publius; who received us and lodged us three days courteously. And it came to pass that the father of Publius lay sick of a fever and of a bloody flux: to whom Paul entered in, and prayed, and laid his hands on him and healed him. So when this was done others also, which had diseases in the island, came, and were healed." This is where Publius lived and where he was converted to Christianity. This is where the earliest-founded Christian church in the world was erected over his house, where the baroque church of St. Paul, that I have just glimpsed, now stands. This city of Melita was the capital in Roman times, it was the Arab capital when they came here in the seventh or eighth century. The Arabs built these bastion fortifications through which we are climbing and they changed the city's name to M'dina. Later it was Citta Notabile when the Spaniards ruled the island but the capital was moved from here in the early sixteenth century: the island was given to the Knights of Saint John of Jerusalem. The Knights, who were themselves besieged in Malta, built Valetta, the harbour that I glimpsed from the air, and this city became Citta Veccia, the old city. Why the R.A.F. call it Rabat my companion hasn't the faintest idea.

We are now turning a hairpin bend at the very top of the incline. I look back down the roadway: it descends steeply down the gorge and trails away across the central valley of the island like a snail track, foreshortening into the distance and glistening amongst the fields and stone walls, all dark and damp in the late evening mist.

The encircling walls close about us, our bus pushes its way across a crowded market place, the driver makes impatient noises on the horn as groups of laughing people move good-naturedly to one side, we cross a narrow bridge, pass under a tall arch into darkness and draw up in the courtyard of a palace.

I stand beside the bus. I look up at the massive silhouette of the palace wings that surround us; proud stone, golden in colour despite its shadowed darkness, a powerful contrast with the cold blue of the evening sky. We enter a hall. This black dampness is not what I expected after glimpsing the pediment curling to a sculptured coat of arms above the door. This palace is enshrouded with history. There was once austere luxury here with Spanish grandees wearing plate ruffs, black armour and rapiers, passing to and fro with wide-skirted ladies, a symphony of red and silver. It is now a vault, with the musty pressure of the walls heavy upon us. With my hand on the cold marble baluster rail I stand watching the pilots climb past me up the wide flight of stairs. I listen to the echo of their footsteps. I watch their shadows, cast by a single hurricane lamp, trespassing diagonally along the walls and creeping silently over the richly ornamented and painted ceiling. As I follow them I am obsessed by the weight of this building, I visualise how the gigantic blocks of stone would hurtle down upon us if a bomb fell. Now, pushed forward in the stream of men along the landing, committed to a long corridor in a strange building towards an unknown room, I stare at the panelling on each heavy wooden door that we pass: if I should open one and step forward would I plunge into a cavernous space already carved by a bomb?

We enter a narrow room filled with pilots chattering together and taking their places for the A.O.C.'s talk. Close to the heavy mahogany table in the centre they are seated or standing, but further back against the walls they appear to be raised up; whatever they have climbed upon is hidden beneath the moving patterns of knees and legs, tilted heads and gesturing arms and hands. The wall opposite is pierced by two deep window recesses backed by closed shutters; there is a pilot already seated in the left hand recess but the one opposite me is vacant: a safe place; I am glad I have reached it: falling masonry would tumble either side of me.

Is it quite stupid to imagine a bomb hitting us? Is it selfishly ignominious to yield to this compelling desire for my own safety? Perhaps it is; but the opposite alternative immediately presents itself: should I flaunt apprehensive warnings of being buried by stone? Should I scorn common sense and take no precautions at all? If I am going to live through the Malta bombing I must use my intelligence, but, at the same time, if I am going to do the job that I've come here to do, I shall have to keep my imagination in strict control.

I smile across the room at other pilots whom I knew by sight on the aircraft carrier, but there are many old hands here as well—I might have met some of them elsewhere in Fighter Command. Good Heavens there's Peter! I haven't seen Peter for almost six months. I never knew he had been sent to Malta. He's seen me too. I watch him closely as we both scramble down from our perches to meet in the centre of the room: how strange it is to see him in khaki shorts; I never knew he had such thin legs, his funny sharp nose and his pointed elfin chin thrust forward with determination are just the same. We clasp hands, but, alas, I learn all too quickly that there's no chance of operating together for he flies from Takali.

"How are the short stories going?" I ask him.

"I'm collecting lots of material," he tells me. "And you?" he asks. "I suppose you brought your paints?"

"Yes; I want to draw the Mad House."

"So you've seen our Château, you'll have to hurry up then, the Germans are just as intrigued by it too. There's not much left of the oriental garden and another large lump came off the building today."

"What's the history of the place, Peter?"

"Well, that's a *long* story, but, briefly, it was built by an old couple to remind them of their honeymoon spent in the Rhineland. A strange couple who must have travelled far and wide for every room is decorated in a different style."

As I listen to Peter's soft voice I find myself awaiting with excitement the unabridged "Story of the Mad House" for he is a writer of great promise, indeed, although only eighteen years old when the war started, he was already on the staff of *The Times*. He is telling me that there are two other pilots from our first squadron here in the room, so, with a promise of some beer together after the A.O.C.'s talk, I move through the crowd of pilots to find them.

Stan Grant was a Flight Commander in the old days and now he's a Squadron Leader. Standing in front of me in his immaculate uniform, yet leaning back away from me with his arms folded, he seems vaguely amused that I've become a Flight Commander myself. Johnny Plagis has now joined us, thinner and taller than I remember him, rounded in the shoulder with a peculiar heaviness. With his hands deep in his pockets he stares sideways at me—a penetrating but unfathomable expression in his pale eyes: I think he expects me to be a killer and resents the fact that I'm not. Strange that I taught him the rudiments of combat flying when he first joined a squadron: now he stands beside me as the skilled Malta pilot and I am the new boy.

I ask them about this morning's raid on Takali, and after an uncomfortable silence that makes me feel that to ask about other people's raids is a breach of island etiquette, I learn that Takali is a shambles, that two good friends of theirs were killed, and that fourteen of the new Spitfires were destroyed or damaged. Fourteen of them? If these figures are true it means that in this first day a third of our reinforcements has been wiped out.

Sudden silence: all the pilots are standing up.

"Sit down, gentlemen."

It is the A.O.C., pausing in the doorway, as everyone settles into their places. My own selected position in the window recess has been taken, so after all I have to stand in the middle of the room.

Air Vice-Marshal Lloyd, C.B., M.C., D.F.C. is now standing behind the table with his arms folded in front of him looking at us. So this is Hugh-Pugh, or Hughie-Pughie as I have heard him called. Medium height and thick set, he looks a picture of confident strength. There's something fatherly about his grey hair, unique in a room full of young pilots: I find myself experiencing the same emotions of respectful affection that senior officers often arouse in me.

I look at his hat lying on the table in front of him: this hat with Air Vice-Marshal rank manifested in the double encrustation of gold leaves on its peak, really is an intimidating barrier between us. As I stare Hugh-Pugh's hand pushes the hat slowly to one side. He leans over the table, looks down, places his finger-tips very lightly on its polished dark surface, looks up again and begins his address.

"I think, gentlemen, that the Germans have welcomed you in a far more striking manner than I could do myself.

"I know the Germans. I fought against them in the last war. I'm fighting them again in this; they're the same lot, cowardly and bullies."

I can hear a faint, rushing, whispering sound, somewhere in the distance. Low down, behind the palace, but in the air nevertheless, and growing nearer. Everyone is listening, even the A.O.C. Whatever is it? The sound is like a thousand old-fashioned aeroplanes with strutted wings and criss-crossed bracing wires, all in densely packed formation diving towards us, all varieties of sound intermingled with a roar as if from one huge approaching engine. Rushing louder it is dropping towards the roof like an express train. I know what the noise must be. There's nothing else it could be—but it's all too soon to die.

I watch our Commander raise his head and follow the track of this hellish din across the ceiling. The first deafening explosion is . . . outside.

As if a tight spring that has held us has snapped: we all start forward; hands push me from behind. Just as suddenly we check ourselves and sway back. The window shutters have burst inwards, and now, as if beyond the bounds of all possibility, there is a second explosion nearer.

More bombs coming; nothing we can do; I resign myself for the final explosion; in this moment which is stretched out in infinite length I endeavour to still my racing heart and achieve communion with God. The sweet serenity is so quickly bestowed that my bowed heart swells in gratitude and love. I am as a starving man in a cold stone cell, yet I have been given a banquet to share with everyone here. I bless all my companions as the explosions continue. I watch the flagstones, wide and flat, leaping in pebbled detail on the floor, I am aware of an ancient supporting arch somewhere far below reaching up towards us from the virgin rock. It is but a quivering sensation of still having life: then silence.

"As I was saying," continues the A.O.C., "the Germans are bullies, and incredibly foolish—the manner in which they are conducting their offensive against the island shows us that."

What's the matter with the German offensive anyway? It's damned efficient only we're on the business end of it. Why don't we disperse:

sixty pilots could be wiped out in here by one bomb? I realise that the
A.O.C. prefers absolute calm. This panic just has to be borne and controlled. The A.O.C. is continuing and I must listen.

"You are here to shoot down his bombers. To make it easier for you
we are going to hit the Hun where it hurts him most. Ten Wellingtons
will arrive here after dark tomorrow evening. They will go out twice
or three times every night for the next three months and bomb their
fighters on the ground. We will not see any great results at once, the
effect will be cumulative.

"You must remember that Malta's main role is an offensive one, to
destroy the enemy shipping and to cut his supply lines. You must remember that in Malta we are all one team. Malta is like the famous statue of
Achilles in Hyde Park, London. Our bombers, torpedo-carrying planes
and submarines are our striking power, like Achilles' sword. Our sword
has been blunted but we will sharpen it. Until then Achilles must rely
on his shield. The anti-aircraft defences and you pilots flying your
Hurricanes and Spitfires are that shield; Malta relies on you.

"The odds are very great over the island for the Germans have more
than five hundred machines in Sicily and you have considerably less than
fifty. You must, however, achieve air superiority. Sooner or later, and
probably much sooner than you think, we must bring in another convoy.
You know what happened to the last one. Only three merchant ships
got through. Of these one was sunk at the entrance to Grand Harbour
and the other two were sunk before they could be unloaded. This must
not happen again. Not only are supplies for our war machine critically
low, but the remaining stocks of food on the island are very short indeed.
Without another convoy we will starve. Whether or not we achieve
this convoy is up to you.

"One last word: in the future you will look back on your time spent
on Malta and you will feel proud you were here.

"Good luck."

Rhodesia, November 1940. Pilot Officer Denis Barnham with his new 'wings' at the Advanced Training Squadron at Cranbourne, near Salisbury.

Biggin Hill, August 1941. Denis with fellow Spitfire pilots of 609 Squadron, which was at that time an international squadron with a high proportion of Belgian pilots. Left to right: Fl. Lt. François de Spirlet, Fl. Off. Giovanni Dieu, Denis and Fl. Off. Roger Malengreau.

London, November 1940. Diana Frith, the future Mrs Denis Barnham, in her ATS uniform (the Auxiliary Territorial Service was the forerunner of today's Women's Royal Army Corps).

Lincolnshire, 24 January 1942. Denis and Diana on the day of their marriage at St. Andrew's Church, Redbourne. Denis carried a copy of this photograph in his flying jacket for the rest of the war.

Biggin Hill, August 1941. Denis is 'captured' by a photographer from the Ministry of Information who visited the station to take photographs of the pilots of 609 Squadron while they waited at readiness between operational sweeps.

At sea, April 1942. Denis, wearing tropical uniform, with sailors and fellow airmen on the USS *Wasp* en route to Malta.

Port Glasgow, April 1942. Spitfires of 601 and 603 Squadron being loaded aboard the USS *Wasp* at Greenock Docks.

Malta, May 1942. Denis in the cockpit of his Spitfire. The aircraft is being refuelled by hand with 4-gallon petrol tins owing to the lack of bowsers, all of which have been destroyed. In this period, in order to maintain constant readiness, the pilots and ground crews were living in their 'pens' with meals being brought out to them.

Malta, May 14 1942. Ju88 M7+CH, shot down by Denis and Plt. Off. Bruce Ingram, burns on Takali airfield.

Malta, May 1942. Left to right: John Bisdee, Denis and Mike Le Bas, an Argentinian volunteer with 601 Squadron. John was Denis's CO in 1941 when the two of them were with 609 Squadron, and he arranged for Denis to be transferred to 601 as one of his flight commanders when he was appointed to command the squadron in March 1942.

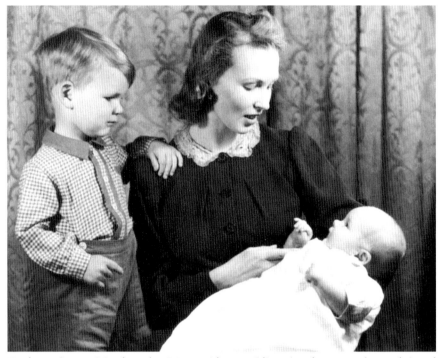

Fetcham, Surrey. March 1947. Diana with sons Oliver (aged 2 years, 4 months) and Michael, who has just arrived.

1956. Denis and Diana.

England, June 1944. Denis sketching. At this stage of the war he was flying operationally and concurrently working as an official war artist. Some of his military paintings can be seen today at Hendon Air Museum and at the Imperial War Museum.

1955. Denis and pupils in the Art Room at Epsom College.

1970. Denis in a typical informal pose – cigarette in hand, and surrounded by paintings.

CHAPTER 5

FIRST DAY

AFTER the A.O.C.'s talk our airman driver plunged our delapidated bus, without lights, down from the M'dina hill top, through a nightscape of peculiar silhouettes and delivered us outside the palace of another hill top town, called Naxxar. By the light of hastily struck matches we groped around for our luggage in the square hall which smelt of cooking fat and drains. We felt our way up the stone staircase before Scotty made a discovery: half a burnt candle. In an oasis of light we moved as a body through shadowed staterooms, picking our way carefully between the huddled sleeping shapes that covered the floor. As empty beds were found the C.O. allocated them to individual pilots, until, finally, there were only three of us left. The Dreaded Hugh and I, as the two Flight Commanders, were accommodated in a small room in the outside corner of the palace, before the C.O., wishing us a silent good night, took the candle and crept away, searching for a bed for himself.

Amongst the bedclothes I lay horizontally vulnerable wearing my tin hat. All night long it went on. I tried to control myself as stick after stick of bombs shrieked overhead. Abrupt and terrible crashes tossed the palace. Silence was of exquisite purity, between avalanches of sound. Heavy anti-aircraft guns, sited nearby, spoke in fury: prolonged echoes roared amongst the hills, fading gradually to be cut short by fainter gun crashes or bomb rumbles in the distance. There was almost continuous droning and gushings of air; gun flashes and bursting high explosive alternately lit up the façade of the golden church on the far side of the road or revealed its proud silhouette just outside the window. I lay as a creature hypnotised. I clutched at the sheets and stared in terror at the flickering line of jagged knuckles on the back of my hands.

Dawn gave us a brief respite: as we ate our breakfast once again the bombs screamed and the palace shuddered.

Yesterday we arrived here, now, mid-morning on Tuesday, April 21st, we are in "G" shelter waiting to play our part in the battle. Squadron-Leader Gracie appears in the narrow entrance at the end of the cavern: he and his parachute seem to be stuck there: bursting through he tossed his 'chute on to one of the wooden benches, then turns and glares at us.

59

"Just shot down two 88s," he snaps; "they fell in the sea in formation."
Fifty Spitfires the A.O.C. said, but most of the Spitfires are already
out of action, some shot down, others damaged, even Gracie's machine
will have to be repaired before it flies again. On our aerodrome there
are three left. The C.O. and I, as the two most experienced pilots of
our Squadron and anxious to get going, ask Gracie to take us up on the
next raid. He agrees. We are committed now!

Overwhelmed by my ignorance of how to fight against odds of thirty
or forty or fifty to one, I stare at Gracie for he is obviously brilliant at
air fighting.

"Sir," I ask him, "what are the best tactics to use?"

Gracie stares at me: I shrivel inside for I'm aware that my question
is hopelessly broad and vague.

"You'll learn," he replies, "but don't go chasing the b . . .s all the way
to Sicily."

"If we are separated from you, with formations of 109s around, what's
the best technique then?"

The C.O. and I both lean forward to listen.

"If you're by yourself weave around at nought feet all over the island,
or better still do steep turns in the middle of Takali aerodrome, inside
the ring of Bofors guns . . ."; he pauses as if surprised at his own advice,
"but don't take any notice of their fighters, it's the big boys we've got
to kill."

"My Spitfire's here," he says, prodding a map of the aerodrome with
his thumb. "Yours," he continues, glancing up at the C.O., "is there,
and yours, Barnham, is up the other end, there.

"Barnham; you'll have to taxi up the runway while I'm taking off
down it, so keep over to your left: I'll take off on the right. Scramble
on two red Very lights."

That seems crazy to me: if I taxi up the runway on the left and he takes
off on the right, we'll have a head-on collision, but Gracie is impatiently
gathering together his flying kit. Blast the take off then, it'll probably
sort itself out.

I attract his attention again: "With the Ju 88s in heaped formation
their return fire must be pretty concentrated—what's the best way
through it?"

"Return fire? Ignore it. Come on, let's get out there."

The C.O. and I each grab parachutes and pursue him up the rock steps.
Gracie is quickly in the driving seat of a Dodge car with its engine
running. The C.O. jumps in front beside him and I climb in the back
on top of the parachutes. This is a mad drive round the perimeter track,
but, bouncing wildly, I'm intrigued by the wavelets of curling dust
flowing out each side of the car. Gracie brakes fiercely and stops: I hand
the C.O. his flying kit. As he steps back Gracie accelerates, past where

Max's Spitfire was yesterday, past the road leading down into the remote valley of Safi and pulls up beside a rock dispersal pen with a dark blue Spitfire in it for me. Hardly have I removed my kit before the Dodge car is disappearing in a cloud of dust.

Left alone in the silence I breathe deeply and look up at the intense blue sky; after all, there may be lots of time before the raid comes in. Looking around I notice three airmen in khaki shorts coming out from behind the Spitfire to greet me.

"It's a good mount, this one, you'll like it sir."

"Mind you bring it back, sir," says the second airman, "the pilot 'oo was 'ere yesterday's 'ad it. We moved this Spit across this mornin'. It's usually a lucky pen, this one."

The third airman with a long bristly face and carrying some black material over his arm doesn't say a word, his round eyes just stare.

"Don't mind Claude 'ere, sir," I am told, "'e's goin' round the bend. 'E's lost 'is screwdriver."

Claude smiles as he offers me a black flying-suit that someone must have left behind. I have never worn a flying-suit in a Spitfire, but I remember as a boy, with my heart full of thrilling sensations, watching the suited pilots climbing into their biplane fighters at the Hendon Flying Display, so I accept the gift and in putting it on feel that I am substantiating another childhood dream.

This corner of the aerodrome is delightful: a tree, from which strange long beans are hanging down, leans over the rock pen enclosing my Spitfire. Its leaves throw a pleasant shade onto some smooth ground where the airmen have been sitting. The tree frames the Spitfire in such a splendid way that I decide to do a drawing.

A faint report from the far side of the aerodrome makes me look round: two red lights are descending through the air above "G" shelter. No time for drawing—Scramble. In the cockpit, I wriggle my head into my new tropical flying-helmet, long tentacles of flame pour from the exhaust ports: the engine coughs into life; clouds of dust spread out behind me as I swing out of the pen onto the rock-strewn road, racing towards the runway.

I am strangely happy: the blue-grey metal of the curved wings sticking out each side of me look good against the delicate colours in the passing brown grass; the mechanical fumes from the engine and the sight of all the ticking instruments are familiar friendly things. Smiling inside my oxygen mask I look across towards a group of Maltese workmen sitting on a rock wall, for, as I turn my Spitfire onto the runway, they stand up and stare back at me. Why do they stand up? A salute to all our pilots perhaps? Bless them anyway. I give them a wave.

Taxi on the left of the runway was what Gracie said. Watch out though: that man's crazy. Swinging my Spitfire from side to side I search diligently: that tiny aircraft trailing a dust plume in front of "G" shelter must be Gracie. The C.O.'s machine is converging from my right. As he crosses onto the runway so his propeller blows a huge dust cloud back at me; dust spiralling above me into the sky, fiery in the sunlight like debris from a volcano: I can't see a thing. From out of the dust—a Spitfire, rushing head on at me along the ground. Swinging my machine off the runway violently over the rubble, the grass and the bumps, I glimpse Gracie's angry eyes. His aircraft was gigantic, but we haven't collided: this Malta is really a mad and wonderful island!

The C.O.'s Spitfire is passing most discreetly on the other side of the runway, tail up for take-off. At last, aware of the general direction in the dust clouds, I swing round and open the throttle wide; gathering speed more and more quickly, and sweeping into the air. Wheels up and a steep turn to see where the others have got to. The landscape floods wide around me: beautiful, beautiful to see the hills and roof tops and churches again, but this is war, down there the sirens must be wailing.

We are climbing higher into a rusty purple void: in all this haze I can't see the island or the sea, only the two Spitfires ahead of me and the glaring Cyclopian eye of the sun staring down at us. Fifteen thousand feet, still in haze—Gracie turning left. I follow in a long stern chase as we dive back in the direction we've come from. I stare through the windscreen at Gracie's tiny Spitfire closely followed by the C.O.'s, both turning slightly right in the distance. In front of the two retreating planes a faint brown trace of the island with bursting anti-aircraft shells is looming towards us. Gracie steepens his dive, continues turning. We are plunging vertically but I can see no enemy planes.

There they are—Ju 88s, top plan view, five, seven, ten, twenty, thirty. No time to count. Still more appear, all sweeping closer. All sizes, extending in depth downwards like fishes in a tank; some very close, some far away below. Take one near the bottom. My Spitfire shudders as I fire two bursts of cannon into a cluster of bombers that get in the way. May have hit one. Can't stop to look. My target is wheeling nicely into position. Ahhhhh! A huge part of a Ju 88, nose and engines, flashes out from under my left wing: must have been right on top of him! Gone now. Easing gently out of my dive, watching my graceful target flying backwards towards me, larger and larger in my gun-sight. Quick search in all directions: lots of 88s but no enemy fighters. Target's wings overlapping my windscreen—I fire. A flash and a burst of smoke from his port engine. He rears up in front of me, steep turning left. Dash the man! Deflection inside his turn. Can only just do it. Fire again. He's swerving to the right. Try for his starboard engine. Fire again and again.

Black smoke puffs on my left wing; balls of orange fire flashing past my cockpit, crackling in my ears. I plunge left, looking back over my left shoulder, for who the hell's hitting me? Nothing there—just an 88 hanging behind my tail. Can't be him. Swerve back again. My own 88 has drawn away a bit; a pretty thing splaying two plumes of smoke that widen as they sweep back towards me, very pale machine and very close to the water. I wonder if it's going to crash?

109s! Two, head-on views, diving from my left, blinking with light. Curling blue tracers strand about me as I turn towards them. A third— got my sight on him for an instant before he went under my nose. Still turning hard left. My helmet's too big for me. Turn pressure pulls it over my eyes. Can't see. Stupid. Push it up and straighten out: that's better. Two more 109s, from the right this time. Turn in towards them. Curl down on the last one. Can't turn sharply enough. Damn the helmet! Another 109 below me. Drop on to his tail. I'll get him all right. A gigantic shape, all rivets and oil streaks, the underside of a Messerschmitt, blots out the sky! Gone. But I'm still on a 109's tail, it's right there in front of me, pointing very slightly downwards. My air-craft shudders and shudders and shudders and shudders as I pour bullets and shells into it. It bursts with black smoke and topples over sideways.

More 109s from the right. Turn. My Spitfire vibrates violently and the sea changes places with the sky. I'm spinning. Opposite rudder and stick forwards—I'm level again. Two more from the right. Once again my Spitfire flicks upside-down. Steep cliffs, and yellow ground hang above my head with black clouds among the buildings there—bombs bursting? Corrective action was immediate, for I'm the right way up once more. Bang! Explosion from my engine—smoke bursting back into the cockpit. Upside down, spinning again. Cliffs very close. Controls don't answer. All gone slack. Can't stop spinning. . . . Spitfire burning . . . out of control. Too low to bale out? Might just make it. Bale out quickly.

But everything is going so slowly, oh so slowly. I can see my right hand coming up gradually towards my helmet to throw it off; I can see my left hand in front of my face, trying to unfasten my oxygen mask which is clamped tightly over my nose and mouth. I watch my fumbling fingers trying, and trying and trying again, to find out where the metal hook is placed. I seem to be slowly saying to myself, oh so very slowly: "You'll have to hurry up, Denis old chap, there's so very, very, little time." But it's no good: I just can't undo all these pipes and wires. I'm too low now. No hope now—can't avoid it: going to be killed.

The scene is strangely peaceful, for unconcerned and apparently un-implicated, I am outside my aeroplane looking back at my body. In front of me is the wing tip, but my attention is drawn back along the upper surface of the wing, back over the painted roundel, to the wing root where the light is shining; above the wing root is the cockpit; within the perspex canopy I can see my own helmeted head with my arms encircling it in such a strange manner! I'm so interested in watching my body over there that I have but a faint impression of the aeroplane's long nose trailing horizontal smoke against a background of dark sea.

Pressure! Controls do respond. Hope. Not going to be killed after all. Smoke's not bad. 109s? Pretend I'm crashing—might leave me alone. Diving, deliberately lurching, down, down, down to white surf at the foot of the cliffs. Rolling sideways I look back at the enemy planes: 109s high up behind me, watching, and, I hope, convinced by my trick. Cliffs towering above me—climb quickly. Sweeping upwards over the cliff brink—the Malta landscape reappears. Another huge burst of smoke from the engine—smoke now pouring from the cowling covers just in front of my windscreen. Throttle dead. Engine dead. 109s after me. Ignore them—got to put this plane down somewhere—but where? Where?

Sinking I drop my left wing: patterns of walls—fields much too small— I'd crash horribly. Searching desperately I drop the right wing. Worn tracks where aircraft have taken off—an aerodrome! Turning and sinking I'm much too close to it. Side-slipping with stick fully back, full top rudder and the wings and body shuddering and shaking, the brittle skeletons of what must once have been huge hangars rush up to meet me. Am landing down wind—overshooting—far walls will break me to bits—no wheels then—belly landing. Turning over the broken hangar, I tighten up the straps—don't want to bash my brains on the gun sight— but floating, still floating—aerodrome shrinking—walls coming—rudder away from that bomb hole—stick back . . . back . . . back. . . . Crump! Nose has dropped—I'm tossed forward but held in straps, tail high in the air I'm hanging in the straps—but now, as the tail drops and we revert to the horizontal in a cloud of dust—what relief—I've done it—I'm down safely.

Reaching towards me—zig-zag across the ground—dust spurts— clattering machine guns, thump, thump, thump of 109 cannons—out of cockpit on to wing I run—but R/T wires, attached to my helmet head, tug at me, dragging me back. I wrench off the accursed helmet and run . . . run for the nearest bomb-hole—all broken white rock—my flying-suit black—trying to be invisible I lie panting, pressing myself down—waiting for the thud of bullets.

I waited and waited. The silence was uncanny. Finally I looked up— it was difficult to believe it but the 109s had gone. The ambulance sped out towards me. Group Captain Thomas, the officer commanding this aerodrome of Halfar, came out in his car and together we examined the bullet holes in my smoking Spitfire. The Group Captain has now brought me to sick quarters. Here, with the spewed bomb rubble beside us brilliant white, sunlit, against the velvet blue, in silence, for the bomb rumble in the distance seems utterly remote, I am at peace. I am drinking a long draught of clear, sparkling water. As I drink I notice through the bottom of the glass, a low wall with figures behind it. As I lower the glass I see it is a group of Maltese peasants watching us intently.

Thanking the Group Captain, I'm climbing out of my black flying-suit: I am surprised to see my own knees reappearing one by one at the end of my khaki shorts. A tall Flight Lieutenant, describing how the fourteen or twenty 109s against which I fought followed me in, shakes me by the hand:

"I've never seen flick rolls used in combat before," he tells me.

"Alas," I reply, "they were unintentional spins."

The Maltese peasants are coming down the road towards us. As they pass, the nearest, a very fat woman, looks into my face with searching eyes, holds my elbow and presses something into my hand. I smile but I don't know what to say to her. As she moves on I look down: it is a small rectangular card, worn and rubbed: her prayer card, marked with a little cross and the words: *Verbum Dei Caro Factum Est.* I look back to thank her but she is gone.

Now the return to Luqa: after collecting my tin hat and sketching things and apologising to the airmen whom we found watching the sky for my returning Spitfire, telling them it would not come back, I follow Group Captain Thomas, who has kindly driven me here, steeply down into "G" shelter cavern. Gracie stares at me angrily:

"So you're alive, are you, you . . ." he says, "you nearly pranged us both at take off."

I stare back at him. Of course I'm alive. And the take off? It's irrelevant to argue about that. Angry at such a welcome, I retreat back up the stone steps. Pancho, Max, Scotty, Cyril, Hugh and the rest of the pilots of our Squadron gather round me in the sunlight; they are telling me how Gracie returned from the action.

"Your C.O.'s had it, Barnham's dead too. I damaged two 88s," was all that he said.

"Isn't the C.O. back?" I ask in alarm.

"No," they reply, "he's missing."

This moment is final, ruthless, inevitable, dead. I look round at the sunlit hillsides which we have trodden for just over twenty four hours.

C

CHAPTER 6

THE MADHOUSE

D AY after day it goes on. We have now flown five of our best pilots and only one has returned safely with his 'plane. Ken has been killed, and other pilots are in hospital. Without our C.O. I am very much aware of the responsibilities that go with the rank tabs on my shoulders.

I step down from the entrance to our Naxxar palace and following a path quietly beside the church I emerge onto a wide expanse of grass. I walk in silence for I am alone. I am festooned with equipment. Suspended from my shoulder by a long strap is my small blue canvas bag containing my sketching and writing things, for I propose to paint if I get the chance; fastened upon it my tin hat bangs awkwardly against my left hip. My heavy service revolver, slung in its holster, bruises my right. I am wearing my round blue officer's hat, a well battered friendly old hat with a kink in front by which I always recognise it; its peak, extending ahead of me like a huge black eyelid, frames the silent landscape into which I am walking.

Stone walls glaring white in the sun recede over the shallow summit of the hill to my left. On my right any view is cut off by the plain and angular outbuildings at the back of the church and by the high-shadowed wall that extends straight out across the grass. Following the wall I can now see hillslopes dropping gently ahead of me towards Valetta: they are covered by a lacework of walls with here and there strange square buildings rising from the corners of the fields. There is a similar building on my own hilltop, just beyond some stunted olive trees, with my path curving through a break in the wall towards it.

I arrive at the foot of this tall rectangle standing up on end without any windows. I am facing its old doors against which the path stops. These double doors were once painted blue, the paint having cracked in the heat and faded to a pale and dusty turquoise, but alas they are both locked. I peer through the spaces by the hinges but it's too dark inside to see what these structures are for: perhaps they are stores for farm implements or perhaps grain is kept in them after the harvest. Standing back I survey the deserted landscape again, for this place commands fine views over the whole island.

66

First the view eastwards, towards Valetta: beyond the swaying yellow of descending wheat fields, and over the top of the heaped white towns of Misida and Hamrun, a line of hills thrusts sharply into the Mediterranean about four miles away. The hills are tinsel-violet with distance, encrusted with the Valetta buildings and almost encircled by the blue waters of Grand Harbour. Ships must once have sailed those peaceful waters with slow and measured dignity, but now the ships over there are wrecked, twisted and gutted by bombing.

By turning round I find I am standing on the brink of a field that plunges almost vertically for hundreds of feet to the south—I look across a few wheat stalks into a vast blue bowl of air; immediately below me there's a walled town while from behind it the central valley of Malta recedes towards other hills. About four miles away is the splendid profile of M'dina perched high on its spur of white rock. I can see the bastion walls, the pinnacles of St.Paul's church and even the citadel palace where we listened to the A.O.C.'s talk. . . . Below that hillcrest is Takali aerodrome, very flat like a sandy-coloured billiard table. . . . And there's the Madhouse, like a bent nail close to the ribbon road. To the left of M'dina, the other side of a rocky defile, I can see the flat escarpment of hills upon which our own aerodrome of Luqa stands, while away to the right, I can follow the humpy-bumpy hill tops, turning round to my right until I'm facing back towards the Naxxar buildings which frame the view to the West.

This, then, is the place where quite alone I try to relax.

By removing my equipment and my R.A.F. hat I feel happily civilian. I stretch myself out on a grassy bank. I feel the heat of the sun on my face and on my bare arms where my sleeves are rolled up. It's difficult to believe that I'm rooted onto this hillside in time, just after half-past eleven in the morning of Saturday, April 25th, with little less than forty minutes before the Germans come back again. I close my eyes.

I am enveloped in a world of luminous orange-pink: this is a sensation of my childhood; it has been the sensation of any human being for thousands of years and will be so for thousands of years to come. The C.O. must have felt like this. Stone and bronze-age man must have stretched himself out like this when Hal Tarxien, Hal Safliéni and other ancient Maltese temples and tombs were being cut into the rock of this very landscape. Legend records that this is the island of Ogygia where the immortal sea nymph, Calypso, dwelt in her cavern. When Odysseus was cast here by the ocean she promised him immortality if only he would stay with her, but he struggled for seven years before he finally escaped. Escaped! No escape for us! I wonder what brutal facts the Odyssey enshrines? Was Calypso some earth goddess to whom Odysseus was going to be sacrificed? Were the "wiles" he struggled against the arguments and persuasions of her priests, as priests in our sister island of Crete may have persuaded men and women to be voluntary and thus more efficacious sacrifices to the Minotaur? I can feel the processional aura of ancient ceremonial here. Perhaps there is a temple carved into the bowels of the rock close to this spot? I feel the barrier of time is flimsy although it is strong. How strange it would be to find myself suddenly beneath the surface of time and walking these ancient hills as Annie Moberly walked in the gardens of Versailles. It is silent here, but with my hand cushioning my head I can hear my wrist watch ticking inevitably forward. But what of the past; the immediate past and beyond it the ancient past? I can hear the rustling of leaves and the hot wind moaning and buffeting over the rocks.

Homer recalls that, "Calypso's cave was sheltered by a verdant copse of alders, aspens, and fragrant cypresses, which was the roosting place of feathered creatures, horned owls and falcons and garrulous choughs, birds of the coast, whose daily business takes them down to the sea. Trailing round the mouth of the cavern, a garden vine ran riot with great bunches of wild grapes; while from four separate but neighbouring springs four crystal rivulets were trained to run this way and that; and in soft meadows on either side the iris and the parsley flourished. It was indeed a spot where even an immortal visitor might pause and gaze in wonder and delight."

Odysseus was not in the cave. Prevented from returning to the home and wife he longed for, he was sitting, "in his accustomed place, tormenting himself with tears and sighs and heartache, and looking out across the barren sea with streaming eyes."

Will I ever see my wife again? Desperately I long for a letter from home—yet several other pilots have had mail and this means Diana's first letter must nearly have reached me—I smile into the singing silence becalming the hilltop.

It is one of those exquisite silences between raids. Although above me is the undisturbed blue: the sky is generally full of bursting shells, diving and wheeling bombers, rising bomb clouds and drifting dust while the 109s blacken the air like bees. I have watched raid after raid from here with aircraft from both sides falling in flames or just falling, looking quite undamaged, until they erupt in black fire in the yellow fields.

I have been on the business end of the bombs too—on the aerodromes—and I am full of admiration for the airmen who are permanently there, while we, when we are not on duty, can withdraw a little from the main targets. Yesterday morning, for instance, when the camp alarm sounded, two airmen fussed me between some trees and into the private slit-trench that they had dug four or five feet deep into the solid rock. There was a third airman bending down and loading his rifle under some corrugated iron that overhung the end of the trench. His two companions introduced him as Ginger, stating proudly that he had the best score of them all. This leader of the three musketeers had apparently shot down four 109s with his rifle, the others claiming two and one respectively. I felt intimidated as I stared at him, for, with all my elaborate training, I have only destroyed three enemy planes so far. The German dive bombers took me by surprise; I saw them suddenly—twenty 88s, high above the tree tops with more appearing steadily from behind the branches, pock-marked by anti-aircraft fire, poised there, noses lifted, about to strike. Ginger grabbed his rifle.

"Come on down, yer great big broody 'ens," he called, "you'll never fly again if you come too near Ginger."

Ginger was wearing nothing but his khaki shorts, his shoes and his tin hat; his nude back was arched and twisted as he yelled upwards. His body was not strong like a Mestrovic, heavy like a Michelangelo, or refined as the Greek—its subtle slightness could be described as "Trans-figured Office English." But the Germans must have seen him for they didn't bomb us, they continued straight on and dived steeply on Takali instead! I felt quite disappointed as I stood in the trench watching the distant bomb bursts rise slowly above our Luqa skyline for I would have liked to have seen Ginger in action. A sudden rush of air—a hundred bombs plunged upon us from a second wave of German planes—I crouched in the hole as the shrill noise of tearing metal went on and on and on; the boulders, stones and pieces of bomb-casing thumped back from the sky as I uncoiled myself and stood upright. Ginger, rifle in hand, was prowling around like a dark ghost searching for aircraft; black smoke swirled overhead and dust was drifting through the branches of the torn trees—but the Germans had gone.

Unlike city bombing, when every missile wreaks terrible havoc, there's nothing much left to knock down on our Malta aerodromes. People at home may think that the two Ju 88s, which crashed fairly close to us on this particular raid, was a heavy price for the enemy to pay for destroying a petrol bowser and putting splinters through a couple of Spitfires. The bowser, however, was our last bowser, and this means that not only will the airmen have to refuel our Spitfires, which swallow ninety gallons each, by hand from five-gallon drums, but also the transit aircraft that call in at Luqa during their nearly two thousand mile night flight between Gibraltar and Egypt: these transit planes, consuming thousands of gallons between them, will have to be refuelled by the airmen, by hand, in darkness with a continuous patrol of enemy aircraft dropping flares and high explosives. Bomb splinters through a couple of Spitfires may sound simple enough to repair: well, one of them, for instance, had a great hole blown through the fuselage just forward of the tail plane and all the control cables and pulley blocks were carried away. We have no spare parts here—they went to the bottom with the merchant ships that failed to reach us in the last abortive convoy—so Chiefy, who mothers our planes, has to search amongst other wrecked fighters to find serviceable pieces, then rob Peter to pay Paul. And it takes time—a grounded Spitfire may be knocked out again before it's ready to fly. I could make a huge list of the things we are up against, but neglect in England is particularly bitter: the new Spitfires we brought with us; guns not properly harmonised, cannon design faulty, even batteries half charged. Take the batteries: all our charging sets have been destroyed in the bombing and, although Chiefy has invented a ropey device to do the job, there's precious little paraffin left to run it. Etcetera, etcetera, etcetera. Then add the fact that the airmen have never worked on Spitfires before; they were trained to service bombers and all the bombers are destroyed.

This, then, is the background to our real job of flying, but there are not enough 'planes for the two squadrons of pilots stationed at Luqa. 126 Squadron has the 'planes from lunch time one day until lunch time the next, then we have them for twenty-four hours. But there are not even enough 'planes in a flyable condition to occupy half a squadron. I have organised our operations by Flights: we are alternately on duty from dawn for the morning one day, an afternoon period the next, then have two days off before flying again.

This time off gives me a chance to paint, indeed I should be painting now. Looking out over the valley towards Takali, staring down at the walled town beneath my feet, a golden town with a domed church and stone walls behind it, foreshortening away into the distance, a golden landscape shimmering with heat. I can hear the nagging artist within me: "Work, work, work," it tells me, "you may not have long to live." Why can't I be like other people and relax? Why should I feel that creative work is the only valid reason for my existence? If this is the so-called artistic temperament it's ironical that I'm not much good at drawing yet, that I'm an immature and interrupted student, with no style in my work and no clear idea of what I want to achieve with it. If I did clever caricatures my companion pilots would think I was a hell of a guy, but instead, although they probably respect me as their Flight Commander, my lust for art is a subject for merriment. Artists just aren't wanted in war, even in peace time they are treated as some kind of freak—in fact, it's probably true to say that I'm shown more respect in any one day as an Officer in the R.A.F. than I'm likely to receive in a lifetime as a painter. And I enjoy being needed; I feel my heart warm to the funny little Maltese children who often crowd around me in the street crying out, "Speetfire Pilot, Speetfire Pilot, Speetfire Pilot."

Some inner daemon forces me to go on drawing, despite the war. I have to put up with the disappointments and utter misery of pictures continually going wrong as an act of faith that one day, I might acquire such skill and experience as will enable them to go right. At times in the past I have been given a taste of "rightness", and when this has happened I have felt caught up in a strange rhythm, a kind of ecstasy, the primitive but highly civilised joy that the Chinese call *Tao*. Although I have only had fleeting experiences of it, I firmly believe that an artist, whether he paints, sculpts, creates music, poetry or any other art, could he but stay in harmony with the Tao from the beginning of his work to the end, the result would show the rhythmic inevitability of every part and be a masterpiece. It's a wonderful adventure to be caught up in this rhythm, but, alas, it's out of gear with mechanical civilisation.

I should be painting now. The fact that I painted the harbour from this hilltop a few days ago does not ease my restless shame about sitting here, so idly waiting for the next raid. To get a good view of the harbour I had to walk out through the growing corn because the pathway ends at the strange tower just behind me. As the crops are very precious to the Maltese I walked along the top of the wall, with the loose rocks wobbling and clonking under my feet. Finally I sat astride the wall painting my picture, listening to the Maltese singing in the distant streets of Naxxar. The sun shone brilliantly and all was peace. Then the sirens sounded. 109s sprinting across the sky made me feel anxious about such an exposed position. Timidly I was wondering if I should retreat but the artist inside me said "No". Bombs crashed down on Takali on my right, while another stick of bombs bursting behind me made me blot my painting in the wrong place. Bomb smoke mounted higher over my head from Naxxar and in the stunned silence, for the singing in the streets had stopped, there was a strange noise. Sis . . . Sis. SisSisssss. Sis . . . Sis. . . . Sis. SisSissss. I looked up at the third wave of enemy bombers droning immediately above me—I thought they were dropping some secret weapon. Sis . . . SisSissss . . . Cling. A jagged lump of shrapnel struck the wall just ahead of me, other pieces were slithering into the fields so I put on my tin hat. I was angry with the enemy and angry with my own utter incompetence to capture the sunlit beauty of the fields with the flat Mediterranean beyond—the painting looked dull. At that moment, all the way along the hillcrest inland from the harbour, a line of black pillared destruction sprang skywards. I attacked my picture with renewed zest—Ju 88s, in twos and fours, were hurling themselves down from above my left shoulder, releasing their bombs and disappearing behind the smoke in the distance. I had to work fast. With the tip of my paintbrush I wanted to catch the character of some of these planes as they streamed past. I watched the next pair: each plane had a long straight fuselage with a tadpole cockpit in front and a tall single rudder behind, while from its wings two huge engines close to the cockpit protruded well forward. I watched the bombs leave the racks of the leading plane, and at that moment, and I assume that an ascending shell hit the bomb load, there was a splitting bang—I was blown off the wall with my painting things scattered in all directions—I lay on my back amongst the corn watching a stationary bubble of fire expand wider and wider in the sky just above me—it turned grey at the edges and disappeared —it was as if the whole plane had been vapourised—I lay there watching other bombers sweep towards the target.

That was the raid during which poor Ken was killed. Although I counted a hundred and sixty-four enemy planes on this side of the island, I saw nothing of the three Spitfires we had airborne. Apparently Ken made the same mistake as the C.O. and I—he chased the enemy bombers for a fraction of a second too long out to sea, he almost certainly destroyed two of them before he was cut off by the hosts of 109s.

There seems to be no escape from the 109s. The C.O. was cut off and outnumbered twenty or thirty to one. Although we all thought he had been killed on that first flight, he was in fact saved by the thin fingers of destiny or chance.

Although his plane, having been hit by enemy bullets and shells, was uncontrollable, he managed to bale out by parachute. Either his parachute was faulty or it had been ripped by bullets because he fell through it. Luckily he was caught up by his ankle, being lowered head first down the sky and into the sea. He disentangled himself, inflated his dinghy and climbed in. He was lucky again, for the 109s, diving down towards him as he sat there, did not open up with machine-guns as I am told is their usual practice, but were content to have a good look at their victim instead. It took the C.O. six hours to paddle his way back to Malta, but, finally, when he was utterly exhausted, he was confronted by the cliffs that rose vertically from the sea for hundreds of feet. He used up his remaining strength paddling out away from the cliffs, trying to prevent himself being thrown against the rocks by the breakers. There came a time when he drifted towards a small bay where, unknown to him, the underwater barbed-wire defences had already torn two pilots to pieces: the waves flung him ashore, dragged him back and flung him ashore again: he must have been washed right over the wire. He clung to a rock but had no strength to stop his head being pounded and pounded against it. By chance a Leading Seaman, who happened to be passing along the cliff top, saw him and, climbing straight down, dragged him up on to the beach. As a final gesture, one of the 88s which were dive bombing Halfar at the time dropped a bomb on the cliff brink and both men were showered with boulders.

This then is the kind of air warfare into which I must lead my boys. With the C.O. in hospital, after which he will be recuperating at the Pilots' Rest Camp at St. Paul's Bay, with the Dreaded Hugh already ill with a kind of dysentery called the Malta Dog which may send him to hospital any day, I am virtually in charge. It seems to me that if we leaders are going to be shot down, killed or wounded, there must be other pilots trained as leaders to take our place. This means I should fly such potential leaders as Max, Scotty and Pancho much more than the others. On the other hand I must get all my pilots, many of whom have never been on operations before, into the air as soon as I can—too long a delay and watching this kind of battle could have a grisly effect on morale.

An additional problem I have to face is that we're not allowed to fly the line astern formation that we used over France and which we have practised; we have been ordered to fly the new line abreast formation which is quite different. We have never tried this before but we are to fly our Spitfires straight and level without weaving, and abreast of each other in a line; each pilot looks out sideways watching the sky in front, above, below and particularly behind his companion, guarding against surprise attack. The method of turning, when the machines cross over one another, and the emergency breaks need practice. But we can't practise—every flight is into action.

Because we've got to become brilliant at our job before even going up into the air, we gather by the Naxxar wall to watch the raids. Oh God—the 109s—they have complete mastery in our sky. They seem to fly in a great staircase or net designed to catch us—first, quite low down, a pair or four, just behind them another pair a little higher, and so on up to thirty thousand feet. Mix it with 109s at low level and they can call twenty or thirty of their friends down to outnumber you drastically within a few seconds. We can never be on top of them, for we are only sent off at the last moment to attack the bombers. The 109 net tries to stop all interception, but if we do get through there are additional 109s that dive with their bomber formations. Even if we get amongst the bombers to do our job then the whole 109 force is called in to destroy us. This is the moment we have our losses. How we are to escape from them I just don't know. Each raid I watch, and I watch for I'm trying to think out some logical advice, some sound factual hope of survival which I can give my boys and with which I can overcome my own dread of going into the sky again.

I am sitting here on this hillside—why is this morning raid late? I throw myself back on the ground and look up at the sky: although I have to screw up my eyes against the glare of the sun, I can see, high above me, a flat white island of cirrus cloud floating quietly against the blue. I feel the muscles, deep inside my body, trying to relax. I stare up at the island of cloud: strange, but if I was flying up there, looking down, this island of Malta would look very much the same—but, oh God, I am flying again this afternoon. Still no sirens. I'll not stay here with fear burning all my courage to ashes, I'll walk back along the wall and wait for the Huns in our usual place.

As I approach, I recognise Pip, one of "B" Flight pilots; I don't know him very well, but his thin figure looks fragile and alone.

"The raid's late," I remark.

"Yes."

He looks palely haunted. His lips smile at me, but his eyes stare. I sense that somewhere inside he is trying to put a blanket over his feelings, just as I am. He is standing quite motionless and he hasn't had a very good shave this morning. I think he is terrified, but if I am mistaken I don't want to sow the seeds of fear in his mind.

"I don't see much of 'B' Flight these days—I hear that you're all riddled with the Dog." I lie, for I haven't heard any such thing, only Hugh who insists in remaining nominally in charge of "B" Flight is ill, but I must say something to this man.

"Have you caught the Dog yet?" I ask.

He shakes his head.

"Have you had a crack at the Hun yet?"

He stares at the ground and seems to be biting his lips.

"What's the matter, laddie?" He remains silent. "If you feel scared don't be worried about it—we all feel the same."

"Do you really?" he asks incredulously.

"Of course we do. We're all human. We're not fanatics like the Nazis, and that's why we'll beat them." I tap my forehead with my finger. "We have more up here to beat them with."

He is smiling gently now, his eyes are relaxing a little.

The sirens have started to wail. I would like to go deeper into Pip's feelings. Has he a faith to hang on to when everything else is stripped away? Does he believe in God? But the other pilots are emerging from beside the church and coming along the path towards us.

We are all assembled, Pancho, Max, Scotty and quiet Cyril, with the rest of my boys in another group to my right: beyond them, further along the wall, the Dreaded Hugh is talking to "B" Flight pilots; Pip is leaning forward attentively from the edge of that bunch. The sky, except for my cirrus cloud which has moved away towards the east, is an uninterrupted blue, slightly reddened by haze. There go some 109s, difficult to see, sweeping inland, and judging from the roar of engines, the rest of the staircase is passing above us. Over the other side of Naxxar church there's some bursting flak. The rumble of engines grows louder, gun crashes more lively, reddish shapes looming through the haze, Ju 87s, Stukas, gathering above us. As the shells burst among them the formation moves slowly but steadily towards Grand Harbour. That's bad shooting: five new bursts well away to one side behind the formation. But no, I'm wrong. It's another formation, Ju 88s this time, passing obliquely behind the first. There go the Stukas diving down, faster and faster, with smaller slender shapes diving amongst them; 109s; with more 109s appearing from nowhere and joining the cascade of dropping planes. The harbour barrage has opened up; puffs of pale smoke writhe in the sky, ineffective in stopping the bomb-bursts all over the city. Luqa is being bombed too! Snap-crack, sharp and loud, set my ears singing: two bombs, heaven knows where from, have burst a few hundred yards behind us on our hill-top; lots of dust and small stones raining down but it's quieter now.

Sudden noise of bomber engines from a new direction, Takali bursts apart like a volcano, bomb clouds leaping skywards, Ju 88s, pulling out of their dive, sweep low towards us. Three, four, six, race above our heads away to the north, but the seventh plane, plunging towards us, is on fire! Smoke is coming out of his port engine, black pieces are falling off him. There's a groan of disappointment, for the flame is going out. The enemy bomber passes above us, it's back on an even keel, looking quite normal, but we all swing round to watch. He's doing a slight turn to the left. He *is* on fire after all: a tiny flame in his port engine is growing rapidly bigger; the engine is all white and dazzling, with fire quickly spreading. The whole bomber is a glistening white pearl with the wing tips and tail sticking out of it black, but it's still flying, doing a slow flat turn to the left. It's beginning to drop. It's going down. It's disappeared steeply behind the hill.

Where have I seen a burning aircraft just like that before? It was long, long ago; a toy glider from my studio steps. I am suddenly ashamed: I never thought for a moment of the poor devils inside; how desperately they must have hoped as the fire went out and how they must have watched with horror from their cockpit windows as the fire, rekindling itself, spread like quicksilver.

The raid is as good as over, the bombers have gone but there's a Spitfire about eight hundred feet above us, just out over the edge of the valley, doing lazy turns in the air. I wonder if he shot down the 88? This graceful shape, indulging the sheer joy of quiet flying, floats along our hillside like a seagull while somewhere in the town below us a clock is chiming the hours of midday.

A howl of engines: razor edged, sharp-angled fighters hurtle from behind the tree clumps. The nearest leaping to the Spitfire sends out ghostly blue fingers. The Spitfire's hit. With a bubbling plume of white smoke pouring from its engine, it plunges towards us, turning on a wing tip steeply into the valley below. Thought it was going to crash but there it goes, trailing smoke into the distance towards the aerodrome. Difficult to pick out the Spitfire because there are four Spits, like tiny model aeroplanes, circling Takali; yes, there it is, approaching the 'drome with its shadow racing along the flat ground. It's going too fast: over-shooting into the walls. It lifts; it's doing a violently steep turn back. It'll make the aerodrome yet. As it passes more slowly over the perimeter track a burst of dust shoots up. We wait anxiously as the dust begins to drift away. The motionless wreckage is now revealed but there's no movement from the cockpit. We wait and wait. At last the pilot, a minute black dot, climbs out on to the wing and moves away like an insect.

"That shook him," says Pancho in a low voice.

CHAPTER 7

"THE KETTLE'S NOT QUITE BOILING"

DOWN at the aerodrome I watch the erks working desperately to get a damaged Spitfire repaired before the next raid comes in. There's no doubt about it, some of our aircraft are in a pretty shocking condition but these men are doing damned well. They are singing. This Easter hymn is punctuated by forceful remarks from grimy lips such as "Lend an 'and and pass that f . . . spanner".

> 'Tis Holy Thursday, let us snooker
> All the blasted Spits at Luqa,
> Fill the sky with every Stuka,
> HALLELUJAH!

> Hail Good Friday! Halfar's turn,
> Watch the blasted Swordfish burn;
> Won't the British ever learn?
> HALLELUJAH!

> Easter Saturday, that's fine!
> Make Takali toe the line,
> Here a rocket, there a mine,
> HALLELUJAH!

> Christ the Lord is risen today!
> Let's bomb the harbour, bomb the bay,
> Bomb the blasted place all day,
> HALLELUJAH!

> Easter Monday, let 'em rip!
> Gosh, we'll give those boys the pip,
> Tear 'em off a Safi strip,
> HALLELUJAH!

I hurry back to my own machine because I don't want to be too far away when the take-off order comes—just two Spitfires left in a flyable condition on the whole of this vast aerodrome; I'm taking one, and now,

77

standing by the huge three-bladed propeller of my own hearse, I watch
Pancho adjusting his kit into the cockpit of the other. Turning round
and leaning on one of the thick solid cannons thrusting forward from the
wing of my plane I stare down the graceful fuselage to my own perspex
coffin. My kit's already inside it. At the end of the fuselage is the delicate
tail plane, while beyond that, high up on the sandbags, is the airman
whom I have posted to watch for the signal. He looks like a happy
carefree child dangling his legs. I wonder if he knows there are only
seven serviceable fighters left on the whole island. What do 109s mean
to him?

During last year's sweeps when over two hundred Spitfires forged out
over the vast area of Northern France, when we measured our flying
times in hours tucked in amongst friends and returned to lavishly equipped
bases, we only saw a few 109s nibbling on the edge of our formations and
I was afraid, but here . . . Of course a few people were shot down during
the sweeps but I never thought it could happen to me; but here . . . With
hundreds of 109s concentrated over our tiny island and having been shot
down once already I have lost all my illusions. We are all cut off, there
are no replacement aircraft as we had during the sweeps. Cut off; there's
no news from home, not a cable, not a letter, not the remotest message
from Diana. Looking at these two remaining aircraft I feel that everyone
has forgotten us. We now know why the Germans have stepped up the
intensity of their bombing, why more and more 109s appear in our sky
with every new raid. Our Reconnaissance Spitfire has brought back
new pictures of the enemy airfields in Sicily. Besides the fleets of bombers
and fighters the photographs reveal crates containing gliders being unloaded from long goods trains. We are going to be invaded. The
possibility of seeing the invasion is remote; everything in the future is
remote except the immediate ordeal of flying. I hope Peter can make
it: I rang him up from Naxxar after the raid this morning. It's a highly
unorthodox request to get him to lead our formation and it may not be
permitted. I can get our tiny formation into the bombers but I want
to see at what point an old hand breaks away from them to avoid the 109s.

As I run my hands along the hard surface of this gull wing I have never
been so aware of the permanence of metal and the yielding quality of flesh
and bone. If this machine is to be broken within the hour and my body
broke with it, the machine will remain recognisably a thing of metal,
people will know that it was once an aeroplane, but this body of mine
may be burnt and charred or jellied beyond recognition. If I must be
killed today I hope I fall into the sea, the ocean is more discreet, people
won't stare at my remains, I won't make them want to vomit or crack
clever jokes over what is left of me.

The airman is standing up, looking towards "G" shelter. Has he seen
something?

"Is it a scramble?" I call to him.

As he shakes his head and makes an impatient negative gesture with his hand stretched down by his side, I hear the noise of a motor-bike coming nearer. As I wander round the front of the pen to see who it is my heart slows its beat of unnecessary alarm. Drawing sedately towards me is a seated figure in khaki. I don't know him, he must be another one of the old hands.

"Hullo, old boy. Got a message from Woody for you. He says it's O.K. about Peter; he'll fly over from Takali and rendezvous with you in the circuit here. That'll make you a complete section of four, won't it?"

"No," I reply, "I've only got two planes at the moment. Tell Woody that Chiefy and his boys are working on a third—they expect to have it ready within an hour."

The newly arrived motor cyclist seems to have plenty of time for a chat. He tells me that there's nothing on the "board" yet, so I introduce myself. He tells me that he's just come out of hospital at Umtarfa.

"What happened to you then?" I ask, provoking him with a smile.

"Oh, the 109s got me about six weeks ago."

"Did you bale out or did you come down with the plane?"

"Baled out, near Filfla, but the 'chute streamed."

"Your 'chute didn't open and you got away with it?" I ask, with a picture in my mind of him falling headlong with his parachute flapping and smacking uselessly in the air behind him, then of his heavy body striking the foot of a rocky wall with a sickly crunch.

"Where's Filfla?" I ask.

"Haven't you seen it?" he replies in astonishment. When I explain that I haven't been on the island very long, he nods his head in understanding.

"Filfla," he tells me, "is a small island out to sea just off the southwest coast opposite Dingli. It's really nothing else but a tall lump of rock and the artillery often use it for a practice shoot."

"Then you fell into the water; but the water's damned hard."

"You're telling me," he replies; "I broke my neck."

"Broke your neck!"

I'm astonished. I always thought that if someone had their neck broken they were automatically dead, on the principle of being hanged. I stare at him, but I hope my bewilderment doesn't reveal too much of my ignorance.

"I suppose the air-sea rescue boats brought you ashore?"

"No, I swam—about a mile and a half."

I continue to stare.

"What are you doing now?" I ask.

"I'm dogsbody. I do odd jobs, until I get a place in a transit plane. Then back to a hospital in U.K. Well, I must be getting along."

I watch him as he looks down for the gears. He has only slight diffi-
culty in doing so despite his stiff neck. He revs the engine gently, lets in
the clutch and drives slowly away in a wide circle. I watch him as he
motors sedately towards "G" shelter. He travels carefully, his seated and
retreating back view doesn't bounce or sway and he steers well clear
of the odd lumps of broken rock. So his parachute didn't open. I know
that the building on the island for packing the parachutes has been blown
to pieces—perhaps makeshift conditions have affected the 'chutes. Was
the C.O.'s 'chute on our first flight really ripped by enemy bullets, or
was it already faulty before he put it on?

Quickly I have my 'chute out for inspection. But there's no time now;
my motor cyclist is back:

"Enemy aircraft are gathering over Sicily," he tells me, "stand by for
immediate take-off."

"Right."

"Sir," says Chiefy, approaching me with my other pilots, "you can
have the third Spitfire now."

"Well done, Chiefy, damn good. I'll take it myself.

"Scotty, you'll join us. Get your kit into this plane. Your call
sign is Pintoe Yellow Three. For God's sake, there go the lights—
scramble."

This line abreast formation's delightful; I look out sideways at Peter's
Spitfire, which joined us before we'd got half-way round the circuit,
with Scotty beyond him and Pancho away in the distance, four Spitfires
leaning up the sky at full throttle. We came out of the haze sheet, which
extends below us like rusty white smoke as far as the horizon, at fifteen
thousand feet, but we are climbing steadily higher and higher into the
cerulean blue bowl. I can't see Peter's face because the brilliant sun is
glinting on . . . what's happening? His Spitfire suddenly staggers. It
drops below leaving black smoke hanging behind it.

"Hullo Denis, Peter here, got to leave you, engine's cut; sorry."

"O.K. Peter, good luck, thanks for coming."

Behind and below us the water grades imperceptably into the haze, an
awful lot of water, with Peter's Spitfire, already far below us, a tiny
silhouette and gliding away towards the north. He'll need good luck
to reach the island, lost and invisible in this Mediterranean chasm.
Eighteen thousand five hundred feet—let's see how we cope with our
very first cross-over turn. Crossing over now, rather a muddle perhaps,
but for beginners . . .

"Hullo Pintoe Leader, there are forty little jobs over St. Paul's Bay,
angels twenty heading south; there's another thirty over Zonkor at angels
fifteen heading south-west. The kettle isn't boiling yet, hang around a
bit chaps."

Seventy 109s prowling for the three of us; there'll be a lot more soon.

What does Woody mean by "the kettle's not quite boiling"?—I can guess—no bombers yet.

"Come in now Pintoes, and come in fast. Grand Harbour."

As I ease my Spitfire into a steeper and steeper dive I notice that by sheer chance Scotty is in the centre of our formation. Splendid opportunity of checking his leadership.

"Hullo Scotty, Denis here, you're the boss. It's your baby from here on. We are your worshipful attendants."

"OK. Denis."

Steeper even steeper, almost vertically into the haze. My Spitfire's bucking and jerking with the speed of our power dive, controls difficult to move. Here comes the island, looming towards us. As Scotty eases us gently out of our plunge, rather low I think, the cliffs, M'dina, Takali flash below us. Lower still across the valley. Naxxar, the hillside, the wall, "B" Flight pilots watching. Abruptly we're over the harbour.

Low over the roof-tops, bombs bursting up towards us, shells bursting among us, while from high above us Stukas are plunging straight down, pulling out of their dive at our level. On my own now, pulling my Spitfire up on its tail, a head-on Stuka is charging towards me, the W structure of its wings perfectly distinct, larger and larger, bombs falling away from its belly disappearing under my aircraft's nose. I fire into its gigantic shape: its enfolding shadow broods for an instant over my head. This is mad, crazy but wonderful. Just below me as I swerve about, I have an impression of angled white houses, with shadowed streets like deep ravines, occasional glimpses of blue water, all of it buried beyond the undergrowth of black bomb-bursts that reach up towards me like a forest of trees. I'm knocked sideways, riding these explosions like a bronco. Ha! Ha! A rolling black cloud leaps alongside me peering in at me with its grotesque dragon face, already gone; shells flash yellow, black, grey, what do I care? This is but the fantastic background to my concentration on the belly of another Stuka, already huge, much closer, winged, round, pregnant, with twin bombs hanging there; head-on detailed beyond the red circle of my gun-sight. Firing steadily I pull my nose carefully upwards so that the enemy machine disappears behind my engine cowlings, so that it must pass through my close grill of bullets and cannon shells, ball, armour piercing, incendiary, everything I've got: a monstrous scarlet shape, a mass of flames, flashes overhead. Another plunging towards me. I pull my aircraft up until it too disappears behind my Spitfire's nose, firing at this invisible thing, that I know is there, rushing at me. Its underside reappears in front of my nose: huge wheels, round matt rubber: I duck my head; it's gone; couldn't have missed him; must have riddled him; guns, what's the matter with my guns? I didn't stop firing but my guns did! With quiet deliberation I look down into my dark cockpit. I place my thumb on the firing button on the top of my control column. I press it for cannons and machine-guns together: there's an escape of compressed air, nothing else. I select for each armament separately but no guns fire. Temperature O.K. Air pressure O.K. But why, why, why? 109s, 109s, *109s.* "Watch out Spitfires" comes the deadly warning.

The thought strikes me as a fiercely moving hand would strike a drunkard. With the sharp-angled shapes flashing about me I'm cold sober now, defenceless with no guns, terrified. I plunge downwards towards the cover of the houses, wrench my Spitfire along a wide street, swerving right, along the main road in the direction of the aerodrome.

"All aircraft cover Laggard Leader about to pancake." That's the call-sign of the Hurricanes. I stare upwards and there, above the familiar hillside that leaps towards me, I can see two Hurricanes circling. Good idea.

"Hullo Woody," I call, "Pintoe Leader going in also."

"O.K. Pinto Leader."

I've closed the throttle and my Spitfire, slowing rapidly, joins the circuit. Craning my head round and searching and searching the sky for pursuing 109s, I feel for the lever and lower the wheels. Damn it, I've overshot the main runway where the tiny Hurricane is landing; never mind, the next runway will do. I turn gently towards it. I'm perfectly positioned for a landing. Slower and slower, in a medium turn, I lower the flaps.

"109s in the circuit": a shrill yell.

I twist round in my seat. My God. Four planes arching upon me. I'm hypnotised by the white blink, the sudden flow of tracers. Missed me by God. The first 109 rushes upwards. I glimpse ahead. I can't possibly go round again with wheels and flaps down, as slow as this, I'd be shot to bits. Helpless I stare back at the second 109 rapidly closing. If I turn I'll spin. I'm dropping fast, runway some distance ahead, I stare at the 109, larger and more awful. My aircraft is sluggish, dropping fiercely: full throttle, for something else is wrong. Oblivious of curling tracers I'm sitting with the nose of my Spitfire pointing skywards. However did I get into such an attitude? Dropping tail first towards a wide square reservoir, a sheet of water rushing up to meet me. A sudden, sweaty black realisation that I'm going to crash.

Rasp of tearing, buckling metal; compressed violently into the seat, compressed further and further, I can feel my bones bending, now I'm riding upwards, riding along on the very top of all the wreckage, slithering diagonally, with frightful noise across the perimeter track on to the very brink of the runway; tarmac, grass, bits of rock, all blurred, but I notice with dispassionate interest that the oleo legs and wheels have come straight up through the smooth top surface of the wings.

Dust and silence. Sitting here I realise with awful horror what I've done: I don't think any bullets struck me: I have crashed a Spitfire through sheer b . . . carelessness. Automatically I turn off the fuel taps and ignition switches. I don't care about the 109s now. Releasing my straps I stand up in the cockpit, my yellow Mae West conspicuous against the blue-grey wreckage. I am on the brink of tears. Where can I hide myself? There's a broken hangar with dark shadows—no good there's an airman there; there's also a car speeding towards me. No escape. I'm caught. The airman driver and another helper are urging me to get in. We're moving off now, faster and faster, the driver crouching low, his head turned flat against the steering wheel, peering furtively at the sky. Through my blur of tears I'm aware of 109s streaking across the aerodrome making another attack. I'm too ashamed to care.

The airmen jolt the car to a halt in the concrete bay behind "G" shelter. They have risked their lives to bring me in, so I thank them although I'm not worth saving. I walk round and face the small black entrance to "G" shelter tunnel. I'll have to go down there. I'll have to face all the other pilots. This is worse than going up into action, but reluctant though I am I've got to go through with it.

Someone's climbing up; I can hear the sound of heavy boots on the steps. A figure emerges into the sunlight: it is Hugh.

"What's happened to the Dreaded Denis?" he proclaims heartily, "were you shot down again?"

"No," I answer bitterly, "I've no excuse. It was sheer b . . . carelessness —totally unnecessary."

This is appalling. We're desperately short of aircraft, all the afternoon I have been nagging Chiefy to get that machine serviceable, the airmen worked magnificently, now I've broken the thing. How can I face anyone? Whatever will they say to me?

Descending into "G" shelter I realise that my Mae West proclaims the fact that I've been flying; all the pilots sitting on the benches staring at me must already know what I've done. I make my way towards the door marked so ominously "Strictly Private. Authorised Persons Only". I hesitate, but finally knock and make my way inside. Senior Officers. Gold braid. Facing the lifted eyebrows of the Group Captain I just can't stop the tears rolling down my cheeks.

"May I have a personal interview with the A.O.C., sir," I ask, "I want to make a personal apology."

"For heaven's sake man, whatever for?"

"I've broken a Spitfire, sir. It was sheer carelessness."

"Don't worry about it. We were watching. Not everyone comes into land with 109s on their tail. Come along to the mess and have a drink."

This is worse than I dreamed of: they're being so kind to me. I sit down on one of the benches and lean forward with my head between my hands. Whatever can I do? However can I get a hundred per cent efficiency out of all my pilots in the face of what I've done. Here's Chiefy too, just standing and staring.

Scotty and Pancho have arrived. Thank God they're safe. They're telling me of the Stukas that they saw plunge into the sea during our attack; several went in apparently, one of them burning fiercely, probably mine—but here comes the inevitable question.

"We saw the broken Spitfire on the edge of the runway, whatever happened to you?"

CHAPTER 8

ROOF AWAY

LYING in bed I light the candle—the orange flame, wavering on its white shaft, illuminates the hands of the alarm clock—twenty-past four; I can give my pilots another ten minutes of sleep. The smell of the candle, the leaping black shadows of this room and the dark cavern of the dormitory stateroom beyond are now part of my life, for I have settled down to the tempo of battle here. I have even thought out my essential advice for our survival in air combat, based on my own experience and presuming that, to be shot down, a fighter pilot must make some mistake. It came to me yesterday when watching the midday raid. I turned to my pilots and said: "You fighter pilots are lucky. The bomber boys over Germany have to face the uncertainties of anti-aircraft fire but you need never be shot down. There are only two exceptions: you may get shot down if you're so heavily outnumbered that you run out of height and air speed, or if you're short of fuel and you're attacked while having to land. There's no other reason to get shot down at all, and if you are—it's your own damned fault."

I am very much aware of the mistake I made last time I crashed, and by the light of the fluttering candle, I read about it and other recent entries in the diary I've started keeping.

". . . Peter crashed on the cliff tops: not hurt. I crashed too—felt frightful about my broken Spitfire—had fuel left—should never have come in to land. Old hands pretend to fight when out of ammo; after all Huns don't know! We learn if we live. Went out for walk in evening—wonderful smells from fields—walking back up the hill watched Naxxar buildings growing taller and taller, swallowing up the stars. Raids all night."

". . . Better trip. Surprised Chiefy by bringing plane back in one piece. Had Max up with me—should make a good leader. We're diving back to island too steeply too soon—result—we come in at roof-top height, under bombers instead of on top. Remedy this."

". . . I let Max take section up. We were heavily bombed, so were Takali and Halfar. Worried about Max and two initiates alone in sky. Sheer joy to see his three planes come back—but he'd flown out to sea too far—by the time he'd dived back it was all over—none of them saw a single enemy plane!"

Looking up from my diary I realise that to make such an error must be all too easy—we've got to get amongst the enemy; indeed, with the odds stacked so heavily against us there's a real art in our air fighting. Everything must be timed perfectly—the climb up into the sun and the dive back into the bomber stream—but then, when one's in amongst the bombers, the break-away is the most vital manœuvre. The whole job's a rapier thrust to do the utmost damage—but no error: once among the bombers the enemy knows where we are—every 109 is after us—every pilot that has so far been shot down has been hit at this moment. I'll lead the formation today—the break-away must be perfect.

Now to wake my pilots. Holding the candle high I climb out of bed. Most of the night-bombing has moved over to the other side of the island—I can even hear the creaking of beds in the big dormitory—but here comes another lot—bombs screeching low overhead burst somewhere outside the town: the Dreaded Hugh's huddled form groans from the side of the room: "Oh, you're the noisiest getter-upper," he complains. Having made my way carefully amongst the black beds I have found Max who, sitting up, is staring at the candle flame with screwed-up eyes. Scotty's awake now, Cyril and Pancho too, but I must take four more: whatever Spitfires are available must be manned with an excess of pilots. Belch and two sergeants, and how about my Baby-Faced South African? I must take him for his first trip today, but where is he? Baby Face's fair hair and closed eyelids are now illuminated below me: the candlelight is glistening on each of his parted lips; I'd love to leave him sleeping but, as I shake him ruthlessly, he opens his eyes, looks up at me and smiles.

The bus, half filled with my silent, swaying companions rattles to a halt outside the tiny mess at Luqa—quickly we eat some breakfast. The cook tells us that the enemy only stopped bombing the aerodrome about ten minutes ago, so I congratulate him on getting our breakfast ready; "bangers" for breakfast, a most appropriate choice. As we leave the building and walk up the road towards the dark smudge of "G" shelter on the skyline, there's an imperceptable lightening of the sky. The muscles in my legs ache as I pick my way over the uneven ground which is difficult to see, stones and rocks loom up in unusual places, dark shapes of airmen are hurrying to and fro in the pale light and there are muttered warnings about delayed-action bombs.

As Chiefy greets me close to the shelter entrance I notice that the dark profile of the stone building where our parachutes are kept is strangely uneven. With Chiefy's torch throwing a broken circle of white light over the rubble we discover our parachutes buried in a tumble of rocks—I am filled with anxiety about the condition of such vital equipment, our parachutes aren't opening properly: I'll get some new ones—but doubt if there are any. We've extracted the 'chutes, my pilots are carrying them

off to "G" shelter, but one thing is certain, if the building is still to be
used as a parachute store it must have its roof replaced at once. I issue my
instructions to Chiefy. He hesitates in protest, then, shouting into the
gloom, orders two erks to search for the missing roof and two others to
climb the wall to secure the rattling corrugated iron that remains. He
stands watching progress: "The bloody roof will be blown off again
in the next raid," he mutters. Ignoring his comment I ask how many
Spitfires are serviceable. There are two. "Come on Baby Face, let's
get out to our planes."

We're both down safely, and well done Baby Face! Although his
formation was hopeless—nearly pranging me in turns, passing low over
the top of my cockpit instead of underneath—he can shoot straight.
Saw puffs streaming back over his wings and huge lumps flying off the
black 88 in front of him. Wasn't much good myself—over careful,
watching for precise moment to break. Baby Face followed me at once—
downwards in direction of sun—best way—can see if one's being followed—109s lost us. But did I break too early? Not much good getting
amongst bombers without destroying any—one's shooting must be
perfect—three or four seconds should be enough. Perhaps I should have
stayed—my chosen 88 was large and staring at me through my gun-
sights—oh, I'm a fool—oh, forget it.
    Since landing, I've been drawing some airmen gathered round me
at the dispersal. I've learned about "Big Eats". Ginger's in trouble
with his Maltese girl-friend—he won't marry the girl and the result's a
bill for all the meals and entertainment he's had with her family! But
now we're down in "G" shelter and I've been talking with Woody on
the phone. He won't let us fly on the next raid. He says there are only
four fighters left serviceable on the whole island. He says he must hold
them on the ground—and the reason: lest Kesselring sends in his airborne
invasion—we've got to stand by! I suppose this means that if we are sent
off—we attack gliders. In my apprehension I've been asking the Wingco
how he'd operate against them. He just laughs. Someone's got to think
ahead—why do people always laugh?
    It's quite a decision for Woody to hold our Spitfires on the ground—
particularly after what happened to Hugh Pugh's bomber force that
arrived here a few nights ago. There were ten Wellingtons and they
went straight off to attack the 109 bases in Sicily. It was a good idea but
the next day, although the Wellingtons were protected by special pens,
six of them were hit in the bombing—they burned fiercely with monuments of smoke hanging above us in the sky. That didn't stop Hugh
Pugh—the remaining four went out over Sicily again the next night—
two more were shot down—the last two were sent back to Egypt. Crews
said, "Nice and safe there!"

The Aerodrome Controller has just poked his head round the door—there's a "hundred and fifty plus" raid coming in but we're not to go up. Prayers for our grounded Spitfires for it's starting—the rock shudders, shrieks and growls—we're all beginning to bounce. What a screeching din! It's like sitting inside an ear-trumpet with giants bawling obscene language down either end. Pancho and Cyril, seated on the other side of the rocking cavern, are very calm. Max and Scotty have their mouths wide open to counteract blast effect. The Wingco, sitting next to me, is splendidly still—has a good expression—probably thinking the communal thought: "Next bomb ours?" I'll do a drawing of him. . . . Blast the bomb quiver—it makes my pen shake.

. . . It's over all too quickly—my loyalties have been divided in wanting the raid to stop for our own safety and for the sake of our Spitfires—and wanting it to go on so that, in my drawing, I could finish the Wingco's hands.

After filing up the steep rock steps we emerge into the dazzle of brilliant sunshine. Just look at that—a huge bomb, black and ugly, squatting on the yellow ground.

"Waiting for us," says an erk. "She must 'ave come skippin' across to nestle 'ere."

Everyone is gathering round to look—the intrepid fellow is even writing something on it with a bit of chalk. The beastly thing gives me the pins and needles of apprehension—I am pleased to withdraw with dignity, for I am picking my way over the rock fragments towards the dispersal point—I want to find out if the Spitfires have survived. Chiefy, on his way back from the dispersal tells me they are undamaged, for Safi Strip has taken most of the punishment. He nods his head towards the centre of the aerodrome where I can see, all too clearly, a large curled up shape of corrugated iron, conspicuously alone on the grass. I glance quickly at the parachute hut: it is once again roofless.

It is Monday, April the 27th. This morning, after I got out of bed, I went and stood on the small balcony outside my bedroom window—it was hot to my bare feet and I could feel the heat of the sun through my pyjamas. The church opposite was in deep shadow, casting a shadow towards me down the forty odd steps and diagonally across the dusty roadway below. Only the two flanking towers of the church, either side of its central façade, tapering upwards, had their crisp edges of baroque stone gleaming with orange detail against the blue. The central façade itself has a colonnade of tall pillars dwarfing the entrance door and rising steadily to support an architrave and pediment, while above the apex of the pediment there is a plinth upon which stands a sculptured figure holding a cross. This cross leaned out towards me and looked down upon me: a silent morning blessing accompanied by the bark of Bofors guns and the whine of engines. I felt terribly sad. I felt cut off from its blessing: the R.A.F. describe me as Church of England while the church opposite, like all the other churches here, was Roman Catholic. I tried to remember that the golden cross above me was a symbol of love far beyond the different interpretations of men and, at last, I found myself smiling back at it.

Further along the flat wall of our palace to my left, a figure, wrapped in a blanket, emerged from the window of the large stateroom and shuffled out into the sunlight on to a similar balcony to mine. Pancho was taking the morning air. Pancho, who was working on a ranch in the Argentine before the war, stood on his balcony like an S-bend, somewhat round shouldered, with his oval face thrust well forward with his usual ghost of a grin on it; the blanket hung from his shoulders in deep folds with diagonal stripes of brown and yellow—he only needed a sombrero to complete the picture of his pampas days. He stared at the church, while on the church itself, in niches, carved stone saints, wrapped in togas, stared back at Pancho.

"Is breakfast ready?" I murmured.

"No cooks, no waiters," he replied, nodding sleepily towards the entrance of the air-raid shelter a few yards down the road.

As we lingered in the sun, we saw a priest emerge from the doorway of the church, a short, plump figure, enclosed in a black robe, wearing a wide-brimmed black hat, looking tiny beneath the lifted façade of elaborate architecture. Raising his robe with one hand and holding it close about him with the other he started to descend the wide flight of steps—he descended majestically as befitting a priest. There was a sound of heavy engines rising to a crescendo as the German bombers, hidden from sight behind our palace roof, plunged towards us—the priest leaped the last four steps in one bound, disappearing down the shelter steps in a flurry of skirts. Simultaneously other Maltese were coming up the steps, streaming out on to the roadside to watch, for a lone Spitfire was attacking. "Don't shoot them down on top of the palace, you fool, we haven't had breakfast yet," called Pancho. My balcony was shuddering with each crash of anti-aircraft fire but, leaning out as far as I dared, I stared upwards to the palace parapet behind which the action was hidden: a wing tip, an engine, then the whole formation of about thirty 88s swept into view. I saw the eliptical flash of the Spitfire and heard the stutter of machine-guns, but incongruously I was intrigued by the Maltese crowds below: gesticulating with excitement, they surged and swayed—all except one huge fellow who stood like a breakwater with his arms folded, only his head turned, following the released bomb-load over the roof-tops.

After the explosions rumbled up from somewhere in the valley beyond, I turned back into the gilded stateroom: Max and Scotty were already thumping and thundering on a baluster-legged table: "Waiter, waiter,

waiter, waiter . . ." A young Maltese, with a sallow complexion, bent double as if in fear of us, came rushing into the room. Breakfast was disgusting: a sooted length of pale bacon flopped lifelessly over a partially fried piece of bread, both coldly congealed to the plate, and a mug of tea. Knowing that we are on semi-starvation diet because of the siege, and knowing also that oil from crashed aircraft, which we have to use for cooking, was responsible for the beastly taste of the bread and bacon, I had to accept it—but to my mind there was no excuse for the tea. If the C.O. was still with us he'd have done something about it, so I stormed out on to the landing towards the kitchen. At the top of the stairs, the mixed smell of oil, cooking fat and dish-cloths was more virulent than ever, stinging my nostrils; I started to descend but I found myself disturbing horizontal layers of blue smoke, and what a splendid effect the smoke made! Silver shafts of light, streaming obliquely through the arched windows, splashed beautiful patterns of gold on the whole flight of steps below me! As I paused to look I became aware that just outside the windows, red and orange flowers were nodding their delicate heads amongst the green leaves. I also noticed that the palace garden was being observed by a man, standing at the bottom of the illuminated gloom, looking out through the last window of all. As I slowly descended I watched his hand resting lightly on the stonework of the window recess with the loose sleeve of his white shirt hanging motionless below his sunburnt wrist. His face remained in profile, puckered by tiny shadows, while the sunlight glistened on his curly black hair. A dish-cloth was hanging from the pocket of his greasy black trousers—he was the cook! My anger had somehow dissolved; I was only aware that as a symbol of authority descending in judgment I was most inadequately dressed in pyjamas!

"You are the cook?" I asked as firmly as I could.

I must have surprised him, for he started back. "Yes, sir," he replied.

"Well, tell me how you made the tea."

"In the usual way, sir."

I liked the man, but I had to get at grips with the situation. Luckily from my silence he seemed to realise that a more detailed account was needed.

"Well, sir," he continued, "water is short. The tap only runs for an hour each day and today's water hasn't come through yet. We are good, sir, we save water just so we can make tea for you. We kept the water that we boiled yesterday's beetroot in and used that."

What could I do but advise very gently and, suppressing a smile, climb back up the stairs?

The Maltese are enduring the battle with wonderful patience; we may be aware of bad food or more particularly that the brewery, which has run out of fuel, has stopped making beer, but the Maltese, who live on a

diet of bread dipped in olive oil, yesterday had their meagre rations cut
by half: the grain stocks are almost exhausted while the olive oil, normally
imported from Italy, has practically run out. I wish I'd had a longer chat
with the cook this morning, but I've been out on an exploratory walk—
indeed I'm on my way back to Naxxar. I'm resting on a stone wall
with the tarmac road in front of me grey with dust because traffic no
longer runs on the island. The road is pot-holed because no one bothers
about repairs any more and it runs through a typical saffron-yellow landscape under a blue sky. There's no one in sight, not a single one of the
two hundred and seventy thousand Maltese who live here. It's strange to
realise that the island is only fifteen miles long and eight miles wide,
smaller in fact than the area of greater London, and, I am told, one of
the most densely populated areas in Europe.

I passed a row of small, flat-roofed stone houses on my way here. Some
windows were boarded up, others sealed by heavy shutters, but even
where the shutters were fully back against the wall, revealing lace curtains in the windows, the blackness of the rooms stared back at me. I
saw no sign of their occupants. I looked at the dust being blown by the
wind past the doors, yet I felt the people were watching me. Does my
Air Force uniform frighten the Maltese peasants? I am not a Nazi to
kick in their doors, but do they fear some frightful retribution from
the skies if they come too near me? I am reminded of a raid the other
day when two 109s came racing along our Naxxar hill so low that I took
out my revolver to have a shot at them. I suddenly felt the presence of a
Maltese labourer and looking round saw him standing watching me from
the next field. He stared at my revolver for a long, dreadful moment,
then turned and ran.

After passing the houses a few minutes ago I came on alone up the road
towards a line of trees and I noticed a Maltese horse-drawn cab, called a
carozzi or garry, standing in their shadows. Now a garry must once
have been a gay vehicle; its four spoked wheels support, by a most
humorous system of half-moon springs, a compartment where passengers
can sit facing each other on two red-leather seats. From each corner of the
compartment a polished wooden pole rises up to support a shallow domed
roof from which bright enclosing curtains hang down. The garry stood
alone in the empty landscape. Its roof was fringed with a dusty crimson
material like an old jester's cap; its curtains were faded yellow, almost
grey. As I came up behind it I could just see the driver's legs protruding
from behind the front curtain. Watching his black trousers stretched
tightly over his bent knees as I drew nearer I felt thrilled that in all this
empty landscape I was going to meet another human being. Coming
alongside I looked up at the driver and smiled. He stared at me. I said
good morning but he just stared—and I felt him staring as I came on down
the road. Perhaps he resented my long searching look at his horse, a

shrunken creature standing motionless between the shafts, its bony head hanging heavily on its thin neck, lost in its harness; a typical example of our emergency food supply. Perhaps he thought that sketch-book in hand I was making an official inventory and that he'd soon be losing his friend the horse and his livelihood as a cab-driver.

Although the Maltese and ourselves share this battle together, the events of this moment of history are so much larger than any of us individuals. As an individual, sitting on this wall with the wind moaning over the rocks, I'm imagining that when the air-raid warning sounds the blue sky may be blackened by the heavy shapes of descending gliders, and knowing full well that there's no one in these open sunlit fields to oppose such an attack, it seems inevitable that I'd be taken prisoner. I feel horribly alone. I feel conspicuously neglected by my wife. Why hasn't she written me a letter? There was nothing for me yesterday when a lot more letters arrived for other pilots; but surely she must have written; perhaps the complete mail hasn't yet been sorted. Perhaps there's a letter waiting for me at Luqa. Perhaps it will be brought back to Naxxar when "B" Flight return from readiness. This glorious hope, which is probably true, makes me leap from the wall and stride forward along the road.

The tarmac has now ended; a dusty track wriggles ahead; I can already see Naxxar in the distance. I am walking along in the valley below the escarpment, below my favourite position near the grain tower; the fields on my right rise in small terraces on to the side of the hill before it becomes too steep to hold them. In the field that I am passing, a most unusual crop is being cut and gathered into bundles by three labourers bending low with their sickles; the foliage, growing vertically like wheat, is deep spinach green topped by gay crimson flowers that bob about in the wind. Flowers in our palace? Why not? Leaning over the wall, and lifting a newly cut bundle, rather sticky to touch, I gesture to the nearest labourer, an old wrinkled sunburnt fellow wearing a wide-brimmed straw hat, to ask if I may have some. He waves a greeting and seems to indicate that I take more, but one bundle is enough. I jump from the slight bank down on to the road again while the labourer, with a happy smile, bends back to the regular rhythm of his work.

The dusty track, glaring with sunlight, is now climbing the hill towards the town. Quite out of breath, with the sticky flowers beginning to wilt in my clammy right hand, I pass the first of the flat-roofed houses. They rise from the street, their wrought-iron balconies hanging above me. There are several fat women in black dresses sitting outside their houses sewing lace, their plump bare legs stretched out into the roadway like hurdles for walkers such as me, and behind them are strong wooden doorways. I am intrigued by the doors for there is a religious text or picture pinned on each of them: many show Saints, but undoubtedly the Madonna and Child is the favourite subject. There is a continuous babble of voices in the street; peasants in dishevelled western suits are passing up and down, children darting to and fro amongst them, while from among the plump girls with intensely black hair, I find myself awaiting, with secret pleasure, glimpses of the slender graceful ones, with young breasts firm beneath their colourful cotton dresses, large eyes and slightly parted lips. These brunette Botticellis have bare feet, and as they walk, their heels twist up little spurts of dust. It's a gay, happy throng of people that surges me into the main street. I hardly notice the damp things, thick with flies in the dust at the side of the road, the odour of human sweat and the fiercely individual smell of the town. Now, the magnificent twin towers of the church are soaring above the bobbing heads, so I make my way over to the left—I must go straight into our palace if the flowers are to survive. I pause in the palace entrance to watch four priests muttering together at the bottom of the church steps for, as the crowd moves by, everyone falls silent; the men lean forward and touch their caps to the priests while the women . . . A sudden mechanical scream from the air-raid siren: some people run forward, others turn round and run back, still more race for the narrow entrance to the shelter. Mothers snatch up their children and yell fiercely at older boys who are still playing games. The hubbub has sorted itself out; the priests have vanished; the streets are almost empty—just a few regulars standing at the shelter entrance staring up into the blue. The flowers will have to wait because I'm on my way down the alley beside the church, out towards the hillside wall to watch the raid.

Here beside the wall there's only one other pilot with me. It is Cyril, quiet and mature, thin and angular, with his long face shadowed under the curved peak of his South African army officer's hat. The raid's almost over: in his usual manner Cyril has been leaning against the wall: arms folded, his left ankle crossed over his right instep, he nodded towards the first wave of Stukas that came in from the north, and gave a slight tilt of his head towards a second wave, also 87s, that approached from behind the two towers of the church. We have watched three waves of enemy bombers converge on the island targets; Luqa and Valetta have both been bombed while, nearer at hand, Takali's billiard table has been ripped from end to end by bomb clouds. With the concussion of the explosions pressing and pulling at our ear-drums we have watched a lorry race across the aerodrome, swerving in and out of tall smoke pillars that sprung up fierce and energetically black. I think it got away with it. Two 87s have been shot down; burning, they passed over our heads to crash a mile or two behind us.

It is silent now and the sunshine is very warm. Cyril taps me on the shoulder: "There's a parachute coming down," he remarks quietly.

"Where?" I shout, swinging round. Cyril gestures into the sky above Luqa. I can't see it, only the red blanket of drifting dust from where the bombs fell on Valetta; above the dust the sky is green crystal, growing blue and still bluer as I look steeply upwards. Yes, there's the 'chute looking pink against the deepest blue of all, descending steadily, descending rather fast perhaps. Will it pass behind the dust? It's already there in white silhouette, dropping much too fast. Something's wrong with it; it's only half open, the rest flapping loosely, and the man is not struggling but just looking down past his feet at the ground rushing up to meet him. The parachute appears for an instant in front of a square house in the valley, then disappears.

The men that we can see moving about down there will ring the hospital; not that the pilot, who may well be one of "B" Flight, could have survived a fall like that. Was his parachute collapsed by the enemy? I hear that it's a habit of the 109s to pull up steeply over a descending 'chute so that the downdraught from their propellers collapses the open silk, entangling the shroud lines, and causes the pilot to fall headlong. I am aware that I'm witnessing total war. Although I could never bring myself to kill such a defenceless man, the inevitable justice of total war is borne in upon me. If we fall by parachute on to our own soil we can go up and fight again: thus we are legitimate military targets. Sorrowfully Cyril and I turn back towards Naxxar.

At the palace I ring through to Luqa and talk to the Dreaded Hugh. I learn that Pip, who I talked to on the hillside the other day when he was so frightened, is missing on his first flight. I put through a call to the hospital: it was Pip in the parachute, but he's still alive; one foot has been shot away and his other foot broken on landing, but he's still alive. Cyril and I wait for the return of the other "B" Flight pilots and the mail. My flowers have not revived in water; they were exposed too long and I've had to throw them away. "B" Flight finally return with the news that Pip has died from spinal concussion and shock. They bring the last of the mail—no letter from Diana—but a large packet has come for Pip and will have to be sent back.

CHAPTER 9

THE SILVER CORD

IT IS now afternoon. The Dreaded Hugh and I are on our way over
to St. Paul's Bay to see the C.O. I look sideways at this sandy-haired
Rhodesian Flight Lieutenant, marching along beside me, rolling to
and fro, with his lengthy khaki shorts flapping about his knees. We have
already passed through the village and, if we've followed the directions
correctly, this next house on the right called Palestrina should be the Pilot's
Rest Camp. After the blinding sunlight the cool darkness of the narrow
hallway is most refreshing—but is this the house? Idly I turn the pages
of a suggestions book on the hall table: "It is suggested that the number
on the house opposite be removed forthwith." Glancing back across the
road I read the number, for it is very distinct: 109!—undoubtedly the
camp for resting pilots!

We have found the C.O. looking very much better, but the air-raid
warning's sounded and he is leading us across the descending lawn at
the back of the house, through a trellised arbour of honeysuckle, down
some steep steps on to a grass terrace commanding a magnificent view
of the Bay. At our feet there is a rocky ravine in deep shadow with trees
growing the other side of it. We look down over the tree-tops on to the
vast stretch of blue water encircled with yellow hills, with the mouth of
the Bay away on our right. At the narrow entrance, which gives us a
framed view of the wide Mediterranean beyond, there is the flat island
where Saint Paul was shipwrecked in the tempest. With the first formation of Ju 88s diving straight at us, and now turning fiercely to drop
their bombs beyond the hilltops on the far side of the Bay, it is difficult
to imagine these blue skies darkly overcast with cloud, to visualise the
scene of driving rain and spray from the boisterous curling seas, obscur-
ing the headlands as St. Paul's ship rode the storm. Yet even as the shell
bursts defile the blue sky above us, following a second wave of German
bombers inland, and as I crouch down as two of the Stukas peel away from
the main stream, diving at us and releasing their bombs into St. Paul's
village, it seemed to me quite natural for St. Paul and his companions,
straining their eyes for a sight of land, to describe this as "a place where
two seas meet." Just over there, the other side of the moving water is the
actual spot where "they ran the ship aground; and the forepart stuck fast,
and remained unmovable, but the hinder part was broken with the

95

violence of the waves." Just above that spot where fragments of St. Paul's boat may still be lying, where "they all escaped safe to land," and where, as they wrote, "the barbarous people showed us no little kindness; for they kindled a fire, and received us every one—" just above it in the blue sky a third formation of bombers is edging into its dive towards a small Maltese harbour.

"Look out—109s." Two black machines, closely followed by two more, turn fiercely over our tree tops and twist away over St. Paul's island: there are five machines arching there and one is a Hurricane, one of our own aircraft, alone and fighting desperately. Oh, well done. The enemy seem to slacken for a moment, their sharp winged Messerschmitts drawing out to sea a little. The Hurricane, seizing the opportunity, dives into the cover of the hills. As it disappears from sight below the hill crests there's a sharp burst of gunfire from the ground. From the ground! The Ground! It was our own guns firing! Our own guns! With terrible anxiety I watch the Hurricane reappear. Its huge shape lifts over the sky-line with part of its left wing breaking away. Uncontrollable it plunges into the rocks; an exploding crimson flame scars the hill, while a smaller black shape, trailing blue smoke, bounces onward down, down, down towards the water; there at the water's edge a second fire bursts out.

"A Hurricane or a Messerschmitt?" calls a Squadron Leader running towards us along the terrace.

"A Hurricane," I reply.

"That's what I thought," he mutters.

The fire, highest on the hillside, has now died down but smoke still oozes from the second. By borrowing the Squadron Leader's field-glasses, which flatten the distant slope and bring it sharply nearer, I examine the wreckage. There is some movement high up in the circular frame: lifting the glasses I can make out several figures urgently leaping downwards from rock to rock. Even from this distance it is obvious that these khaki figures are well aware of what they have done. I lower the glasses and hand them back. None of us says a word.

Twenty minutes later—a sudden wail; a Maltese barkeeper giving the All Clear on his hand siren; the sea and the sky remain a motionless blue; the distant hillside glitters in saffron yellow, with smoke drifting away from it; there's a sound of footsteps approaching on the flagstone path from the lawn. Three Army officers in smart uniforms emerge from the honey-suckle archway, descend the steps and the Captain, who leads them, holds something towards me: a burnt fragment of khaki battledress and some charred pieces of paper are thrust into my hands.

"They were all we could get from the Hurricane pilot," he says, "he was burned about the head and had a cannon shell through his pelvis."

In bewilderment I look down at the khaki fragment, in the centre of it, simple, undamaged and without adornment of medals, is the brevet of R.A.F. wings; the papers appear to be a letter to his wife or girl friend; while on another scorched and brittle envelope I can read his name and rank of Flight Sergeant quite clearly. Hugh, producing a scissors, takes these intimacies from me. He cuts the brown fire traces from the wings and puts them in an envelope into his pocket. He adds the fringe of burnt material to the other papers, and, before I can stop him, hurls them over into the deep ravine. I stare down into the darkness.

The Captain is talking to the C.O., in fact the whole party, with Hugh following, is climbing back up the steps towards the house. As they pass out of sight I hear the Captain's voice: "What do you want us to do with the body?"

"Good luck, Flight Sergeant," I whisper inwardly.

The sun glares down from the empty sky; the trees do not move; the perfume of the honeysuckle is sickly sweet in the warm air; the other Squadron Leader, stands motionless, still gazing out at the distant hills; brilliant flowers are growing in the grass to the very brink of the dark ravine. My fumbling thought is in the presence of great mysteries. The Flight Sergeant has gone, yet he was a human being like myself; if something of him has gone out into the world of spirit such a part must have been with him yesterday as he walked the island paths. We all have the same constitution, so what is this inner part of me by which I send a blessing to him without words, this strange sensitivity close to my heart? In so far as I think deeply and love deeply it may be with the eternal part of my nature that does not die.

My physical body is fixed on this hillside in time and space, the ground is hard under my right foot when I stamp, I feel pain as I pinch myself. Even if I survive to-morrow's flying I know that there will be another ordeal and another and another—my own body may soon be entangled in burning wreckage—it may be pulped, a bloody mess, a broken thing. Other people will say: "What do you want us to do with the body?"

But what of the inner life that does not die? Although I shamefully neglect it, I feel that joy after death, or life after death, is in proportion to the degree in which we love God, his creatures and his creation; in proportion to the degree in which we experience this fuller life while we are still here on earth; in proportion to our obedience. I feel that we are here to grow the wings of love and that when the ugly moment comes, when our bodies are broken and smashed, we soar out joyously into new life. Yet how are we to lead the good life—to love in a world gone mad with war? My whole being is obsessed by war and all my actions too. If I am hit while flying, with my mind focused on tactics, combat and deflection shooting, will I be granted a moment of silent communion before my aircraft strikes the ground?

D

The Squadron Leader, having lowered his field glasses, is walking slowly towards me—I can't just stand here and stare at him.

"What happened to you, sir? Were you shot down like our C.O.?"

"Yes, I was shot down. I came out of hospital just over a week ago—since then I've been staying here. Delightful isn't it."

"Yes, but tell me something, please. You know those strange moments when flying, when there's a sudden emergency, did you ever find that you had changed gear in time? Have you suddenly found yourself on a different time scale, thinking and feeling so fast that the speed of normal life appeared in slow motion to you?"

"I think most of us feel like that in an emergency. Why?"

"Well, you've been shot down. Did you ever find this experience carried a stage further? Did you ever find yourself outside your own body looking back at it?"

"Yes," he eventually replied, "it's strange that you should ask that."

He pauses again; he seems reluctant to continue: I think he realises from my urgency that I'm earnestly seeking for something; perhaps he's on his guard against "shooting a line", accursed inhibition that always prevents us learning from someone else's experience in the R.A.F.

"After a bang with 109s," he continues slowly, "I think my tail was falling off, but I don't quite know, I had some control and I tried to bring the plane down. I was approaching the main runway at Luqa from the Safi end when she started to dive. It got steeper and steeper but I couldn't stop it. I watched a ravine with a stone wall on top coming up to meet me: it was no good, the controls didn't answer: I gave up. Suddenly I was outside the aeroplane watching the whole thing happening. The aeroplane with my body inside it went on diving but it didn't hit the ravine, first it crumpled and bounced on a great angle of rock and I watched my body being tossed about, then it went sideways in slow motion through a wall, somersaulting on its broken wing across a small field and finally burrowing into another wall under some trees. It didn't catch fire although I expected flames. My body looked like a discarded marionette entangled with the wreckage. I watched the blood wagon arrive, and I watched them hack me out. I was outside myself until long after my body reached the hospital; I didn't go back until half-way through the operation."

A Ju 88 reconnaissance plane is approaching from high up over the sea. The Squadron Leader climbs the steps into the shadow of the honeysuckle arbour and I join him in the hiding place as the peering photographic eye passes across above us. What happened to him is the same as what happened to me on my first flight only he was outside for very much longer. It's the moment of resigning oneself to death that seems to trigger off this kind of experience. Is it the spirit's ultimate association with the material world? In this moment of detachment do we have a chance to think on God once again? Is such a moment prolonged after we have died. Yet while we live, staring back at ourselves, we must be attached to our body in some invisible way.

Yes—"the silver cord!" The lovely verses from Ecclesiastes float into my mind with new meaning.

"When the silver cord be loosed, or the golden bowl be broken, or the pitcher broken at the fountain, then shall the body return to the dust, and the spirit return to God who gave it."

This morning, despite my fear of air battle I felt confident about my tactics—I was sure that I'd be able to deliver our American pilot called Tilley, and Warrant Officer "Belch", who I was taking up for their first Malta trip, accurately into the bomber stream, that we'd be able to shoot down several enemy planes, and that I'd get them safely out again. I had led them steeply up into the sun and was diving back when it happened—great spurts of oil came splashing back over my windscreen and flooding all over the side panels and hood—it grew darker and darker inside my cockpit—then the oil froze in solid black waves—couldn't see out. Tried opening the hood—it ran an inch then jammed. Tried to get Tilley or Belch to take over—not their fault they couldn't hear me—my transmitter went faulty. Could hear Woody all right as I dived; couldn't tell him I was in trouble. "Big jobs on Takali," he called. By the time I found Takali, through a small gap in the oil—nothing but dust. "Grand Harbour" called Woody—couldn't find the harbour in time. "Halfar now." Managed to get a brief glimpse of the German bombers—could no longer see them as I turned—charged blindly on. Got amongst them all right, 88s first. Then 109s—tried to make myself a difficult target, twisted and turned, nearly collided with a 109—prayed fiercely—seemed to be two people: the pilot flinging my Spitfire about and some other impersonal awareness of what was happening—a brief fiery glimpse as a 109 went down in flames—the battle seemed to go on for hours. Finally, when I landed my plane back at Luqa poor Chiefy came and stared at it—not many bullet holes.

During lunch at Luqa there was another raid—the mess was straddled by bombs. As the guard room collapsed on top of our bus I am late in getting over to St. Paul's Bay for my second visit. Well done, Tilley: I've left him over at the aerodrome, hunting for the Intelligence officer, trying to get his victory confirmed, for he shot down the 109—said it was sitting on a Spitfire's tail. It may have been sitting on Belch's tail or perhaps mine—I didn't see much of the action.

Here at St. Paul's Bay I walk across the lawn at the back of the house, I descend the steps by the honeysuckle, and now beside the ravine, so dark and deep, I walk the whole length of the wide terrace and follow the path downwards into the cool dark shadow of the trees. All around me in the subfusc light knuckled tree roots clasp the rocks while their trunks, twisting upwards, branch out over my head into a translucent fan vaulting of green leaves. I walk slowly, but all too soon I re-emerge into hot sunlight radiant from a cobalt sky. Still going down, across a precipitous slope of sunscorched grass, making my way carefully for, if I slipped, I would plunge headlong into the motionless water about a hundred feet below. Now, by the safety of a rock wall, I look out over the blue bay towards the lemon yellow hills on the far shore.

Passing through a gap in the wall I descend a flight of steps towards a concrete platform built only a few inches above the lapping water. There are several pilots down there stretched out on white towels in their bathing costumes; in a hot sleepy fashion they glance up at me as I approach: most are strangers but two familiar figures, the C.O. and the Dreaded Hugh, roll on their sides and wave a greeting.

After telling them that I've initiated the last of my pilots and that Tilley has destroyed a 109 I look around this silent restful place partly shadowed as it is by the cliff. How I'd love to bathe; the transparent water looks so cool and clean; I must bathe for I haven't been fully immersed in water since I left the aircraft-carrier,'my hair is thick with dust, my clothes are sticking to me: but I have no bathing costume. I would not like to offend the Maltese, but no, this place is not really overlooked, the "stranger" officers tell me they don't object, so I peel off my clothes and leap to the water's edge. My watch! I nearly forgot it in this new delight of refreshing nakedness. Once again I stare down into the crystal blue world rippling with sheets of light; at the rocks below the surface swayingly enfolded by green and vermilion.

"Is it really deep enough?" I ask.

"It's ten feet there," smiles the C.O.

Further out the surface of the bay is deep blue; St. Paul's tiny island, low against the sea in the distance, is gay yellow, dappled with the palest of violet shadows; beyond that is the firm horizon. I feel joyous and newly born as Adam must have felt in Eden air, so I take a deep breath and dive in.

The water is icy, but I am gliding downwards with my eyes wide open watching the changing patterns of sunlight. I roll over and over as I rise to the surface, then splash lustily with my feet beating up and down in the churned white water. Tiring quickly I swim out to sea instead. I am stung by a jellyfish: the sudden searing pain of a narrow red hot iron across the width of my back astonishes me: it continues to burn despite the water so freezingly delicious. Swimming around the pain gradually passes away and finally, growing happily exhausted, I make for the shore. Standing up by a tall rock, with the sun burning the salty drops of sea water from my shoulders, I look down at my body as yet unmutilated by war: I'm astonishingly slim, half starved, I suppose, my tapering sunburnt legs turn blue under water and my feet appear to float above the rocky pebbles. Feeling vividly alive I climb out and rub myself briskly with a towel.

"Air raid warning's gone," C.O. tells me.

"What does it matter, we can watch from here."

"109s machine-gunned us this morning—we don't want to get caught again."

"Surely not here"—but Hugh's pointing out the chips in the rock and some flattened bullets lying on the concrete.

I dress, but it seems a pity to climb the steps and crawl up the steep hillside, yet that's what we are doing, our breaths quick and urgent from the exertion—the 109s are already murmuring above us. In the shadow of the trees the C.O. suggests that we all go into St. Paul's village and have a really large fish supper in a bar restaurant that has been recommended to him. Emerging on to the terrace I'm not surprised to see Max, Scotty and Baby Face for they said they might come over: they're staring up at the sky and, glimpsing us, they point out two waves of enemy bombers coming in from the north. Smoke-splashed by anti-aircraft fire, about forty bombers are passing above us and heading inland towards the aerodromes. There is no sign of the three or four fighters that the island could muster in defence; Woody may be holding them on the ground again; it is with unspoken anxiety for our few machines that our large party, after climbing up to the house, sets off down the road towards the village.

During our ten minutes walk we have watched the 109s sweeping the sky in twos, fours, and eights with the sound of others higher up, but now as we arrive at the small harbour with its angular jetties sticking out into the bay, we are greeted by a Maltese whirling the handle of the siren for the All Clear. The aerodromes may be a shambles but, still indulging our afternoon off from war, we enter the restaurant and each down a draught of fiery sherry. The C.O. searches out the cook and having organised six plump fish to be ready at seven o'clock turns to us with the suggestion of visiting other taverns for drinks while we wait. The others agree, but I'm staying here; I've got to fly again tomorrow and the view over the bay is so beautiful. Alone now, with another glass of sherry at my elbow, I've seated myself on a low wall close to the harbour entrance. The sherry, a blend of liquorice and vinegar, is really rather horrid, but the silence is real refreshment, with the lap of water, the quiet stealth of the fisherman manœuvring his red and green gondola boat and catching crabs that I can see scurrying along the bottom, the great blobs of silver reflecting from the descending sun, the village foreground, the romantic castle high up on the cliff top behind it, and the whole sky suffused with light as in a painting by Turner. I try to catch something of its mood in my drawing.

All too soon it's seven o'clock, the others have returned, the fish is ready for us and we enter a back room to take our places at a wide rectangular table. I have managed to get a seat close to the open door through which I can watch the water, the hillside and the rapidly changing effects for I seem to be tied to their quietude. My companion pilots, however, are laughing and full of fun; I join the noise and chatter as best I can but I am overwhelmed by the silence beyond the door. The sun has gone down, the hill with its wonderful buildings gorgeous with colour, is dark against the sky, the sky is a quiet mother of pearl, and the gently moving water is still an unaccountable royal blue; although the buildings are grey-brown, huddled into the dark indigo hillside, each house has turned one pale face towards the light to catch the last blessing of the day.

CHAPTER 10

TIP AND RUN

Diary: Wednesday, April 29.

Yesterday's flying hell but flying has to be faced. Trying to forget about it quickly, trying to lead a normal life despite the battle—I've come over to St. Paul's Bay again this morning: sketched wayside shrines—strangely silent walk—no early-morning raid.

On swimming platform—hardly expected "life" drawing on Malta—most swimmers have discarded costumes now. Twelve o'clock—still no raid—everyone apprehensive.

3 p.m.—been drawing "Uncle" Bosworth, officer-in-charge here. With his plump figure in khaki shorts and shirt overflowing lounge armchair, he stared at me, pebble eyes through horn-rim specs.: asked me what Huns were up to—I don't know. 3.30 now, still no raid—don't like it. Uncle sat very still: flies crawled all over him, played hop-skotch on his tattooed arms, polished their feet on his bald head—he didn't move—just an involuntary twitch of his curled moustache. 4 p.m.—eerie silence continues.

5 p.m.—sun hot—been swimming—still no raid—now looking at Diana's photo—always carry it—it might get buried at Naxxar—difficult to believe really her—remote in some other world.

A faint hum and Sirens!—five tiny planes in stratosphere crawling overhead—thirty thousand feet? Reconnaisance? No 109s, no 88s, no 87s—all clear sounding already. All bewildered. Some pilots say Eyeties—others say England raided last night. Have Huns withdrawn from Sicily? "Genned-up" pilot, just come down steps, says "No". Recce Spit reports two hundred Ju 88s., one hundred and fifty 87s, more than a hundred 109s and gliders. Invasion? Lull before storm? Two thousand tons of bombs dropped here last month, seven thousand this month, may be pre-invasion softening up? End of April, beginning of May, always time for Spring Offensives. Genned-up pilot says "No"—says "Huns daren't invade us"—tells us "official figures"—one hundred and ninety-two enemy planes destroyed and damaged last month, almost three hundred this month—says "enemy can't stand such losses." But could six fighters we have left stop invasion? Gen man replies that Hun won't invade so long as we have any planes left. Why not?—horribly uneasy about silence—am going down to St. Paul's village, to paint.

11 p.m. Naxxar, in bed. Dusk at village more beautiful than ever—painting a failure—tones and colours changed too quickly. Moonlight followed dusk—soft blue light over cubic houses cast long grey shadows—saw lovers under palm trees—thought of Diana—no news of her. Walked back along cliff tops—sea pure viridian green, sky a dark cold blue with stars, uncanny silence and nostalgic smell of hay from fields. Beyond window above church can see lines of moonlit clouds—do write to me my darling. Sirens. Sirens breathing, moaning, screaming, rising and falling, enemy planes coming, sky full of engines, bombs coming——Oh, my God.

Diary: Thursday, April 30.

Bombs and bombers screeched all night long—seemed as if all pillars of air were being flattened violently, one against another, until they crushed our ear drums and left our heads ringing—couldn't sleep.

Diary: Friday, May 1.

Same again—no sleep at all. If enemy flies three sorties with his bombers we've had a thousand bombers on each of the last two nights—feels like it. Readiness at Luqa but not sent up—ack ack followed five Eyeties at thirty thou. Why sudden change in attack? Everyone uneasy. Uneasiness spread to Army this evening—guns all loaded.

Diary: Saturday, May 2.

Third night without sleep—bomb crash with flares descending over Luqa—whole enemy bomber force committed to night attack. C.O.'s just come back—he's taking us down to dawn readiness. Some new plan —all of us go.

What a day it's been: I've done absolutely nothing but I'm tired out. We found Luqa a shocking mess, cratered like the moon, and not only craters, but crack—crack-crack, delayed action bombs kept sending columns of black smoke bursting sky-wards from runways, perimeter tracks, stone walls, and dispersal points. Searching for our Spitfires, which had been moved to safer positions, we skirted clusters of red flags where other bombs were waiting to go off—we could see figures working desperately on the main runway, trying to fill in holes, trying to remove or defuse the bombs that were still there. All had to confess it—the aerodrome was out of action. I watched the C.O. and two other Spits fly off to Takali to do their readiness there, but as my Spitfire was slightly bent I had to wait while Chiefy and the boys worked on it. I sat on a white rock, jerking violently as black thunderslap pillars shot up against the white galleon clouds moving in from the north. When my plane was ready I received final instructions from Woody that there was no enemy activity of any kind and that I was to take off and land immediately at Takali. I climbed into the cockpit, bundled my sketching things and tin hat on to my lap, then, avoiding bomb holes, thundered off the Luqa escarpment.

In the air I was sorely tempted to explore the caverns of creamy cloud, that slid over the top of my cockpit canopy, the first cumulus clouds that have covered the sky here, but obeying orders I closed the throttle and started the wide descending circle. Approaching Takali I banked leisurely round the dome of Mosta church—this third biggest dome in the world rose towards my left wing-tip with a smooth, full bellied curve, its upper surface enriched with a design of palmettes—the ornamental Byzantine crown which topped the dome sailed past my cockpit window, then, as I floated out over the hollow-walled gardens of Mosta village, I lowered my wheels. With the aerodrome grass widening in front of me I put down the flaps—I heard Woody's voice in my earphones: "One plus, enemy aircraft, fifteen miles north of Gozo."

I was by then slowing and taxi-ing back towards the parking place; I was convinced that such a small plot was an enemy reconnaissance plane at thirty or thirty-five thousand feet, too high and too far away to worry about, so switching off the engine, I climbed out on to the wing root. I was astonished to see all the airmen and pilots stampeding away from me. Diving from a gap in the clouds were the straight wings and under-slung engines—an 88. I began my dash for cover when—snap-crack: a ringing blow seemed to pierce all the stretched membranes within me. It must only have been a few minutes later, the dust was falling back, some airmen were running to help me, there was a ringing, ringing, ringing in my head—staggering to my feet I must have started running, running in the same direction as before. Overwhelmed by a single desire to bury myself deep and safe in the rock I found myself jolting down a steep rocky incline into a kind of pit. I gazed into the mouths of tunnels but my imagination, conjuring up visions of horrors in the darkness, must have helped me to pull myself together. Hunting for deep shelter instead of developing the open-air slit-trench technique for being bombed is the beginning of blind panic that makes one "bomb happy" or "round the bend". Ashamed I turned round at once and walked back.

Once on the aerodrome, with considerable pain in my ears, I felt responsible for the whole incident—despite my old friend Peter assuring me that everyone was astonished at this first tip and run raid they had experienced. I tried to forget the incident by talking with Peter and a friend of his called Mac, a delightful fellow—we discussed line abreast formation—they were telling me variations of the basic pair whereby enemy planes could be lured to destruction—but they were sent up to intercept another raid. The same happened later and I thought it hardly fair that we Luqa pilots should be held on the ground.

We watched a formation of 88s slide mysteriously out of the clouds then turn steeply to drop their bombs on Valetta, we also had our first sight of Italian fighters parading the sky. Sporadic raids all day but the C.O. kept us for fourteen hours instead of the normal seven-hour shift. I wandered about, restless, lifeless, still ashamed of myself, and thoroughly upset by the unusual rhythm of battle. In a desperate effort to settle down I got Johnny Plagis to act as my model: he looked much the same as at Hugh Pughs' address of welcome, glaring sideways at me with his strange eyes—I had considerable satisfaction in accepting the silent challenge of the man and imprisoning him in my pen-and-ink drawing. Later I wandered along the perimeter track to sketch the untidy wreckage of a Spitfire—its undamaged propeller hung over the edge of a bomb hole while the rest of the scattered pieces, protruding from the fire-stained earth, looked like a squashed insect—with the dome of Mosta church behind it and with cumulus clouds riding the Mediterranean horizon, I hoped it would be a souvenir sketch of our first and last Takali visit. This evening we flew our Spitfires back to Luqa. I was the last to land—I hung about in the twilight sky hoping that the night bombing might begin early, that I might have a chance of redeeming my ignominy by shooting something down—I banked through tiny cumulus clouds that rode the blood-red sunset—but it was no good. I'm tired out.

Sunday, May 3: yet another night without sleep. Luqa was wrecked again and we've been operating from Takali, flying this time and fighting with 109s who have come back in hordes—I'm hot, sweaty and very tired—but there's no water to wash in. As our bus squeezed its way back here to Naxxar, I looked out through the glassless window frame at the Maltese getting on with their simple, good lives—after fighting for my own life I loved them: old women, wearing their sombre black head-dresses, clutched voluminous black garments around them as they pressed themselves up against the walls or sped on in front of the bus like bats—particularly I loved the young girls of thirteen or fourteen who looked in at us with delicately innocent faces, such fresh innocence after hell was like a draught of cool water.

Tired though we all are there's no rest—the C.O. back from his convalescence is buzzing like a dynamo, embroiling everyone in abundant plans and projects: people are rushing to and fro carrying furniture, blankets and bedding. Undoubtedly moving our rooms is the best scheme. In our new room with simple whitewashed walls at the back of the palace there are two other beds besides mine: one is for the C.O. and the other is for the Dreaded Hugh—but Hugh will be away in hospital for some time yet for his tummy complaint, Malta Dog, is much worse. Opposite our door are real bathrooms, while the promise of water to run for half an hour each morning and evening will be luxury. Also

luxurious, is the hope, from time to time, of electric light instead of
candles and evil-smelling paraffin wicks protruding from beer bottle tops.

My work in all this activity is the decoration of a huge area of wall:
in fact I am standing in the centre of a small room that is being fitted up
as a bar. Paint brush in hand I am staring up at the Squadron crest, a
winged sword, almost completed high on the wall above the bar counter.
I can't complete it now for I've run out of red paint. Another job
unfinished is the Squadron score board—three columns, headed respectively "Destroyed", "Probables" and "Damaged". But what the devil
do I put in these columns? Although we have shot down at least fifteen
enemy planes since our arrival we have no official score. I don't think
our Intelligence Officer, a bomber type, in what had originally been a
bomber aerodrome, has much idea about how to follow up fighter
claims—time and again Takali appear to have been given the credit for
machines we have destroyed.

I don't know what to put on this score board. I'm packing up—going
to join Scotty and Max—they've just carried a large settee in here and have
gone through the french windows on to the flat roof outside.

This is certainly better: this sun-scorched roof is enclosed by a balustrade
against which I'm leaning; although Naxxar rooftops block the view
south and the tall palace walls behind me block the northern and eastern
skies, I am looking down over the garden, out towards the western hills:
The garden wall is smothered with purple bougainvillaea and the flagstone path stretches away through the palm trees towards a wrought-iron
gate into the fields. Swinging round I look back at Max and Scotty;
they are sunbathing on their blankets; Baby Face, more modestly clad in
khaki shorts, is spreading out his bedding on the hot flagstones. I'll get
my bedding and join them.

I have just settled here but the air-raid sirens are screaming, the guns
have opened fire and we all watch the sky. Emerging from behind the
palace wall a formation of tiny Italian bombers, high in the stratosphere,
is moving majestically across the blue spaces between the clouds; their pin-
head shapes, shining against the blue, plucked with white puffs, are
vertically above us. "Don't frighten them," calls Scotty towards the
gunners, then, tipping his dark-blue Australian hat to a jaunty angle on
his head, he gazes skywards again. The bombers are steering straight for
Takali but because of the roof tops we won't be able to see the bombing.
Wirr-rr-rr-ssh-ssh-ssh rushing of air; Max snatches for his pants; Baby
Face and I jam in the french windows, break through and fall flat; the
bombs are rushing upon us, this is the end. I hug the sofa, finding comfort
in its round plump shape; Scotty sprawls across the dusty floor, sliding
until his face is within an inch of mine; I have an impression of Max's
heavy body with his pants on, but the thump of his arrival is lost in the
roar of bombs . . . a continuous splitting roar . . . more coming. . . .

more coming . . . splitting and tearing in our ears . . . more, more, more.
The last one arrives with a rush and a flop into the garden, a dud or a
delayed action.

We sit up, laughing at ourselves, we are smeared with dust; dust fills
the room; and dust hangs in the air above the flat roof outside.

"Listen," says Max.

There is shrieking and moaning and crying out from the streets below.

"Come on," I call to the others for I am instantly calm, surprisingly
calm. Hastily donning my clothes I lead the way down the stairs and
out into the street: Maltese policemen are running in all directions,
running out into the square and back again; there are children crying
and women tossing their arms, clasping their hands, sobbing and shrieking
in hysterics. No one has taken charge. Although some smashed stonework, blasted out from a narrow street on my right, lies across the road,
a quick glimpse does not reveal excessive damage. I grab one of the
Maltese men who has been standing and running and staring.

"Where exactly did the bombs go off?"

He seems delighted to have found someone in uniform. He leads me
down another side street, partially blocked, into the hallway of a house,
then runs away. Downstairs rooms thick with broken glass; up the stairs
—crumbling first floor rooms empty—so out on to the street again. A
gap between the houses, a field, yawning with bomb craters like red boils
—crimson earth and objects scattered everywhere—pieces with long
shaggy hair on them—goat, not human. Back in the street, running and
peering through all the open doors, suddenly a hallway, white with
tumbled rock and rubble leads incongruously through to white daylight.
Where are my pilots? Running back into the square I glimpse Max,
Scotty and Baby Face heading back towards the church.

"Where the hell are you going?" I shout. "Work for you this way."

They join me in the hall of the house. We discover tall closed doors
on our left, bulging out at us, bulging with the weight of wreckage.
We peer through a splintered hole where a rock has burst through the
panelling: the room, which is open to the sky, is packed tight with white
dust and stone blocks. We hear a noise underneath it all, a ghastly
inhuman noise, muffled and strained, then silence. Watching the rivulets
of dust that curl down the sunlit walls we hear the noise again. We are
stunned by its inhuman anguish. Baby Face seizes the door and, struggling
with it, wrenches it open: we leap back as huge blocks, broken stones,
rubble and splintered wood spew out upon us. Inside there is a second
pair of doors that we cannot move. Together we lift a coloured marble
pedestal that has been standing in the hall and batter a gap large enough
for Max and me to climb through.

That noise again, then silence. Listening intently we decide to begin
near the middle of the far wall. It's a struggle for us to lift the huge

blocks, but one by one they are put to one side as we dig deeper and deeper into the white dust with our hands and fingers. One after another we lift more blocks aside. Finally, from the rubble and other angled rocks, a round object protrudes, red on top, white with dust, white dust falling away from it as it turns slowly towards me; one red watery eye blinks open, staring at me. More dust falls away and the thing has lips.

Baby Face takes over my job at burrowing as, straightening up, I yell to Scotty in the hallway to have a glass of water sent. Waiting for it, I look around the room and notice that, on two matchstick beams that sag across the open sky, a great stone rock is balanced and wobbling just above our heads. I call out quickly to Scotty to stop heaving his chopper: yes, the gap in the door must be widened to get the victim out, but he must work carefully. The glass of water now passed through to me looks clean and fresh; from my hip pocket I draw out my small flask of brandy that I have always carried with me for occasions such as this; adding a little to the water I moisten the lips of the head, then, supporting it with my left hand, I let it drink a little. It is an old man who talks to me in broken English. He is miraculously alive and so far, as we continue to dig, his body seems intact.

A Maltese fellow had leapt down beside us. He is digging feverishly. He looks up to tell me that the old man is his father; apparently he left him sleeping in an upstairs room. The man now pauses to wipe away the remaining dust very tenderly from his father's face. The last rocks removed, the old man is freed, and we lift him on to a stretcher that has been squeezed through to us. A woman, shrieking in the hallway, has to be carried out in a fainting condition before we can move the old man from the building. Now, I'm walking alongside the stretcher for he talks to me and I hold his hand. We pass red-eyed neighbours, who, peering from their doorways, cross themselves as we approach the square where the ambulance is surrounded by an excited crowd. In the ambulance the old man talks to me for a few moments, then, relaxing his grip on my hand, he dies.

All last night I lay with my tin hat on my head watching the great stones in the ceiling as the bombs screamed down on us. Luqa's out of action and this afternoon we operate our Spitfires from Takali yet again. It is mid-morning of Monday, May the 4th; the C.O.'s exploring somewhere in the island trying to buy drinks to stock the bar; Max, Scotty, Baby Face, Pancho and Cyril are here on the hillside with me; 109s have already swept overhead; the harbour anti-aircraft barrage is going mad for a Vic formation of five Italian bombers is lumbering in from the sea.

It's a crazy height to fly, five thousand feet straight and level, into the bursting shells; the gunners can't miss them. One plane wobbles violently, falling out of place, but it's climbing again and closing up; the self control of those pilots and crews is magnificent; bearing a charmed life the planes are still coming on, but where are our fighters? From high in the blue there's a noise of cannon fire; we can't see the dogfight but our fighters have obviously been cut off by 109s. With the flickering shells having no effect at all, the bombers continue past us; if they were trying to hit the harbour they've missed: there go their bombs, blanketing the valley in a long line towards Luqa: still unharmed the bombers turn away behind the rising curtain of dust, their engines fading eastwards.

Above us, in the undisturbed blue with the sun glaring out of it, the dog-fight's still going on: we can hear long bursts of heavy canon, the remote clatter of machine-guns and the rising and fading moan of turning aircraft. Quiet now; but Cyril's seen something: two dots curving downwards, two fighters swinging round over the bomb dust heading towards us, Spitfires, but they're too late, the bombers have gone.

Approaching our hillside the Spitfires start to turn: I'm not particularly impressed by the way they are crossing over. Look out! A black shape is hurtling upon them; swerving, but it's going too fast: it can't bring its guns to bear. Its engine howls as the 109 passes low in front of us; it wavers as the pilot twists in his seat to see if he's being followed, then, with sudden power, it bounds forward, behind Naxxar's square buildings, reappearing above the skyline in the distance, a tiny dot streaking away northwards.

A 109 by itself? Never. Where's its number two? We all search the sky. The two Spits are climbing in vic formation much too close together, tactically vulnerable; why doesn't the second Spit take up its wide line-abreast formation for mutual protection? If there is a second 109, watching, these Spits are asking for trouble; there's nothing we can do to help them. They circle left, still in tight vic formation, and with their engines murmuring lazily they pass above us. The second German! With horror we watch a black dot dive vertically down the blue just this side of Valetta; it eases out of its dive about two miles away, and now, low behind the grain store, it's rushing towards us. The Spitfires haven't seen its angled shape growing larger and larger; they can't hear its roaring engine. Turn, you fools, turn . . . turn . . . The 109, making for the second Spitfire, lifts gently over our heads, then, swerving towards the leader, opens fire. Although the second Spit breaks violent right, the leader continues straight and level for that critical instant longer: a flash of a shell striking below its cockpit before the 109 streaks upwards and away.

The Spitfire circles to the left, wobbling a little, trailing a wisp of smoke, but now, as both machines level out and pass slowly over our heads, the smoke has stopped, the leader's engine is running smoothly, it flies steadily while its companion, after making an inquisitive turn towards it, moves out into wide line abreast where it should have been all the time. The section heads towards Naxxar, lucky to have escaped; but no, the leading machine trembles as if an uncertain hand is holding the controls. It steadies itself again. It's turning. It's nose is dropping. It is plunging straight down. Pull out . . . pull out . . . pull out. . . . With engine roaring it seems to hang for an instant between the twin towers of Naxxar church, then drops out of sight. Scotty puts his fingers in his ears: wuump, a sprout of black smoke is mounting higher and higher above the buildings.

I turn to my pilots: "Have you learned the lesson from that?" I demand angrily. "Number two's fault, he was too damned close. If you fly like that in our Squadron, I'll shoot you down myself."

The second Spitfire is circling the smoke pillar. We run—but what is the use of running? As we pass the church we are joined by a crowd of small boys. I find myself heading a strange party through the narrow streets and out along the road beyond the town, for the plane has crashed near the army camp. Although a platoon of soldiers is called to attention as I pass, I know they salute the officer who has just died. Nearing the place I send back the children; I also tell my pilots that there's no need for them to see the wreck, but they follow me; over the stone walls towards a gully where a dark red flame fringed with black smoke gushes up. It is a place of humped rock, disturbed red earth and burnt grass; there are a few pieces of telescoped metal; everyone looks very tall; a Sergeant Major and a Corporal are shovelling earth on to flames near a flat disc which may have been a wheel; two other soldiers are searching amongst scattered fragments, while a private next to me with a rifle slung round his shoulder stares down at a twisted piece of propeller mechanism. My pilots are climbing back towards the road, but I am sketching this scene in my diary. It is silent but for the fire which crackles and spurts. As I stare down at the wreckage, drawing unrecognisable pieces, I seem to feel someone I know, I seem to be in the presence of Mac, Peter's friend. Quietly, in inner silence I bid him farewell.

A car has drawn up on the road above us: the short plump figure of Gracie, now a Wing Commander at Takali, is climbing over the rocks towards me. Two Army officers have joined him and now all four of us stare down at the pieces. As Gracie prods a large lump of earth, the soldiers hand him their finds: a wallet, a photograph of a girl, two post-cards from England, and a ring which have miraculously been thrown clear. Again Gracie prods the lump with his foot; with horror I realise I could have been standing on what is unrecognisably Mac's body.

"What do you want us to do with it?" asks the Army Officer.

"Dig it in," says Gracie.

"No. Don't dig it in," I interrupt hotly; an air battle is waging but invasion has not yet started, the soldiers must have plenty of time to bury him. "His girl in England," I continue, "or his family may want to visit his grave one day."

"Any monument in a cemetery will do," replies Gracie.

"Don't dig it in—give him a proper burial," is my only retort. I am much junior to Gracie, I don't know if I will be obeyed or not. Gracie's only concern is with the efforts of the living to save Malta, and he's magnificent at that; Mac's dead body is now irrelevant. I know it is a discarded thing, empty of essence, but for the sake of those who come after us please God let a stone or a cross mark the actual spot where this moist earth is finally laid to rest.

It is now afternoon; down here at Takali aerodrome we've just had another raid—not that we're doing much good dressed up as pilots in our yellow Mae Wests, yet being held on the ground. I am sitting on a rock close to the dispersal point with the wide expanse of aerodrome in front of me. Over there I can see the caves and, on top of the craggy hillside, the bastions, domes and palaces of M'dina, lovely buildings shimmering in the heat, gold and violet vibrating together. Below them, on the far side of the aerodrome, smoke is swirling up from a burning Spitfire or perhaps an ammunition dump, for I can hear the crackling of exploding shells and bullets, but except for this, and the noise of the old bus grinding its way up the hill to fetch us some tea, there is silence and my Spitfire waits for me.

Life here is a mixture of horror and effort with odd moments of reflection thrown across the pattern of battle. I want to face it four square, to extract from this experience its full measure of truth—but I feel dreadfully alone. I envy my companions their magnificent spirit but I seem to have nothing in common with their gaiety and laughter. Perhaps I feel cut off because I'm married—I'm too young to tell. I've always been bewildered by my fellow men—have never understood them, have always shrunk into myself. I am not by nature or structure a fighter pilot, I'm not a boxer or an athlete, I'm an artist. If only I could believe in war—it seems the most incredible foolishness. I am suspicious of intellectual explanations about it; instead I feel with my heart; I am appalled and saddened. If only I could live abstracted from it as an artist, but instead I have to play a violent part. Perhaps it is a test, perhaps there is something I must solve here, perhaps I must achieve some inner victory. But over what must I be victorious? Over my fear? Over myself? I suppose an anguish of selfishness cries out in me. Selfishly I long for my wife, for the natural birthright of being together, for even having news of her. . . .

. . . Two Spitfires are racing across the aerodrome, long dust-plumes stopping abruptly as, lifting from the ground, they climb away into the distance. We Luqa pilots seem to be held on the ground again. Last night Woody told us why. He considers that the daylight bombers are a bait to lure us into the air; into the air so that the hordes of enemy fighters, that appear simultaneously, may destroy the last of our machines. He considers this the final German strategy before sending in their invasion. But he won't be drawn; he sends up a couple of Spits from time to time to convince the enemy that we still have some left, otherwise he holds us deliberately. It's an effort to convince myself that he's right, but one fact is certain: a few days ago we only had four aircraft left, now, however, due to first-rate efforts by the airmen, the island can boast fourteen!

109s—Look out!—109s sweeping towards us at low level, four, six, ten, as I run for the nearest bomb hole, shallow hole, white, much too shallow, I squirm lower into the rock as the engine roar is strung with a claaattttter of guns. Head down, nose bent in the hard dust, eyes closed, waiting, waiting, claaaaaaatttttter, moaning engines, others coming back, roaring lower—I must reach the trenches where the airmen are firing back. As I gather my legs under me for my fifty-yard spring I glance upwards: two 109s just above me, black machines, long yellow noses, helmeted pilots staring back at me along the foreshortened surface of their wings; they stare with such indolent superiority that I feel singled out in my shallow hole for their next attack—as they sweep past—I run. Nearer and nearer to the trench—claaaattter—claaatttter—claaattter—but as I jump down amongst the airmen I notice they have put down their rifles. The airmen are gazing skywards: Spitfires firing, Spitfires sitting right behind the 109s; the enemy fighters opening up their engines shoot away —the Spitfires just don't have the speed to follow. I sit down on my white rock again, all jumpy, red-eyed and tired—things are pretty desperate for 109s to penetrate our weakened defences, then escape unharmed.

Tuesday, May 5.

Hugh-Pugh and Woody called a conference for all Squadron and Flight Commanders last night at M'dina—tired out, both the C.O. and I went over. After driving back through the bombing after midnight, I found that some damn fool had taken the candle and alarm clock from our bedroom—of all times to play a practical joke. It didn't worry the C.O. because he could sleep late, but I had to lead on dawn readiness—just dared not sleep, lest I overslept—fought my tiredness for the three and a half necessary hours. In pre-dawn dark Pancho appeared with the candle and clock; doing my job for me; he had assumed that the C.O. and I had both been killed in the bombing; he had taken over command—felt bitterly angry with him but he was right—had to commend him for his initiative. Went to Luqa—found it out of action—same as Monday we went to Takali. Held on ground again. Repeated attacks by 109s.

Wednesday, May 6.

Same again—no sleep—bombed all night—held on the ground at Takali—Eyeties bombed from thirty thous: rush of air—fell flat—whole carpet of bombs fell in Attah village. 109s—but Bofors fire balls didn't hit any. 109s got lone Spit coming to our rescue—burning fiercely it streaked down the sky—long black plume stretching out behind it before it burst on the hill. Pilot, F/Lt. Johnson, Takali type, baled out— his fouth parachute jump here—horribly burned this time—in Umtarfa hospital.

Thursday, May 7

Same again—brutal night bombing—no sleep. 109s brought bombs to plaster us—thought they were long range tanks—seemed to release them by firing their guns.

It is Friday, May the 8th, I'm trying to write a letter to my wife, but what can I say to her—I have only battle to write about. Even now, just after lunch, bombs are screaming down, the whole place is shaking with the crash of explosions, there's a continuous stuttering bark of bursting shells. I'm still feeling sick from this morning when Woody, in utter exasperation, sent us all into the air. A hell of a fight. The Italians were bombing us at the same time—there was a gush of black smoke along the Naxxar hillside beyond my wing tip. The fight took place at low level all round Takali, with Spitfires chasing 109s up into the sun while other 109s dived in from other directions, a free for all, but despite being outnumbered four or five to one, only one of the Hurricanes, whose landing we were trying to cover, was hit: I glimpsed it staggering to the ground crashing on its belly on the edge of the aerodrome—the pilot got out unhurt. Tilley destroyed two enemy fighters but I was not much good: chased a 109 up a rocky gorge, into what was probably a trap, for two other machines pounced upon me. Watching the 109s I almost collided with a bridge that spanned the gorge. I glimpsed my original 109 swerving back to the aerodrome, probably laughing at my predicament, when an ascending glow of Bofors shells blew his tail right off; he hit the ground in a pillar of smoke near the brewery chimney. Total this morning was five 109s definitely destroyed, with another five probables—perhaps ten altogether—without loss to ourselves except for the damaged Hurricane.

Invasion may be imminent, our island may be on its last legs but, if all goes well, very different events will happen in the next two days! Even now as I lean on this table, three aircraft carriers are nosing their way into the Mediterranean towards us. Sixty-four reinforcement Spitfires will fly off their decks at dawn tomorrow morning. This is the first step of a plan to run a convoy through, for our need is more extreme than urgency—food and fuel for only a few weeks longer. Our ammunition shortage, for we will run out within two or three days, is so extreme that it cannot wait for the convoy: it is therefore planned that the *Welshman*, a very fast merchant cruiser, laden with ammunition, shall run unescorted to our island during darkness tomorrow night. As it is planned that the daylight unloading of the ammunition shall take place under the protective umbrella of our newly arrived fighters—everything depends on the Spitfires' safe arrival and our ability to refuel them and get them into action quickly. Without doubt the Germans will strike immediately and, having lost one third of our April reinforcements within the vulnerable refuelling period, we have made careful preparations for the reception of this lot.

These Spitfires already know their destinations; Luqa, Takali or Halfar. On the perimeter tracks or in the fields surrounding these aerodromes special pens have been built for their protection. Alongside each pen will be two slit trenches, for stores of fuel and ammunition, and ground crews respectively. Further stores and meals will be delivered to each pen by army lorry, for we are to stand by from dawn to dusk as long as the battle lasts. Each of us pilots has his own crew, and, as there is apprehension in some quarters that airmen may run off to deep shelters in the heavy bombing that is expected, we have been given orders to shoot them if they make the attempt. Ridiculous order—the airmen are grand.

Each new Spitfire arriving will have a large number clearly painted on its side; we each have our own particular aircraft to meet; no matter what bombs are falling at the time, we are to run out on to the open aerodrome to guide it back to its own specially built pen. Whatever rank the new pilot may be, we oust him and climb in ourselves—he is under our orders. Refuelling must be as swift as possible and we stand by for immediate take-off. We must expect to take part in every raid, six or seven sorties a day without relief. If our plane is damaged in combat we are not to return to the pens in the front line, but take it along new taxi tracks through fields, over rocky hills, and valleys, to repair pens built in the rear. If we are not wounded, we are to return to the aerodrome at once and there take over a more junior pilot's plane. At all times the senior Malta pilot will have priority in flying the dwindling number of Spitfires that remain. As a Flight Commander I must expect to fly to the bitter end.

It is with this knowledge about what is going to happen that I'm trying to write this last letter to my wife. I suppose it's because I'm exhausted with little or no sleep for so very long that a weak, unaccountably childish, cowardly part of my nature quails at the future. It seems to cry out inside me "Leave us alone. Don't send us any more Spitfires; we're doing quite well as we are." I know this inner protest illogically

ignores the facts of starvation and the ammunition shortage; I suppose
it's rooted in fear that the Germans will attack us more fiercely than ever;
I suppose it's my imagination breeding terror from what has already
happened here. I must pluck out my timidity. This must be faced, but
God, I'm tired.

As I lean back in my chair there's a growing sound emerging from the
bomb bursts, a great roar of German aircraft passing low overhead—a
long clatter of machine-guns. A Maltese waiter running across the room
knocks against the table: my fountain-pen falls to the floor. Damn him,
damn him, damn him; he has, yes, he has broken the nib—the pen that I
use for all my drawing. How am I going to draw now? I can feel my hot
temper rising inside me. The Maltese looks all upset, pale, cringing, with
his elbows lifted in apology. I am standing up stiffly tense staring down at
his silly white face—try and control this monstrous anger.

The C.O. enters. He chuckles with laughter. I'm in no mood to be
laughed at so I swing round towards him, more furious than ever.

"I've just been machine-gunned in the garden," he tells us, "by the
rear gunner of a Ju 87—but look—he missed!"

The C.O. holds up his round blue ceremonial hat, bullet-torn on one
side.

PART THREE

FOREGROUND

CHAPTER 11

THE PRICE OF VICTORY

EXCEPT for the battle-dressed soldiers, who have joined our ground-crew teams, laughing together with sun-bronzed airmen, there is silence on Luqa aerodrome as we wait for the reinforcements. An apprehensive silence for the enemy must know what's happening—last night not a single bomb was dropped on the island—the Germans are probably watching our approaching formations on their radar screens—sending off their bombers to catch our new Spitfires immediately after arrival.

We stare westwards into the empty sky above the distant Takali hills from which our Spitfires will emerge. As I glance round at the newly constructed pens, empty and waiting, five minutes pass, ten minutes pass. These new pens are more elaborate than the old ones, each has one of its projecting arms lengthened and turned across the entrance to give the new planes greater protection against bomb blast—it's going to be difficult to manœuvre the Spitfires in and out. The pens are built of old petrol cans filled with earth—sunlight is reflecting on their silver-white metal—horribly conspicuous—indeed the whole aerodrome, not only appears adorned with a necklace of silver, but has pendant ornaments stretching back into the rocky landscape along the new taxi tracks.

Fifteen minutes—we all move restlessly. We are standing at the opening of one of these tracks which extends back from us towards a hill-top crested by a look-out tower among the olive trees; it is flanked by glittering pens all the way. My own particular pen is up there by the tower but the two soldiers of my crew have erected their gas-operated machine-gun well away from the trees with a wide arc of fire towards the north.

Sudden roar—four Hurricanes in line abreast, surge overhead having just taken off from neighbouring Halfar; there go the air-raid warnings. Amongst the white clumps of ack-ack that appear abruptly over Valetta, come the 109s, already banking across above us: simultaneously, low in the sky, to the right of the shimmering hills, cruising slowly towards us, we can see the first formation of Spitfires. This first lot has started to turn in the distance for they are to land at Takali, sixteen, perhaps eighteen, Spitfires circling there, short of petrol after their long flight, some already dropping down to land. Through a diagonal stream of flak the enemy fighters plunge straight towards the circling planes; there's a rattle of machine-guns and four dots streak vertically up into the blue.

Another formation of Spits circles above us, with their wheels swinging out from their wings passing in single file towards the other end of the runway, but some enemy fighters are manœuvring into the sun. Our first Spitfire settles gracefully on to the runway. The second is holding off a little too high. "Look at that Spitfire—oh, be careful of that Spitfire." It drops, bounces drunkenly but now, at last, with its Merlin engine throttled back and popping sporadically, it's running smoothly along the ground. Scotty must have spotted his number, for there he goes, racing out on to the aerodrome, his little legs criss-crossing as he runs, his right hand clutching his tin hat on to his head. No sign of my number yet— but what a din! The clatter of gunfire is louder than the engines, but we can't see a thing: clouds of dust, red-brown in the sunlight, stirred up by the taxi-ing aircraft, blot everything out! Ah-h-h! we've just been covered with dust—gritty in our noses and mouths.

Carefully reopening my eyes, I find that a Spitfire has turned into a nearby pen; the pilot is climbing out and Scotty, plump with his Mae West, climbs in. As the airmen tip the glistening petrol cans, so the original pilot, a young officer, jumps down from the wing root, radiant with smiles.

Above the drifting dust-clouds I glimpse two Hurricanes as they race overhead—too late—109s have swept through another larger formation of Spitfires: a Spitfire drops out: the formation continues towards us leaving the column of black smoke behind it. The new Pilot Officer's face has changed from smiles to an expression of astonished bewilderment.

With their wheels down more Spitfires are passing overhead one after another towards Halfar aerodrome on our left. Two have passed and we watch the third, the details of its wings and ailerons silver against the blue; two 109s whirl towards it: a splutter of gunfire as blue tendrils of smoke leap from the leading Messerschmitt. Both enemy aircraft swing away, low over the tree-tops and round the look-out tower: another burst of fire from the ground—my two soldiers, I think. The Spitfire's disappeared. "Was it shot down?" I ask the new Pilot Officer— he is clutching the sandbags, his body crouched, head lifted, eyes staring— he doesn't answer.

Another Spitfire, lowering its wheels and flaps, with probably only a gallon or two of petrol left, creeps towards us through the shellfire; it's descending slowly, oh so slowly straight and level; a 109 is racing towards it—but a Hurricane leaps on to the 109's tail! The 109 and the Hurricane turn viciously; as they twist back towards us there's a blink of white light as the Hurricane opens fire—"Look out". Shoving the new Pilot Officer into cover from the bullets we all fall into a heap. Lifting my head I watch the Spitfire continuing straight and level over the trees.

Thus, one by one, our reinforcements made their individual landings with much less opposition from the Germans than we expected. I have collected my machine. It has been refuelled. Fully equipped I sit waiting in the cockpit. Any minute the German bombers will arrive. Any second the take-off signal. The inner pads of my flying helmet encircle my ears, cutting me off from the noises of battle. The sky looks empty. Sirens? Lifting my ear-flaps, suddenly aware of the heat of the sun, I am astonished, but the All Clear is sounding. Why the All Clear? Where are the German bombers?—should have been right behind the 109s. Even if they weren't, the 109s must have wirelessed the news of the Spitfires' arrival. Enemy bombers *must* be approaching in force.

In the phoney silence I look around my tiny cockpit, at the black instrument panel, with its dials, hiding the huge petrol tank with ninety gallons practically resting on my lap; I look at the pale-green metal ribs of the fuselage that enclose me; I look at the heavy control column between my bent knees and away into the darkness where my feet in black shoes are resting lightly on the rudder-bar. I look at all the hard pieces of functional metal and I wonder, as I always wonder before take-off, which of them will puncture my body if I crash. Having checked my instruments I stare forwards past the motionless propeller blades: in the field opposite there is a labourer cutting hay.

Two red lights fired from the tower behind me. As I switch on my airmen leap to the starter trolley. The sirens wail. I have a swift impression of the Maltese labourer throwing down his scythe, jumping the low wall and pedalling away on his bicycle.

Two red lights, only two: it is the signal for the other squadron to take off, not us. As the minutes pass I lean forward in the straps examining the northern sky: there's more haze, a few small cumulus clouds have formed, and a large formation of Ju 88s is sliding through the ack-ack bursts; they're turning and dropping towards Takali. Blast it—they have disappeared behind the tin wall that encloses my Spitfire and me. Ginger, one of my airmen team, high up on the wall gives me a running commentary, but it is quickly over—the All Clear is sounding again— the Maltese labourer returns to his work.

From my cockpit I watch the labourer, wearing faded blue trousers and a white shirt, scything with long, horizontal sweeps. Between the two of us there is a stone wall, and just this side of the taxi-track the slit trench with supplies in it. Looking down on the heaped petrol cans and wriggling belts of ammunition, it occurs to me that should a fierce battle develop this supply trench would be a target for strafing 109s— better camouflage it. Calling Ginger up on the wing root I instruct him to go over to the labourer, present my compliments and ask for a few handfuls of straw. I watch Ginger and the labourer talking.

The trench is now camouflaged, but here's Chiefy on his bicycle—I call out to him. Catching my eye he swiftly props his machine against the wall of my pen and, climbing up, tells me the news. I learn that he's in charge of the repair pens further back; that several Spitfires have been damaged already; that one new arrival, who tried to join up with a 109 over Grand Harbour, thinking it was one of our machines, had a lump blown out of his fuselage for his ignorance; that a new Flight Commander, having just landed at Halfar, saw his inexperienced pilots being attacked by 109s as they came in to land behind him: he tried to take off down wind to go to their rescue: his Spitfire, striking the top of a dispersal pen, blew up. The sirens are wailing again: Chiefy jumps on his bicycle, but he is quickly overtaken by the labourer.

The sirens are quickly sounding the All Clear—a false alarm—I've never heard one on Malta before—everyone's strung up. The labourer is quickly back, his brown arms swinging rhythmically.

Following his example I get out my sketch-book—but what shall I draw? I can only wriggle an inch or two in my seat and although I'd like to draw the labourer he has moved behind the propeller blade. In the mirror over my windscreen I can see the top of my moving helmeted head: adjusting the mirror I can see the whole of my face. Self portrait—my face is framed by the rim of my sliding cockpit canopy behind me, and, what is more, the two parts of the tail plane of my aircraft, still further back, stick out each side of my flying helmet like horns, as if I were some Viking warrior. I'm no warrior, I'm just an artist suddenly intrigued by an amusing subject. The stupid sirens are at it again. I suppose we'll get orders to fly now that I've got interested in this drawing. My fountain-pen is giving me trouble after its knock—there's also a formation of Ju 88s crawling up into the sky above the top of the mirror. I can't incorporate them into the picture because the upper part of the design is now fixed. I have got to decide how much of my shoulders to include. The 88s are diving over the top of us now—Halfar, I think, not us. Having completed the harness straps, the parachute straps, the oxygen mask hanging sideways and the wriggling twisting tubes and wires, I develop the face itself. After ten minutes of effort it's still giving me trouble—it's difficult because the eyes are screwed up against the glare of sunlight. Strange face in the mirror; I'm an artist but that fellow up there is festooned about with the paraphernalia of mechanical war. Sirens again, and the labourer, leaving his field, waves to me this time.

As I wave back I'm astonished to realise it's the warning, not the All Clear. Although I'm alert for the take-off signal the succession of sirens has become bewildering—one thing is certain—this battle is a complete fiasco—it's not developing as planned. It's damned uncomfortable sitting here—I could be back in a few seconds—come what may, I'm getting out for a stretch.

" Along the hillcrest inland from the harbour, a line of black pillared destruction sprang skywards."

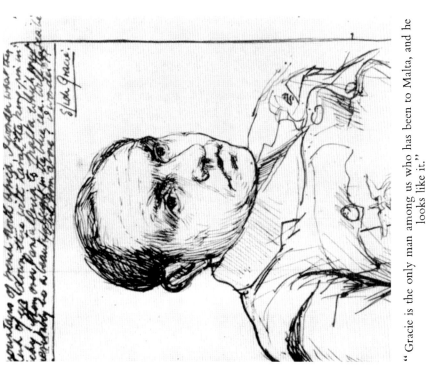

The Dreaded Hugh.

"Gracie is the only man among us who has been to Malta, and he looks like it."

One of the airmen ground crew.

"Thinking the communal thought: Next bomb ours?"

View from the Naxxar hilltop—with a Ju 88 falling in flames.

"Uncle sat very still; flies crawled all over him."

"The great blobs of silver reflecting from the descending sun."

Crashed Wellington.

Spitfire resting—view from the sandbags at the back of the pen.

Pilots resting—the swimming platform at St. Paul's Bay.

Paul's Bay, the deep blue water and the main hills on the far bank; to our right was St Paul's island and the monument at the point he had landed centuries ago, and beyond it the open sea. That was the direction in the Germans returned to Sicily and many were the enemy aircraft that were confirmed to crash into the sea from this terrace.

" I wandered along the perimeter track to sketch the untidy wreckage of a Spitfire."

High in the air over the western Mediterranean.

Now the sun is rising out of the sea behind the tailplane, while through the rusty haze the rocky mountains of Algiers look golden as to pass slowly along the port windows.

How pleasant it is to walk round the side of this pen and increase the scope of vision: the fine buildings of the harbour in the distance, yellow and violet against the blue Mediterranean, while in the immediate foreground old delayed-action bombs which haven't gone off lie where they fell, half-buried in rock.

Sudden gunfire—roaring engines—shrill scream and rush of bombs—into the trench—the rock is splitting, splitting, the very fibres of air are wrenched and flung apart. Invisible pieces of rock thump back from the sky, clanging erratically on the corrugated iron, two objects slither along the ground towards us, stopping short in a vomit of dust. Suddenly overhead, in a small gap between pillars of dust and swirling bomb clouds—Stukas, with Spitfires standing on their tails, rolling on their backs, in a wild dance of fire and return fire: a Stuka bursts into flame, rears up, topples over sideways and plunges into the labourer's field. I look up from the flaming wreck to find that the battle has passed almost out of sight, just a few dots twisting away into the distance. Climbing out of the trench I glance at the objects in the dust: two huge pieces of bomb casing, twisted silver, gleaming in the sunlight. The All Clear is sounding and here comes my labourer wheeling his bicycle. I join him and we stand together looking silently across his field: we watch the smoke rising from the black heap of broken aeroplane, we look at the red earth craters and we shake our heads over his scattered crop.

I can't sleep. I suppose all day long I was strung up for battle and no real battle came—even when we took off in the late afternoon we did not see much action. After dark we gathered in the aerodrome mess, waiting and waiting for our evening meal: lying in the arm-chair to which I had dragged myself, I cursed whatever delay kept us from sleep. Finally we ate the meal and, after a jolting journey in the bus, fell exhausted on to our beds. I felt frightful: my breath was bad as if I had turned putrid within: I seemed to be building up for a bilious attack, of all ridiculous times to have one. Since then I have been tossing and turning; I threw all the bedclothes off, being dreadfully hot. Now, just after 2 a.m., I'm freezing cold, hunched in the bedclothes, shivering. Enemy aircraft drone overhead. A bomb falls, more bombs fall, but I can't take any interest in these noises. So the night passes. It's pitch dark, but it must be time to get up for I can hear the C.O. cursing that the electric light has failed again. He gropes about, strikes a match and lights a candle.

Hot now and lifeless, my body won't obey my will—yet I must get up. With a great convulsive effort I'm out, standing on the floor. I can't move swiftly. What about washing and shaving? Surely if I throw cold water over myself that will suffice. The shock of the cold water is refreshing. Dressed now, my body shivers. The C.O. leads the way down the stairs with a candle, but I don't feel right—it must be this unshaven state—sapping all my self-respect. "I'll be with you in three minutes," I call out as, tearing off my shirt, I rush into the bathroom to scrape the whiskers from my face.

In the bus now, and I can't understand why I'm not enjoying the cold air that blows through the smashed windows, cool on my hot forehead, like a bathe in an icy mountain stream. The bombing has stopped and we are racing through blue-grey darkness across the valley: ahead of us the Luqa escarpment of hills is a solid black silhouette below the phosphorous pencil mark of the waning moon. My uneasy body seems turned in on itself; I feel no quiver of its usual response to such loveliness.

On the aerodrome I have been put in charge of the Squadron, because the C.O. has had to go and see Woody in Valetta. I have been watching the eastern sky gradually lighten, the hills to the south of us are re-awakening to their rounded three-dimensional existence with pale light flooding across them. But my body is rebellious: from time to time a great hand within my stomach seems to grip, squeeze and crush all my inner parts. The sun rises inch by inch above the horizon. A wave of heat engulfs us. That pain again, sharp and intense. I bend forward to ease it.

With the sun higher above this golden landscape I've had to rush several times behind the rocks searching for a place, yet I daren't go far lest the take-off signal is fired. I hate this kind of problem, but should I fly with this unknown factor of what my body may do to me next? Should I put someone else in charge? Because I am frightened, I want to fly, but should I go up when I am responsible for the leadership and safety of my boys? Will I be able to think and act quickly enough? Will my tactical judgment be impaired? Doubt is eliminated by putting the question in a different way: have I a pilot available who would do the job as well or better? I naturally think of Max, a stout-hearted leader and fighter pilot. I call him over. Agreeing to take over the formation, he moves his kit into the C.O.'s machine, then we sit together discussing probable tactics.

It is now almost nine o'clock; the sun glares down upon us. I'm sitting in an arm-chair made of petrol cans covered with sacks. I'm utterly lifeless; I may be developing the "Malta Dog" that has laid low many pilots and kept the Dreaded Hugh in hospital, so I ask an airman called Grimes, who is sitting on an arm-chair next to me, about the illness. "The bloody Dog b . . . up Christmas for me; walking down Safi Strip I was sick seven times," he tells me. As I haven't yet been sick I feel a complete impostor. I glance towards Max, sitting a few yards away on a pile of yellow sandbags talking to Scotty; his brilliant Mae West has the words "Spitfire—British" painted on it in startling black letters lest he has to bale out and gets manhandled as he lands. I stare with mixed feelings—he's an experienced pilot, but I should be leading the Squadron.

On my right a crowd of sunburnt erks is shaking with laughter, happy fellows without responsibilities. In the midst of them the story-teller, an Australian Sergeant Pilot, one of the new boys who brought a Spitfire from the aircraft carrier yesterday. . . . Four lights—Scramble! The airmen leap to their positions, Max jumps for the cockpit of my Spitfire, up the taxi-track other Spits are being pushed rapidly out of their pens into more accessible positions for starting, propellers turning, dust swirls skywards, the engine of Max's Spitfire chokes twice before bursting with life. As he begins to taxi out I run impetuously round the wing tip; leaping up beside the cockpit in the slip-stream blast, I hang there for a moment shouting good luck to him. He smiles but I can't hear what he says; he lifts a perpendicular thumb as I stand back; lowering his goggles he races away in a dust-cloud. One by one the Spitfires lift from the ground and, thundering overhead, turn steeply on their wing tips, chasing Max, joining formation and climbing away into the distance. The sirens wail from Luqa village; the Spitfires have gone.

I wander up the empty taxi-track to join my old crew near the look-out tower, but on hearing the growing sound of a Spitfire we turn quickly. It races low over the tree-tops and away; silence for a brief moment before there's a sound of a different nature: two ugly looking Messerschmitts are after it. "Man the guns," I call to the soldiers. The machine-gun rattles as the 109 leader flashes past. Was he hit? Black puffs of smoke choked back into the air behind him. But the Spitfire is returning, cannons and machine-guns clattering as it charges at the enemy like an angry dog. The second 109 pulls steeply upward, but the leader noses over behind the trees: instantly a smoke cloud explodes into the sky. All is silent again but for the whispering of the Spitfire's engine as it circles round the monument of its victory—or ours?

Something very strange is happening over towards Valetta: over Grand Harbour a grotesque fog of greeny-grey smoke is spreading wider and wider: the Harbour smoke-screen is vomiting upwards from huge canisters to cover the target area and shield the ammunition ship. Above it stretches the tall belt of thick bronze haze, leaving only a small space of clear blue sky steeply above us. The guns have started to erupt, spattering the blue with shell-bursts, and there, in that confined area of sky, a procession of enemy bombers has started to arrive; five, ten, sixteen, seventeen, twenty-three Stukas, with more emerging from the bronzed obscurity; forty of them now, fifty, their pilots obviously straining their eyes downwards trying to get a glimpse of the target ship through the smoke cover. One after another they are beginning their dive. Suddenly, without warning, a second and third umbrella of black smoke appear at two distinct levels above the harbour; flickering and twinkling with light, barrier roofs of bursting shells—a continuous violent sound like fire crackers, bursting and roaring—more and more explosions split their steel in the gathering murk—still more guns open fire, converging their contribution over the harbour. Hundreds of enemy aircraft are diving into this inferno with Spitfires, appearing suddenly in the blue, following down behind them; black dots dropping like stones behind the Spitfires: 109s! What an aerial monument of courage this scene is.

Simultaneously other Spitfires, in wide formation roaring across our aerodrome at tree-top height, hurl themselves towards the harbour; more fighters are taking off behind us; Hurricanes and Spitfires streaming away in twos and fours into the mushroom smoke; still more machines from behind us, I can see the frail pilots in their bright Mae Wests settling into their seats, bending forward in their straps, peering ahead as they ride their thin-winged mounts into battle. Some of them climb high into the smoke but others sweep down to lower level to pounce on the surviving German bombers that pull out from the bottom of the maelstrom.

"An 87 down," someone cried out.

"There's another," shouts a different voice, "and another."

High up in the blue still more enemy planes are appearing, searching, plunging downwards. More Spitfires are after them. There goes a Spitfire—leaping on to its prey—it's hit by a bursting shell—Oh, God—snapping in half, the Spitfire gyrates violently and disappears. A parachute has opened in the middle of the holocaust, it's floating, floating, slowly floating through the dark luminous layers of bursting shells, down, slowly down towards the bomb-bursts.

It looks as if it's all over now: the anti-aircraft levels are no longer boiling with movement, there's an occasional flicker of a shell, the enemy planes have gone . . . but look! One solitary Stuka is arriving in the blue! It must have been miles behind the others. As the barrage re-erupts into fury it is calmly positioning itself for its dive. In a strange way, although we are anxious for the safety of our precious ship, all our hearts are with the enemy plane: we are witnessing an act of superb courage. He's starting his dive. He's plummeting vertically downwards, down, down, down, down. He's hit. The whole tail has come off—the mass of the machine veers for one drunken moment sideways and upwards—the right wing snaps in two places—the fragments drop untidily behind the hill.

Time moves on and on and on. Wearing my yellow Mae West, for I have taken over leadership, I wander away from the pen and seating myself on the brink of a bomb-hole stare down into its rocky depths in silence. I glance occasionally towards Valetta reappearing from its smoke pall in the distance—but I can't put back the hands of the clock. Two of our machines have not come back—one of them is Max. There's no news of him after he positioned the Squadron magnificently: I think he is dead.

The bus has just arrived with lunch so I join the queue of airmen. Old Greg, the Catering Officer and several of his helpers are handing out plates of food and mugs of tea through the splintered window-frames; there's also free beer and free cigarettes, but I cannot face the food: a cup of tea is all that I need. As I sip the hot tea I notice an Austin car, very square and upright, drawing up in a cloud of dust: out gets the C.O.

"The battle has gone well, many Huns have been shot down, the ammunition ship is safe and unloading is well advanced," he proclaims.

I quickly tell him. Hearing it he withdraws into sudden silence. I've got to tell him more, although to mention my own trivial troubles in the same breath as the death of a gallant comrade overwhelms me with self-disgust.

"I was not flying; I had some tummy trouble." I'm aware that I'm blushing with shame, so, in order to soften the ghastly ignominy of my statement I add that "I'm better now."

The C.O. contemplates me in silence.

"You don't look too well and you're not to fly," he replied, pausing in thought. "When you've finished your tea take the Austin and report to the aerodrome controller in 'G' shelter, he'll probably find a job for you, but take it easy, we don't want you laid up."

I've been asleep—oh, heavens, I must have fallen asleep. I force my eyes wide open. An airman, standing by a steaming kettle in the corner of "G" shelter cavern, is watching me intently, but the Wing Commander controller has gone.

"Where is he?" I ask sharply.

"Up on the roof, sir."

I'm aware that the shudder of explosions has stopped. I glance at my watch: nearly half-past six; I've been asleep five hours. The airman presses a hot cup of tea into my hands, but I haven't got time to drink it. As he has made it especially for me I ask for some more condensed milk to cool it down.

"What happened in the raid?" I ask him.

"Which raid, sir?"

"The one after lunch."

"The Wingco said that two 88s and four 87s had been blown to bits over Valetta, but when the Spits came down they claimed seven more. That makes today's total well over thirty. But there's another raid on now, sir."

Thanking the airman, I run up the steps into the sunlight, making my way towards the M/T Section. Four 109s racing across the aerodrome lead my eye to our dispersal pens: they are empty—the C.O. and the boys are airborne again. When I was last driving the Austin, its starboard front tyre had been exploded by a jagged lump of shrapnel: it has now been repaired, so I hasten to "G" shelter roof. Standing in front of the Wing Commander and feeling bitterly ashamed of falling asleep, I report that the car is ready for action again. I am given the job of visiting the pens to interview the newly arrived pilots, to find out how many operational hours they have done: we are going to keep only those pilots who have flown over fifty and preferably over a hundred hours in action against the enemy—inexperienced men will be returned to England.

Having covered half the aerodrome I am driving fast towards the next pen containing a Spitfire; there's a considerable noise of enemy aircraft and odd bursts of flak towards the north. As the Austin slithers to a standstill I see the new pilot about to jump down into the slit trench—I call him over.

"I want your name, your total flying hours, your total hours on Spits and your operational hours."

I am shocked by what he tells me; another babe with no operational hours at all. Of all the pilots I have so far seen only two qualify to remain here. It looks as if we'll *have* to keep some of these babes as replacements. As the young pilot looks at me, he glances furtively up at the sky: a formation of enemy bombers, high up over Grand Harbour, is heading towards us. I know he wants to get into the shelter but for both our sakes I want to appear indifferent to the immediate situation.

"Did you ever see an enemy plane before you arrived here yesterday?"

"No, sir."

"Well, those machines up there must be your first Italians. They're Cant Z 1008s. I think the twin rudders on the dihedral tail plane look very pretty, don't you?"

Then, giving him a broad, mischievous wink, and hoping not to spoil the impression by crashing the gears, I accelerate vigorously down the perimeter track. The approaching formation, with shells bursting furiously round it, is much nearer. The Austin bucks and jumps over the potholes. With wheels locked I slide into one of our empty dispersal pens. I join a party of airmen and soldiers staring into the sky. The Italian bombers are no longer there: two have gone while the last one of all is dropping below a long trail of flaming débris—a huge machine, already quite low, tumbling over and over sideways in a series of convulsive jerks. Suddenly gushing with flame, it disintegrates into a shower of sparks. The blue sky is empty but for a white parachute not properly open, which, flapping and streaming behind the struggling figure, is plunging down into the harbour smoke-screen.

There is a sudden glint of wings, a howl of Merlin engines as the victorious Spitfires race steeply round the aerodrome. One by one they come in to land. The C.O. taxies his machine towards us. As he climbs out of the cockpit we learn that it was but a brief encounter: our Squadron has destroyed the whole Italian formation.

The day is ended. We are all back at Naxxar listening to the news broadcast from Rome Radio: we want to compare our claims with the losses the enemy admit. The Italians report "that a powerful naval force has been attacked in Grand Harbour". Fantastic; the only ship in the harbour was the *Welshman*; she was not hit, the ammunition was successfully unloaded and she has sailed away under cover of darkness. "Thirty-seven Axis aircraft have failed to return from operations over Malta." Interesting—just a few more than our defences claim. "Axis planes," Rome Radio continues, "have shot down forty-seven Spitfires."

Forty-seven Spitfires! Never before have we been in a position to recognise such a flagrant propaganda lie. We know the facts: only two or three machines and only one R.A.F. pilot have been lost today. The Spitfire that I saw blown in half in the harbour barrage was one of our Sergeant Pilots called Dickson: the straps holding him into the cockpit snapped and he was thrown through the perspex roof—he is safe with a gash on his leg. The price of our victory is Max. Reluctantly he is posted missing, believed killed.

E

CHAPTER 12

THE ROYAL MALTA ARTILLERY

I T IS the early evening of Monday, May the 11th, and I've just had a complete day off. I've just walked back through the countryside and through the town. I've arrived at the palace entrance, and I'm filled with an ecstatic desire to work, to paint, for the loveliness of things possesses me. When I woke up this morning the sheets were all screwed up after a night of restless tossing; then, suddenly, I remembered that the C.O. had ordered me to take a day off to get my tummy in order. I could hardly believe it—I didn't have to get up—so I lay back among the blankets quite unable to realise that I had a whole day to myself. I lay there for hours. "Let the day just happen. I'm too tired to paint, to study, to plan anything special, just let it happen."

At lunch-time I roused myself and, still clad in dishevelled grey pyjamas, got up and ate some food. I washed and shaved carefully, donned my best khaki uniform, of shorts, poplin shirt and tunic, deciding, as an afterthought, to wear a tie for the first time in Malta, then, with my friendly blue hat at a jaunty angle on my head, I set out.

Baby Face and Sergeant Harris, who, not required for flying, were on their way over to Umtarfa to see the Dreaded Hugh in hospital, accompanied me through the narrow streets of Naxxar and out on to the road that drops down into the valley towards Birkirkara, Hamrun and Valetta. The white surface of the road was throwing up so much heat, that when a small telephone repair lorry stopped alongside and offered us a lift, I quickly forgot my best uniform and climbed into the back with the others. Sitting on some ladders I looked at the two Maltese workmen that were there: their clothes hung loosely about them, they had red faces, sunburnt feet and they seemed to be covered all over with a strange white powder. When the lorry started up and whirled onwards faster and faster along the craggy road I found out why: the white dust rose up behind us in such dense clouds that we were soon as hotly powdered as the Maltese.

We hardly saw Birkirkara because of the dust, but by shouting loudly we got the lorry to stop by the arches of the aqueduct just this side of Hamrun. We thanked our Maltese benefactors and watched the white dust-cloud roll off down the road towards Valetta. Baby Face and Harris's road towards M'dina and the hospital went off at right angles.

Giving them a message for the Dreaded Hugh, to the effect that I might, but I hoped that I would not, be joining him in hospital with the Dog, I banged the dust out of my uniform and, deciding that Valetta might be somewhat unhealthy, having been visited by three or four hundred bombers yesterday, walked back the way we had come.

I not only felt very smart as I walked but happy. I was alone with the rest of my afternoon stretching out joyously ahead of me. Carrying my inevitable blue canvas bag containing writing things, sketch-book and Diana's photograph I grew frightfully hot as I strode along: the sun scorched down, the air was like fire as I breathed. On reaching Birkirkara once again and on looking around for a café I was astonished that there were hardly any shops at all; there were ruins of course, heaps of rubble with the tall adjoining buildings brutally cracked or opened up so that bedrooms and bathrooms, in yellow, violet and pink, were poised above me in the blue sky; business seemed to be carried on in the front rooms of houses that were left. After passing a long queue that edged slowly into a room where a fat woman was weighing out meagre rations on a pair of skeleton iron scales, I stopped at the next house. Its wares, displayed at the roadside, tempted me to go in. The wizened old lady, dressed in black, who explained the Maltese lace trade to me, was so delightful with her wrinkled toothless face that I imagined many such ladies, all over the island, sitting in their darkened rooms or perhaps outside their front doors in dazzling white sunlight, all working busily with ancestral skill. I was shown some beautiful things, sweeping cobweb folds of lace with Maltese crosses worked intricately into the limitless patterns. After buying some of this work for Diana I was still feeling frightfully hot.

The old lady directed me towards a café and when I arrived there I was delighted to recognise the quality of the Maltese lace festooned across its windows. The bell shook on the door as I stepped inside. I would have liked an ice or a hot cup of coffee, but I settled for the only drink available—goat's milk flavoured with almond. Standing at the counter I took a sip and on finding it delicious, finished the glass. Sitting down at one of the round tables, I ordered another. The proprietor, in black striped trousers and a white shirt, having brought it for me sat down astride a chair and, leaning forward on the back of it, introduced himself as Joe.

"Ah—yesterday we all enjoyed," he stated in his broken English.

"None of the Maltese went to the shelters," he continued, "they stand in the streets to watch it all. That Italian bomber, how nice she fall in flames at the very end. Good shooting by the gunners, wasn't it?"

"Wonderful shooting by the gunners," exclaimed a chorus of Maltese sitting at other tables. "They got him plump in the middle: woof!" they expostulated, mimicking the falling bomber with their hands.

Now I liked Joe and I liked his Maltese customers; they were very justly proud of the achievements of the Royal Malta Artillery, especially after the fantastic barrage yesterday, the heaviest concentration of ack-ack there has yet been in this war, but I felt proud of our Squadron's achievements so I had to correct the error:

"The Italian bomber was shot down by my C.O.," I told them. "In fact, pilots from our Squadron destroyed the whole Italian formation." I paused, wondering if I should clinch the point by explaining what a nice piece of deflection shooting our C.O. had made, but instead I veered from the subject a little:

"In the first raid," I asked, "did you see the Spitfire have its tail blown off and the pilot come down by parachute? He was Sergeant Dickson, another of our fellows."

"Ah, he was exciting." Joe leaned forward with zest, his dark eyes glittering in his egg-shaped face, a face with a blue-black chin, a tint that was carried up either side to his curly hair, a face that would have to be shaved twice or three times a day to keep it in that condition. His next statement took me by surprise: "And it was *The Royal Malta Artillery*, Joseph Azzopardi, a gunner in *The Royal Malta Artillery*, who rescued him from the sea."

A spontaneous cry of delight from all the Maltese in the café.

"Touché," I confessed, "we're a team!"

Joe brought another round of goat's milk and drinks for the others who had gathered round us. I pressed him to tell us more about the rescue.

"Well," he said, "all the guns were firing, all the sea was splashing with pieces from the sky, all the people were cheering when someone call out: 'Fighter coming down'—and there he was, parachutist. He go into the sea about a mile away, so Joseph and Tony push out in the boat; David Angus and Joseph Camenzuli of Lower Valetta take another boat in case the first one sinks. There were lots and lots of people, a thousand watching, perhaps more, and when they see the pilot isn't hurt they all cheer. Karmel Palmier brings down whisky from his bar as they put the pilot, all laughing, on a door from a broken house as a stretcher. Wonderful day, with lots and lots of bombers shot down. It is a fine victory and perhaps the Germans do not come back again."

Intrigued by Joe, I stayed talking with him for an hour or more. He told me how before the war there had been delightful hotels at St. Paul's Bay and other resorts round the coast, how lanterns lit the terraced dance floors high above the sea and how, late into the night, orchestras played. He described his own big café in Valetta: how when it had been destroyed by bombing he started a new one in Hamrun: apparently that too had been wrecked and he pointed out details of how he had built his present café from a small disused garage. With a shrug of his shoulders he apologised for the scarcity of food and drinks.

After our talk I settled at the table to write to Diana, but I was in such agony from the bites of the colossal flies that buzzed around us that, despite Joe's assurance that I would get used to them in time, I could stand it no longer. Laughing uproariously at my inglorious departure, we all shook hands before I set off up the road again.

I hadn't gone far when I noticed a flustered old gentleman in another front-room shop. He told me in apology that he had just moved in and was trying to sort the stuffs that he'd managed to rescue from yesterday's bombing. I don't know if this news stimulated the customer in me or whether it was the sudden picture of Diana that floated into my mind; Diana tall and stately in an evening dress, her head with its fair shining curls lifted proudly on her long slender neck; but I determined to buy something. Perhaps I remembered that good materials are impossible to get in England now, but, visualising an evening dress, I searched among the rolls of material. As I lifted a roll of heavy Chinese silk it moved across the light, a wave of opalescence sweeping across its surface like a rainbow. I stood with beating heart as he measured it out: there was enough for a full evening dress with a little over.

Happily laden with parcels, yet armed with the resolution to buy no more, I continued my walk up the road—but I was not happy for long. A window filled with paintings caught my eye; thus I met the Maltese artist who has become famous throughout the island for his painting of the dive-bombing of H.M.S. *Illustrious*. I was jealous of him. Not of his success but of his opportunities. He must have had considerable success, for he owned his own gallery in the fashionable Strada Reale before the war; he must have had his tragedies too; his gallery was opposite the Opera House. As the Corinthian pillars of the Opera House are now thrown down in the rubble, blocking half the street, I assumed his business had perished by the same bomb; despite this he is still able to be painting all the time. Realising that I may not survive to paint on a real canvas ever again I felt utterly overwhelmed by war.

Perhaps it was to cheer myself up, perhaps to satisfy my curiosity about a Maltese cinema or to indulge the nostalgia for films which I associate with home and England and peacetime, that when I noticed placards outside the local cinema, advertising that *Green Hell* was showing today, I walked across to the grille, behind which a fat red-faced man in shirt sleeves was selling tickets, paid my one and fourpence and went inside.

I waited on a hard seat in the balcony for the show to begin; a breeze shook the tarpaulin that was stretched across a gaping bomb-hole in the roof, letting long narrow shafts of dusty sunlight pierce the gloom; sunlight also streamed in through the door below as more people arrived. I watched some giggling girls take such a long time in seating themselves in a row of stalls. I watched some young men in dirty lounge suits and trilby hats sauntering to and fro in front of the girls. Finally some impatient children tugged a reluctant curtain across the door. There was a thunderclap of noise—from the gramophone! First some military bands playing marches, followed quickly by hot dance tunes. Now I have an absolute aversion to military music and I do not like jazz, but I was astonished to find myself inhaling the music like a perfume—it was beautiful. Next came a repetitive noise that rasped and rasped and rasped and rasped until someone scurried over to lift the needle. Just as suddenly the film began. I was bewildered to see the flickering images in black and white and grey: I couldn't understand what was happening, but after a time I rediscovered the idiom—but the music, the light orchestral music that accompanied the film, it overwhelmed me. I was so over-come, as I leaned back in my seat, that tears burst from between my closed eyelids, rolling down my cheeks. Not having heard music for weeks and weeks and weeks, I continued crying silently; the music seemed to be wrenching my starved soul in such an agony of ecstasy that I could stand it no longer: I had to open my eyes and look.

Film stars. Faces like old friends from home. The film was about an expedition through a jungle swamp, which my imagination, frustrated by the black and white flickering screen, rendered in squelching green and soggy brown. Friends indeed—within a few minutes they were busily at work, indulging that noble pastime of blasting to pieces the sculptured relics of an ancient civilisation, in their greedy hunt for gold. Monument after archaic monument toppled, shattered on the moonstone steps. As the hero rested from this vandalism, with the heroine nestling closer and closer into his arms, "Intermission" was flashed in front of us.

During the interval I grew vaguely annoyed at some children climbing over the seats for, as my row was not fastened down, I sat in imminent danger of a back-somersault. I also glimpsed several soldiers cuddling Maltese girl-friends in the rows behind me. I thought of the dilemma of the soldiers: returning to England early in the war, after a full tour of overseas duty, they have got caught up in this Malta siege; they must be despairing of ever returning to their wives, fiancées, and sweethearts again. The black and white screen reawoke to a close-up of pouting lips and continued passion: just as suddenly the ominous words: "Air-Raid Warning" were flashed upon it. My heart turned sick but the film continued. It showed the ancient ruins decimated, the gold found, a bloody battle with natives hurling poisonous darts from one side of the screen and the explorers firing their hot guns from the other, and it ended peacefully with a picture of a well-timbered Elizabethan drawing-room, with the Europeans, uncomfortably clad in dinner-jackets, lifting their glasses in a toast to "Adventure". Outside anti-aircraft guns were firing salvo after salvo and we could hear the fainter clap, clap, of shells bursting high above us.

As I put my tin hat on my head and took the road towards Naxxar, I noticed that high above me was the most astonishing sight for Malta: a towering storm-cloud with its threatening purple-black base dominated the sky over Luqa. As I looked two 109s, then four more, were silhouetted for a moment thousands of feet above me before passing into the side of the white vapour. I had barely gone another twenty yards when a formation of Ju 88s slid through a gap behind me. They dived through a sudden barrage and were disappearing into the gloom when there was a roar of engines low over the house-tops: six Spitfires were turning in behind them. I was staring southwards, trying to see what was happening in between the houses when I became aware that someone was standing close beside me. I turned and looked down: happy eyes glittered back at me from a lined, intelligent, middle-aged face; the man wore khaki uniform with corporal's stripes, but his feet were bare in the dust. Glancing at his shoulder flashes I was immediately intrigued: a member of the Royal Malta Artillery!

"Would you like to come up on my roof, sir?" he asked me. "We could see much better from there."

So up we went. As we listened to the crash of bombs falling on the distant aerodromes, I looked up at the cloud peaks, the avalanches of curling whiteness and the thick stygian gloom of mauve and purple air— a fantastic battle-ground for the Spitfires and 109s rushing through it all at high speed. We saw one brilliant piece of shooting by a Spitfire with one of our Squadron numbers on it. A 109, which had just dived on a bunch of Spitfires, pulled up sharply when, much to my astonishment, for they were flying much more slowly, a Spitfire pulled up after it. The Spit hung there poised in the gloom at a violent angle and, with one burst of cannon it smote the German. The enemy fighter flicked over on to its back and belching smoke blacker even than the thunderclouds, it started coming down in an inverted attitude. I then witnessed a sight which I have feared for a long time might happen. Obviously anxious to claim it as their victory, two Takali Spitfires raced from opposite directions on to the tail of the falling German. So anxious were they to claim this machine, which incidentally fell into the sea despite their stupidity, that not seeing each other they crashed together with a frightful report. Glued together for a moment in the dark sky they broke apart, two parachutes opened, and a gleam of sunlight flickered on a detached wing doing a dance on its own as it fell silently earthwards. The pilots were safe but they didn't deserve to be. So much for Takali and their claims!

Leaving friendly and enemy fighters stalking each other, perhaps more warily in the gloom, the Corporal led me down the spiral staircase to the upstairs landing, down a straight flight of stairs into a whitewashed hall dominated by a large aspidistra in a brown pot, then into his kitchen where he brewed tea. We talked, and after the best cup of tea I had yet

tasted in Malta, he illustrated his domestic life by showing me his garden.
He showed me his "grapes tree", his "plums tree", his "lemons tree", his
"orange tree" and his "tangerines tree" too.

"My plums tree isn't so good," he told me, "he had the garden wall
on top of him." In explanation he climbed up on to the long heap of
white rocks and pointed out seven huge craters in the field beyond.
He showed me the chicken-house where his brown and white chickens
strutted with indignation at the rubble that filled their pen. He showed
me his water supply and described how the rain-water falling on the flat
roof of his house in the winter was guided to the reservoir beneath the
flagstones of a little courtyard for use in the summertime. I was sampling
an icy draught of this sparkling water when I realised how late it was
getting. Next, when he was showing me the rich abundance of his
flowers growing in the front garden I told him, most reluctantly, that
I would have to go. "A minute more," he said, rushing away behind
the square house. As I waited amongst the palm trees I thought of his
way of life and of the gallant way in which the Royal Malta Artillery
are defending it, but he wasn't long; running back he pressed into my
hands three large bunches of heavily perfumed arum lilies. "For your
room," he said, and being members of the same team we smiled at each
other with understanding.

With complete happiness I continued my walk towards Naxxar. I
looked into the brilliant eye of the sun, hanging low in the sky between
two mountains of flattened violet cloud, their edges fringed with silver;
I looked across the central plain, all golden with light, stretching away
towards the shadowed hills near M'dina; I was thinking of the beauty of
the island and of the Corporal's home, when I noticed that on a small
knoll over which I would soon have to pass, was one of those windmill
stumps or look-out towers with a large rectangular building as its base,
similar to the one at Luqa. Considering it would make a splendid studio
I began to imagine myself as an artist working in Malta in peacetime. I wouldn't have to sell many pictures to pay the rent of twenty
pounds a year, in fact my wife and I might well have money over to
spend on trips to Italy to see the masterpieces of painting that we know
so well in reproduction. Looking up at the windows high above the road
I imagined a large studio music room with delicately tinted walls, and
gorgeously coloured carpets on the floor as a setting for Diana playing
her grand piano and myself painting at a huge easel. I imagined pictures
that I had already finished, large oil-paintings thick with brilliant colour,
decorating the walls. Diana could have happy Maltese servants to keep
the house spotlessly clean, we could have our own ice-cold water supply
under our own flagstone courtyard, while in the garden we could grow
our own vines and oranges.

As I walked on I wondered about the pictures I would be painting in this joyous life, for painting all the time, my pictures would quickly improve. I wondered what kind of style they would have, and this made me think of the great masters of the past and what they might make of the Malta life if they were here. I was passing a cornfield, still vibrant with heat, and I visualised Vincent Van Gogh striding towards me with his flaming red hair and intense eyes. Pieter Breughel would love it too, particularly the peasants whom he would depict with penetrating caricature. As I thought of Breughel I was astonished to see a flock of goats being driven down the road towards me—it was like a vivid Breughel painting. Breughel, painting in allegory, might also have something to say about the torture of war on Malta, about the cumulative strain of action, about the strange madness of the "bomb happy" ones; he might even paint the horrors of crushed bodies and torn limbs in another Triumph of Death. As I walked I shook my head, dispelling, with an effort, the image from my mind. I thought about the romantic Delacroix and how he might stand, sketch-book at the ready, amid the firing guns and falling bombs, to depict the fighting men in noble attitudes. The pride of war is so stupid that I cast away the Delacroix images. It seemed to me that I have more sympathy with Goya, for as I reached the foot of the hill up to Naxxar, I felt his presence in the evening shadows standing quite alone.

As I entered the narrow streets a few minutes ago, at the end of my slow walk home, the sun had dropped behind the western hills, the clouds were floating serenely, while the houses were bathed in pale light, all luminous in their tender shadowing. I looked in through several of the open front doors and thought how Rembrandt would have loved the orange candlelight and the women sewing behind stout tables. Approaching the palace, I was once again struck by the young girls' faces, of the delicacy of their modelling, of the simplicity yet subtlety of contour. If I love the riot of Malta colouring, still more do I love the quietude of evening moments; Botticelli is my closest friend. Thinking of him as if this town of Naxxar were Florence I seem to hear the Catholic people all around me whispering together: they seem to be saying how scandalous it is for him to use a minx like Simonetta, Lorenzo's mistress, as a model for his Madonna.

I'm standing on the palace steps; I'm filled with an ecstatic desire to work, to paint. I'm going to rush up the stairs to my studio and I couldn't have a more beautiful model than Diana. But what's this stink of burnt fat and dish-cloths? The odour hanging in layers of blue smoke at the foot of the filthy marble stairs? Now at the top I turn towards my bedroom, next to the bar—but in my present mood I don't want to talk to all my companions.

"Hullo, Denis," the happy faces smile a greeting, "did you hear what happened to the Eyetie who baled out of the burning bomber last night?"

I shake my head. I don't want to know. I can guess all too easily. The picture of the tumbling bomber and now of the poor helpless figure with streaming parachute, is starkly vivid in my mind.

"Well, he came down on top of a fountain and the spike went up through his arse hole and impaled him there."

I am back in the R.A.F., a member of a war team.

CHAPTER 13

RESCUE BOAT

EARLIER today, anxious to put up a good performance after having a whole day off, I sat beside him on top of the sandbags as we waited for our turn to fly. At twenty-two I felt such an old man compared with him—he looked so very young. He confessed it with a shy smile: he too was married; he had been married a fortnight, just a few days before leaving England. Sitting in his cabin in the aircraft carrier, bringing our recent reinforcements to us, he must have looked at his wife's photograph and gazed back over the wake of the ship just as I did last April. Three days ago, after delivering his Spitfire, this young Pilot Officer jumped down on to the Malta dust for the first time; I remember his happy face—there was real achievement in his eyes. The fact that his expression changed to utter bewilderment, when he realised that a battle was taking place round the aerodrome circuit, was only natural for he had never seen enemy planes before; nevertheless, I was impressed this morning as I gave him my distilled experience of the enemy here and explained the formation and tactics we use. He seemed to grasp the essentials at once.

I do not know what he was thinking as we listened to the moan of planes battling high above us for, staring at the burnt wreckage of last night's mail plane which had been pulled clear of the runway, I was obsessed with my own thoughts: shrapnel had exploded a tyre as the mail plane was taking off, throwing it out of control; although the thirteen occupants had got out alive the mail was destroyed, the parcel of Chinese silk, together with some landscape sketches and a long letter for Diana, were burnt. Perhaps the young officer was thinking about his wife, perhaps he was grappling inwardly with his fear as we waited; if it was fear, he controlled himself very well. We watched a white spot high in the blue lengthen into a beautiful spiralling plume, then the Spitfire, which had been hit in the glycol tank, attempted to land down wind and crashed through the stone walls on the far side of the 'drome. Chiefy, riding by on his bicycle a few minutes later, called out to us: "The pilot's all right, but he was shot through both legs." The young officer accepted this state of affairs quite normally. I felt perfectly confident that, flying as my number two on his first operational trip, he would be safe—I did not, however, anticipate the fiasco of the take-off.

As we taxied out I was amazed by the fantastic number of Spitfires converging on to the runway as well as mine; nevertheless, we'd had our signal so off we went. I was turning back over the aerodrome, waiting for the rest of the Squadron to come up into formation and watching two Spitfires, like toy models taking off on the runway below—when they hit each other; the tangle of wings and slithering metal bodies disappearing into a gigantic burst of dust behind me. Were those two mine? I had no time to worry.

"Exile Leader airborne," I called into my microphone, "what orders?"

"Exile Leader, you are all to land immediately and with extreme care."

A strange order. I checked it before relaying it to the rest of my aircraft. Landing through the dust and over the wreckage was tricky, but turning off the runway and twisting in my seat to watch how the new boy and the others would manage it, I found, to my consternation, that my Spitfires were not landing at all: they had disappeared.

"Hullo, Exile Blue One," I called to one of my section leaders, "where the devil are you?"

"Angels seventeen—going up."

I had no idea what was happening or who had blundered, but orders or no orders I was not going to have my Squadron and, particularly a new boy, wandering around the sky without me. I remember the astonishment on the airmen's faces as I swept past the empty dispersal pens. At full throttle I lifted over the wreckage and pulled my Spitfire steeply upwards; with the yellow island shrinking below and a layer of clouds dropping down towards me, I called again:

"Hullo Blue One, where are you now?"

"Angels twenty-eight, about to engage."

With the Squadron twenty thousand feet above those clouds I knew it was quite hopeless—I would never catch them. If I had known what was going to happen to the young officer I would have made that long climb in lonely silhouette against the cloud layer—but, and I must face it—I would have been too late anyway.

My own flight was not without interest. Scanning the sky with continuous apprehension lest I was attacked by the hordes of 109s that were being reported, I determined to patrol just below cloud height to pounce upon any enemy aircraft that might come through from on top. Hunting alone in the Malta sky is a perilous game. I chased an Italian bomber well out to sea—a crazy thing to do: by flying out to sea the C.O. and I had been shot down and Ken and many others killed. With a feeling of naked vulnerability I headed back—suddenly, as I was re-crossing the coast at St. Paul's Bay, my mouth went dry: three dots were rushing head-on towards me. Three dots; 109s? three dots with white smudges above them! Parachutes! I turned quickly to avoid those three white parachutes—three Italians, swinging to and fro and drifting southwards with the earth far below us. Circling round and round them was rather fun, for the three Ice-cream Men, one slightly higher than the other two, appeared to go up and down like figures on a merry-go-round. As I watched them I became aware that they were staring back at me in terror: probably thought I was playing with them, that any second I would come in to attack them with blazing machine-guns or fly over the top of them to collapse their 'chutes as the Germans do to us—I gave them a wave. Immediate response—they all waved back, sinking towards the ground, yet jerking up and down as they waved. It was a glorious display of Italian friendliness! The lower we got the more and more swiftly the ground came up to meet us. I edged away, so that they could concentrate on their landings, for they were very nearly down on the cliff tops near Dingli. A gust of wind blew them over the edge and they fell another three hundred feet into the sea. I was powerless to help them, but, to make sure they were safe, I dropped down from the sky and my view, as I raced along the wave-crests, was limited to the blue-green water sliding under my wings and the tall cliff rushing past. There they were: three white silk stains drifting in the swirling water; a lot of splashing too. I pulled up in a steep climbing turn over the cliff brink and back across a deserted landscape to dive again for another run past. A quick glimpse revealed the three of them trying to climb up on a ledge. On the third run I saw them all standing safe and sound. They were waving happily.

Once more patrolling over the centre of the island I heard a radio message from Woody: "Anyone short of gravy is to land." As I came down on the runway, sweeping past the wreckage, I remembered the take-off fiasco. I taxied quickly to my pen and switched off the engine.

"Are those two broken Spitfires ours?"

"No, sir," replied the airman, "someone said they were Halfar Spits."

"All right," I gestured towards the tank, "have her filled up as quick as you can."

The others, including the new boy, had not yet returned so I watched the sky: a Spitfire, lowering its wheels, raced into the circuit; other Spitfires were coming back but 109s were whirling amongst them: there were long, brutal, unhesitating bursts of cannon fire. I rounded on a soldier leaning aimlessly against his bicycle.

"Go to 'G' shelter; ask the Wing Commander if I can be sent up on aerodrome cover; pedal as fast as you can."

As the first Spitfire landed I waved it into the nearest pen. Sergeant Harris, leaning from the cockpit, called out to me:

"Three Spits are down in the sea, perhaps more."

"Hurry up then, for God's sake, get your machine refuelled."

The soldier, returning slowly, was doing idle twists and turns round odd lumps of rock; I ran towards him.

"The Wing Commander isn't there," he said.

"What do the others say?"

"I didn't ask them."

I had a frenzied desire to knock the man flat, but instead, loosing a string of oaths, I grabbed the bicycle. Hunched over the handlebars I felt stunned by what had happened to my men. Lifting the ops-room phone I asked urgently for Woody.

"Woody, can I do an aerodrome cover?"

"Have you two aircraft refuelled and rearmed?"

"Yes."

"Good work: then go as cover to the rescue boat just leaving St. Paul's Bay."

"O.K. We'll call ourselves Black Section. By the way, there are three Eyeties on a ledge below the cliffs a mile north-west of Dingli."

"Right-ho, Denis, we'll look after them."

Quickly followed by Harris and oblivious of the aircraft coming in to land, I controlled my racing fighter plane out along the runway, dragging it into the air. Turning viciously round the look-out tower we swerved out over the valley.

"Black Section airborne."

"Well done, Black Leader, watch out for 109s, there are lots around."

A long white trail across the blue waters of the bay ahead of us, revealed the rescue boat bouncing out past St. Paul's Island towards the open sea. It was very conspicuous with its brown cabin, yellow rescue markings on its deck, and its brilliant white wake. I tried to work out the best way of defending it. The sun was dead astern of the boat, giving the enemy a tactical advantage.

"Hullo, Black Leader, four 109s up sun of us now. They're coming in to attack. . . ."

It is dark and we've just arrived back at Naxxar palace. Harris and I covered the rescue boat after a fashion, it was neither sunk nor damaged, but as bullets from the 109s came perilously close to it I cannot help thinking we could have done our job better. Because we were out-numbered two to one it was a difficult situation: if we had each gone chasing a 109, the other two could have attacked and sunk the boat while we weren't there; so we didn't chase them, we hung about behind the stern and harried them as they came in to attack. They did not succeed, but we had no spectacular success either.

I don't yet know who blundered the take-off. The aircraft that collided were certainly Halfar Spits, their Squadron having been moved over to Luqa for some reason or other. I have discovered that the Halfar

Squadron usually take off on four red lights on their own aerodrome, the same as us, so someone ought to have changed the respective signals; of course they may have done, but I was not informed about it. I don't yet know why my boys did not respond to the order to land, nor do I know if I could have saved the young Pilot Officer if I had been with him at twenty thousand feet.

The young Pilot Officer was shot down. He made the error of lagging behind, of being inadequately covered by the others, shot down because, like the rest of us, he had never flown the line abreast formation before and had had no opportunity ever to practise it. Although his plane was hit he baled out successfully by parachute; indeed, falling in to the sea, he was the pilot for whom the rescue boat put out. He must have inflated his dinghy successfully and climbed in—but he was dead when he was picked up. From the condition of his body it was obvious that the 109s must have come down and cannoned and machine-gunned him as he drifted helplessly.

One by one our companions pass from our daily experience. If we feel something of the spiritual joy that lies beyond death we cannot grieve for the traveller who undertakes this journey. In our air fighting we are alone; on the ground we are too exhausted, without time to get to know each other intimately, and rarely knowing each other, we cannot adequately lament the loss of what our companions might have become had they continued to live. The loss of this young officer, this bridegroom, whom I only really talked to for the first time today, makes me realise that grief is for those who are left, a man's intimate friends, his parents, his wife and his family; for them the throbbing wound in their daily lives, for something very precious has been wrenched away. I am sure that the bereaved ones will one day remember with pure compassion instead of pain, but, at the moment, they must be wounded with grief.

The C.O. has just come in, looking very sprightly after his day off. I'd better tell him the news—but he speaks first:

"Were you covering the rescue boat?" he asks me.

"Yes."

"Well, what the devil was the matter with you? You put up a bloody poor show."

Wednesday, and I'm walking along the tree-lined road towards St. Paul's Bay. It seems to me that if we'd gone chasing the 109s the C.O.'s reaction might have been different. We might have destroyed one, perhaps two of the enemy fighters, but the boat would have been sunk by the others while we weren't there. Everyone would have said: "Damn shame about the boat, but you did damn well in the circumstances." The boat was not touched but the fact is that success here is measured by the number of enemy aircraft a pilot shoots down. I may be wretchedly alone but I'll show them; I'll make my mark somehow; according to my own standards I'll be the best fighter pilot in the squadron.

Silence on this empty road; a prison of solitude as I walk. I had hoped for a friend in the young Pilot Officer: I felt we could have silently supported each other in the face of the obscenities of this battle—but he's dead. When the others tell me, with thoughtless laughter, that people in Valetta did a boisterous dance round the body of the Italian impaled on the fountain, I seem to be alone in my horror and lament for humanity. Even my drawing separates me from my companions. Surely they too must be ravished by the tenderness of evening light and the wonderful lines and shapes and constructions of things—can't they realise that it's the simple love of life that makes me want to draw?

I walk slowly on—sudden engines, a rasp of machine-guns, dust flies up all round me, white scars appear on the stonework of the walls; I fling myself into the cover of the wall as two 109s, leaping towards me, tilt sideways over the tree-tops; they're banking round for a second attack. Am I the target? They're coming round, sweeping back towards me—a Bofors gun has opened up, thank God; ascending red fireballs streak into the sky then kick backwards, in black puffs, close to the enemy planes. My God, shells bursting on the tree-tops, shrapnel tearing its way through the leaves, slithering into the earth beside me, thumping on to the roadway behind, clanging on the wall against which I cringe in terror. They've gone! I'm walking back towards Naxxar with a beating heart and hands trembling—the fact that the landscape is empty is appalling to bear—I want to be with the other pilots. If only I could return to the companionship of a letter. I want a letter from my wife, but no letter has come. I have nothing from her pen, from her mind, or from her heart; nothing but the photograph I carry with me. I stare at it trying to draw some comfort from it—but without a letter there is none.

In this isolation I am aware that strange things are happening to me. It's a peculiar sense that things have a pattern in them—a kind of parallel or repeat, that something that has happened, happens again, the same but different. I am sitting on top of the sandbag pen at the opening of our taxi-track. I am wearing my Mae West for we are on readiness. Thursday, May the 14th, my day to lead the Squadron, for, whatever the C.O. may think of me we still take it in turns to lead. When we are sent off I take another new boy up for his first operational flight. He is sitting with me, just as the young Pilot Officer sat with me two days ago. I have been briefing him about combat here in much the same words. Both of us stare upwards for another battle wages invisibly in the pools of blue.

I dreamed last night, not the usual nightmare, but a good clear dream of aerial combat. I was completely confident. In my dream the sky was partially covered by flat patches of white cirrus, very high up: as we climbed for height, in danger of being attacked from above, we stayed under the areas of cirrus so that the enemy were in sharp silhouette above us; on the other hand, when we had thus obtained our altitude, we moved out into the blue areas to be invisible. Cat and mouse tactics and highly successful in all the subsequent details. It was a splendid dream and the strange thing is that the sky over the aerodrome is just the same now! If we have to take off I know just what I'm going to do, indeed I may have lived this whole action already.

The new officer and I, each with our own thoughts, stare upwards: the blue areas seem to palpitate in their glaring intensity of colour. I can just make out four aircraft, golden against the blue and growing steadily larger: four Spitfires, looking as if they've had the worst of the battle up top and beating a hasty retreat, are spiralling down towards us. They swoop down over the aerodrome and now one of them, joining the circuit, is banking leisurely round the 'drome, descending slowly in a medium turn. How beautiful it looks, as graceful as a bird, yellow brown on the top surface of its elliptical wings—now pale duck-egg blue on the underside as it passes us and murmurs away again. Round and round, getting steadily lower. Lower and lower. It's getting very low, dangerously low. I jump to my feet as it disappears behind "G" shelter—a roar of flame, a bubble of fire fifty feet high, searing its way over the grass in front of us, a monstrous trail of exploding petrol with blackened fragments being spewed out of the bottom of it. It's plunged into the valley—it's gone—no trace of it, not even a wisp of smoke, just the roar, now silence.

Red lights—Scramble—as I strap myself in I think of the new boy—ghastly for him to witness that before his first trip. Surging from the ground, passing over the blackened plumb line of debris, I find the horror of that pilot's fiery death obliterated by the sensation of pure smooth flight: the earth slides away and my companions sweep into position each side of me.

"Hullo, Woody, Exile Leader airborne."

"Hullo, Denis, as much height as you can into the sun."

Sun in the blue—no good. Climb under cloud. Westwards under pathways of cloud, ten thousand feet, thirteen thousand; out over the sea; turning back, back across the island, traversing cloud. Tiny aircraft high above—109s—two lots of four—they've seen us—turning towards the sun are they? I'll move farther over to my left—they'll have to cross the cloud to attack us—they'll be clearly visible.

"Exile Leader, 109s behind at five o'clock."

"All right I can see them."

They're coming round, manœuvring round behind us—going to attack while they still have height advantage. Would like to avoid combat, don't want a brawl, want to keep cohesion and gain height, want to catch bombers later. They *are* going to attack. Must keep cohesion. Must keep cohesion. How about defensive circle? Years out of date but Huns may have forgotten counter-action.

"Aircraft line astern, Exiles, line astern—go."

109s bewildered? Drawing off a bit? No they're not! I throw the Squadron on to the turn.

"They're coming down now, Exiles, just tighten up the turn and stay put."

"Hullo, chaps, Woody here, there's a big party, forty plus, thirty miles away heading south towards Grand Harbour."

Thirty miles—just time to cope with 109s first. Stupid Germans joining our circle—two just in front of me. Throttle wide, creeping into position behind them—turn pressure pushes me hard into seat—109 nearer, three hundred yards? Gentle follow through—deflection in front of him—no hurry, quite easy, gently does it: my aircraft shudders as machine-gun bullets and cannon shells stream out towards him. Why doesn't he catch fire, blow up, disintegrate? Another burst. Tilted enemy flies steadily on. Blast my bad shooting—some error—too much deflection? Not enough? Damned if I know. God I'm hot. Got to get him. Closer still. . . .

"109s behind"—a shrill cry.

I flung my Spitfire violently in the opposite direction. Fool that I am—some nervous reaction—we'd have all been perfectly safe in the turn—who the hell called out like that? All my Spitfires are following me out of the circle—109s above in clear silhouette but we're moving into the blue now.

"For God's sake stay under the cloud"—that shrill panicky fellow again.

"Shut up."

He's damn right though—would like to stay under white—we've got to go out into blue—out into sun—must surprise approaching bombers. My Spits in single file—crazy—keep turning. Black 109s, yellow noses, low overhead, pulling up again—ugly—ugly—must keep turning—must stay in blue—lengthen turn slightly right. St. Paul's Bay below us, waves lapping against rocks down there, resting pilots must be watching, it's got to be good. Where the hell are the 109s? Must keep turning.

"Hullo, Woody, where are the bombers now?"

"Practically on the doorstep, Denis, you should be able to see them, angels one seven." Woody's voice is loud but remote.

On the northern horizon the blue sea meets the sky in a belt of white haze—suddenly, against the white—three tiny dots. Why only three?

Must keep turning—where are those 109s? Approaching dots under my
right wing—dots reappearing—certainly only three bombers—Ju 88s?
Keep turning—bombers behind tail—turning—bombers on other side
now—nearer—level out—check sun position, finger up, shadow slightly
left—keep over to the right—must stay invisible—this attack must be
perfect. Blurrs round the bombers—109s in close escort! Bombers under
wing. Tighten circle a bit—must stay invisible. Bombers reappearing—
hell of a strong escort—thirty, no forty 109s flying in twos and fours.
Bombers behind tail—must go in quickly—enemy force reappearing—
ideal position—this is it.

"In we go now, Exiles, each man cover the man in front. Destroy the
bombers first. Straight in and straight out."

With the 88s parading past in vic formation I'm diving fast on to the
tail of the nearest, black against the blue sea, black against the white
houses of Valetta—109s alive to our attack? No—still flying steadily.
Harbour barrage—shells burst red and black, friendly shells, fired by our
side. Bomber growing larger, backwards towards me—gun sight spot
on his port wing—200 yards—on his port engine—fire now: quick white
flashes along the wing, one, two, three, four on the engine—a great
burst of black smoke gushing back. Swerving right and tilting—enemy
fighters? No. Over my left shoulder the sky filled with shellbursts;
Spitfires behind other bombers; 109s breaking up too late from their tidy
formation. Nearest Spit sliding up behind my burning bomber—
strikes all down the bomber's fuselage, strikes along near wing, starboard
engine splits into flame, bomber dropping below, tumbling downwards,
pyre of blackness.

Our machines are being refuelled. Happy erks pass brimming cans of
petrol to their comrades standing on the wings. Sunlight glitters on
wrinkled metal foil as cans are tipped; they're flung aside empty into
clanging banging heaps. Snake belts of pointed shells and bullets are
loaded into almost empty ammunition boxes. A smoke pall hangs over
Takali in the distance for the 88 that one of my boys and I have just shot
down fell close to the perimeter-track there. Both other bombers fell
into the sea. The new boy, standing next to me, is highly excited although
he quite forgot to fire his guns. None of our planes has been damaged—
refuelling is completed. Back on readiness; lights from "G" shelter—off
we go again. . . .

In our second flight this afternoon preliminary skirmishes with 109s
upset my positioning for a surprise attack—in order to get at the bombers
which were about to dive on our last repair shops at Kalafrana, I had to
lead my boys straight across in front of thirty or forty 109s in close
escort on the bombers. With the Vic of three 88s, tipped up big and black
in front of my windscreen, I prayed hard for I expected we would have

casualties. As I settled on to the tail of the nearest bomber I was aware of of a 109 creeping into position behind me—I fired a steady three second burst, hitting the bomber all the time, watching cannon shells and bullets ripping into his black wing, a cascade of flashing white sparks just inboard of his port engine—then, breaking violently left, flashed past the attacking 109 astonishingly close: saw its bright red propeller spinner, oval shaped like an elongated egg with a rippling highlight, rotating in strangely slow motion. The German pilot jerked his head up to look at me— then open sky and sudden panic as other 109s fastened on my tail. Did an aileron turn downwards, pulling fiercely up again. Saw the bomber dropping from the dog-fight above: its port wing, where my cannon shells had torn into it, had snapped off and was fluttering high above, while the rest of the machine, quite flat with flame gushing from its broken wing stump, was gyrating round and round, a gigantic Catherine wheel. 109s on me again—we all had a hell of a fight to get home.

We have driven back to Naxxar and I am tired out as the C.O. greets us in the bar. I tell him that my boys and I have destroyed five Ju 88s, severely damaged another and shot down two 109s without loss today— he chuckles at our success but he refers to that damned score-board again. I still haven't painted any swastikas on it, nor do I know what to paint there. I am bitterly angry and full of distress. I need some encouragement and so do my boys—I thought our successes today would have helped us a bit but our efforts have been thrown back in our faces. For instance the 88 that I've just destroyed has been credited to the ack-ack gunners—credited to them despite the wing snapping off just where I hit it, despite the rear gunner, who baled out by parachute, confirming that I, the Spitfire Leader shot him down. Not only that but the earlier 88, the one that I, and Ingram flying the Spitfire behind me, destroyed after circling above St. Paul's Bay, the one that fell on Takali—it has been credited to a Takali pilot. Officially credited to him despite the fact that the C.O. and "B" Flight pilots watched the whole actions from St. Paul's Bay, confirming everything we did, then went over to Takali to take photographs and bring back Sqadron trophies. I should be ashamed of my distress—people say "what does it matter who shoots down the enemy planes so long as they never fly again"—but it does matter: If I can be blamed for things going wrong I want some kind of credit when things go right.

CHAPTER 14

TOTAL WAR

I HAVE three things to hang on to in this nightmare island: my wife,
although I have no letter; my art, although I'm too tired to paint;
and my job as a fighter pilot, even if I am considered a failure. Today,
Saturday, May the 16th, is my official day to lead the Squadron but here
I am, at four o'clock in the afternoon, clad in pyjamas, lying on the sofa
in the bar with the C.O.s raincoat wrapped about me: I am feeling
wretchedly ill with the Malta Dog again. I thought the earlier bout that
hit me a week ago had been thrown off successfully, but this morning,
when I tried to get up I was shivering again. The C.O. forbade me to
fly. All morning I lay sunbathing on the flat roof outside discovering
that the hot sun on my body got rid of the dreadful fits of icy fever; I
watched the sunlight glisten on the beads of salt sweat that rose on my
bronzed skin; I also glimpsed at the sky for Ju 88s, Messerschmitts and
Spitfires were racing to and fro across the blue and in and out of the clouds
that started to build up. The whole sky is now obscured by heavy cloud
so that the wind blowing in through the open french windows is refreshingly cool. The pain in my stomach is at the moment nothing worse
than a dull ache, although from time to time it clenches my intestines.
I'm feeling dizzy with a splitting pain inside my head: it seems to splash
like acid inside my skull.

A refreshing wind; it blows my hair over my hot forehead as I gaze
at the whitewashed walls that surround me: I am glad the sun has gone
in for the dazzling light on them made my eyes ache. High on the wall,
above the bar opposite, is the Squadron crest, the flaming sword that I
painted there: it's a diabolically awful colour, a dark crimson, like dried
blood. To the left of the bar is the accursed score-board, still a blank
despite the C.O.s instructions to fill it with swastikas that nobody agrees
about. On the bar itself are a few bottles while Manuel Galea, our Maltese
barman, is waiting behind the counter—ghostly replica of Manet's "Bar
aux Folies Bergère", but without the glitter or gaiety. The erotic touch
in this place, engrimed as it is with dust and dirt, is given by a calendar
advertising a firm that used to belong to a "B" Flight pilot, another pilot
who was killed the other day when his parachute failed to open; it depicts
a provocatively naked blonde standing up with her purple back towards
us and the rest of her body tantalisingly, but not quite, revealed in a

half-length mirror that is cunningly placed in front of her. Pilots pay more attention to the huge rudder of polished wood that fell clear of the Italian bomber that the C.O. destroyed, filling the corner behind my left shoulder, and to the dull black machine-guns, buckled and twisted, from one of my abortive 88s. These guns are pinned, high on the wall above me. They look like black embracing snakes. Manuel Galea still stands waiting but no one is bothering to drink anything. There are hundreds of flies crawling silently over the bar counter, blackening the discarded glasses; there are more flies buzzing round my hot face. I wish the damn things would leave me alone.

Squadron Leader Barton, commonly called "Sailor", the C.O. of the other Luqa Squadron is also off duty today, also suffering from the Dog; he's shuffling across the dusty floor, clad in black leather flying boots and an old silk dressing-gown, but there are many other pilots lying ill on their beds in the next room, most with the Dog. Mike Graves, of the other squadron is in there, too, he shot down an 88 yesterday but his Spitfire, flying into the disintegrating wreckage, blew up; although Mike escaped by parachute he is somewhat shaken. This bar is now empty but for one other companion, lying back on the opposite end of this sofa, exhausted and silent: Pancho isn't ill, but he looks awful. His usually happy face is drawn and worried and there are drooping bags under his eyes. Pancho, leading the formation this morning instead of me, had to act quickly in a tactical situation that was as ugly as the one I faced on my last trip. He did the only thing possible by turning straight into a large formation of Italian Reggiani fighters—he is blaming himself for what happened to Sergeant Harris. Harris's Spitfire was hit in the glycol tank— he tried to bring it back, he was too low to reach the runway, his machine hit a stone wall, cartwheeling across the aerodrome, tearing off its wings. He is in hospital with the base of his skull split. Doubt if he'll live.

There's activity by the french windows: the C.O. and Scotty are coming in, unwinding a drum of electric cable behind them. Scotty looks ill, a changed man since Max was killed: all the sparkle of fun behind his eyes has gone, his lifted eyebrows give his wizened little face a bewildered expression.

"Whatever's that for?" I ask him.

Scotty tries to smile: "It's a Floozie phone," he replies, "you'll soon be able to ring up all your floozies and things."

Presumably a civilian telephone line is being brought into the mess. A Floozie is a girl friend of a particular type. I wonder how many of us really go into action with these girls? Some do. One of our newly arrived pilots had his first experience of a woman in Valetta last night; he told me this morning he was terribly ashamed.

Late in the evening, with this persistent pain in my head and wretched uneasiness in my stomach, I'm lying on my bed in darkness; I am dropping into semi-consciousness; I know I'm dreaming. A long dark tunnel of earth, pitch black, but someone else is in here with me: all the muffled noises, the groans and exertion tell me that some companion is climbing with me up this dark tunnel. In continuous darkness, crawling on our hands and knees, we grope our way forward with the heavy roof pressing low upon us. How long have we been climbing, heaving ourselves along with endless labour? We've got to keep on upwards although there's no sign that the tunnel will ever end. In the packed earth wall, just a few feet in front of me, a great wooden door is suddenly thrown open: glaring light floods out over the floor, radiating from some source that I cannot see—white light, pure and dazzling. Although I crane my head sideways and peer into the opening it is still impossible to see whence it comes. But my companion can. He is a few steps ahead of me, opposite this unknown place, head turned as he looks inside: the light has caught him, frozen him in an attitude of stepping forward into the blackness, his groping hands recoil in terror from what he sees. As his shoulders lift high from his ribs, glittering beads of sweat break out all over his back. His eyeballs stare fixedly, his nostrils twist, his mouth drops open, the nape of his neck twitches, his hair moves. Watching him in horrified fascination I feel the same terror overwhelming me. I cannot breathe, my heart is pounding wildly, sweat's oozing out on to my forehead. Paralysed with terror I'm fighting desperately to get back to the walls of my bedroom. Fighting, fighting my way back. My bedroom, my bedroom. My clutching hands gradually relax their rigid hold on twisted sheets. My heart is still thumping while my breath is coming in great gasps. I lift my head from the sweat-soaked mattress. It is nearly dawn and on the opposite side of the room the heavy body of the C.O. is tossing in his bed.

The C.O. tells me that he's not well this morning; I don't know if I'm better or worse, but it's irrelevant, for someone has got to take the pilots down for dawn readiness. I am quickly dressed. By the fluttering candle-flame I wait for the others. Why did I feel such terror in the night? I don't think I'm frightened of the unknown that lies beyond death—such fear then is unaccountable. After good clear dreams of combat the other night the flying that followed was highly successful— what's going to happen after this nightmare—am I going to get killed, or is someone else?

We are close to our Spitfires in readiness. The Group Captain Station Commander has just been over to see us in a polished American car, reminiscent of peacetime, I thought to myself, as I held the door open for him.

"Barnham," he said, "I hear you are suffering from the Dog. Woody says you are not to fly. By the way, tell whoever you put in charge to use the call sign Ratter instead of Exile for flying today."

His visit is an unnecessary complication: I don't want to fly, I'm feeling wretched with a splitting head pain—and now I've been ordered not to. But with the C.O. ill, the Dreaded Hugh in hospital, somebody has got to lead the formation, somebody has got to pilot the eight Spitfires available—I don't know how long we can go on like this because I'm not the only man who has spewed up his breakfast in the last half hour. I'm not, however, going to send another Max to his death.

We are in the air now; we've been orbiting at twenty-seven thousand feet for almost half an hour but the raid that Woody expected to develop on Grand Harbour hasn't materialised—oxygen's diminishing fast, our petrol's short. In order to conserve fuel I'm leading the formation at a very slow speed—we are wide open to 109 attack. Impossible to search for enemy planes in the violet blue with the dazzling sun piercing my perspex hood with opaque prongs of white light—I've shoved the hood fully back—icy air blusters about my open cockpit, brutally cold. Far below us, Malta is a brown blob in a vast sea; seventy miles away in Sicily I can see the volcano of Etna, its snow-covered crater clearly below our level—if we stay up here much longer, with our dark, strong shapely Spitfires floating together in the pale void and dressed as we are in shorts and shirts, in a temperature of thirty degrees below zero, we'll all die of cold. Shivering in convulsive jerks from the shoulders I search the sky —my companions turn their trusting pink faces towards me, alert for any manoeuvre I may make.

"The Eyetie raid is coming in from the northwest. Over Gozo at angels thirty. Gain as much height as you can, Sailor."

An Eyetie raid approaching, but Woody, calling me Sailor, must think I'm Squadron Leader Barton—of course, he doesn't know I'm flying! It's with a sense of truancy that I smile down at the tiny island.

"Going up Ratter Squadron—keep your eyes open."

From thirty-four thousand feet I steer the Squadron in a shallow dive to one side of the approaching enemy. I can see five big bombers packed tight, their wings, angled tail planes, and fragile vertical rudders over-lapping neatly. I can see their fighter escort, forty Italian fighters—but in such a stupid formation: a long diagonal line on the far side. I am going to try out a new manoeuvre, based on what I learned against the 88s the other day. I am leading four Spitfires in line abreast with another lot of four Spitfires, Blue Section, just behind me. "O.K. Blue Section, turn into the bombers now," I order, twisting round in my seat and watching them go The enemy fighters, as they turn to attack Blue Section, will, I hope, like all good fighter pilots, look over their shoulders first—my four Spitfires, called Red Section, will be right behind them. In order to defend themselves, those forty fighters should turn quickly into us: Blue Section, without opposition should be able to destroy the whole bomber formation.

Blue Section are closing with the bombers—the enemy fighters, having seen them, are moving to intercept—I am coming round behind. But have the enemy seen my four machines? Am I too far behind? Have I misjudged it? No—it's working perfectly—the enemy fighters have seen us—the whole lot are turning back towards us, clumsily, one after another—Blue Section is having a free run in! One enemy fighter jerks across my nose in a steep turn—about to follow him round I glimpse right—alongside me is another Italian machine, with its huge white cross markings on fuselage and tail—beyond it many more Macchis are deploying to attack us. Pulling back on my control column I roll inverted high over the top of them—we've drawn off the whole hornet's nest—ten to one against us—no real need to stay. I glimpse a Spitfire with its guns firing on a Macchi's tail.

"Come on out of it, Red Section," I call.

Rolling out and diving behind them I watch the bombers flying onwards—flying steadily onwards, quite unperturbed—Blue Section must have muffed their attack. In anger at our failure I stare at the bombers; four of them; four of them; one is missing but only one. Far below there are dots of smoke on the tiny island—their bombs going off.

"All Ratter aircraft reform with Ratter Leader—Angels thirty over St. Paul's Bay."

I wait and I wait—I want to have another bash at these Italians. The plan worked beautifully—I gave Blue Section the plum rôle yet without opposition they muffed it—should have done the job myself. Where is everybody? I wait and I wait—my men are probably short of fuel—too late now—the enemy have crossed the coast.

Anger consumes me as, kicking on bottom rudder and throwing over the control column, I plunge vertically earthwards. Down, down, down, down, down—I'm making this blasted Spitfire dive vertically as fast as it will go. My anger is matched by the mounting speed, the solid buffeting air around my open cockpit and the fierce pressure needed to control this machine. The rising detail of individual hills and houses is blotted out by sudden frost on my windscreen—down, down, down—controls rigid but the aircraft is bucking, wriggling and making strange noises—something's wrong. As I start turning the trimming wheel to ease me out of this dive a wave of heat engulfs my feet and legs. She's on fire. The aerodrome runway flashes past and heaving with all my strength on the controls I race low round the buildings of Valetta and out over the blue harbour—the sudden heat is nothing more than the contrast between the icy temperatures up top and heat radiating from the sun-scorched landscape below. Luqa aerodrome swings past a second time. Slowing, with dispersal pens and parked Spitfires streaming past my bounding wing-tip, I feel the sudden onset of pain in my stomach: it doubles me forward in my seat. Slow enough to lower my wheels and flaps I slide in for my landing on the long runway. I taxi up to a group of my airmen, switch off the engine and start climbing out; as the airmen push my aircraft back between the protective walls of the sandbag pen, I stagger to the ground and am sick.

Back to Naxxar—to the pilots talking in the bar:
"That 88 you shot down on Takali the other day," a "B" Flight pilot tells me. "Bloody good show! We watched it all then went over to have a look. The German pilot was draped over the top of the wreckage—all burning—as the flames consumed him, so the muscles contracted in his right arm bringing it up in a Heil Hitler salute. Interesting to watch."

"Yes," says another pilot with a bitter laugh, "four more unhappy families in Germany—let 'em all sizzle. Have any luck today?"

"Yes," I reply, "we destroyed an Italian bomber and a fighter."

To have destroyed only two machines with eight Spitfires isn't good enough—if only we could have re-formed again and had another go—I must think out some plan. It was not Blue Section's fault that they only destroyed one bomber—the pilots' hands were frozen solid—they couldn't move their fingers to fire their guns—Baby Face has gone to sick quarters with frost bite.

My companions are a grand lot of men but all of us are ill, gaunt, with dark eyes, fiercely strained and living on the edge of frayed nerves—we are numb with war. I am hardly more than sorrowful that a German pilot dies in the wreckage of his plane that I set fire to—although it is ugly, ugly to think that I am responsible for the distress of his family. But I must protest about war. I protest about hate. Why must senior officers who I know to be good men come here to tell us to hate. We may be fearful in our cockpits, but this is just a job to be done and most of us must surely be serene and quiet in our attitude towards the enemy. Cyril, for instance, how could he be anything else? Why then must we hate? Why must we be set on a downward path towards barbarity? How much do we have to accept? But people are beginning to hate—"Four more unhappy families in Germany," we say, "good show—watch the Germans sizzle." A pilot in my Flight gave me a story he's written about himself: "Staccato machine-guns and his face in the mirror—his lips drawn back over his teeth in a snarl." Hate, hate, hate and proud of it. Where can it all end?

There is terrible news: news of the Italians, the three ice-cream men who, less than a week ago, I watched descending in their parachutes and landing in the sea; the ones I watched standing alive and well on the ledge on to which they had climbed; the men I watched waving to me and trusting me. Some persons unknown arrived on the cliff top before the rescue party—or did the rescue men themselves commit the crime? I do not know—but all that was found of the Italians was crushed bodies, pulp and blood—someone had deliberately rolled rocks over the cliff top.

I am in hell—those Italians were personal to me—I loved them as they swung down the sky waving and kicking their legs like young children— I looked forward to meeting them some day—they are dead. Atrocities are true then, and, Lord forgive us, there is laughter in the mess, laughter. . . .

"Now we won't have to feed them."

"They shoot us in our parachutes and dinghies—we'll do the same to them."

. . . And to my protests—laughter, and one single remark:

"Denis, you need re-educating, this is total war."

What is happening to us? I can bear the laughter no longer. Beyond the open door is the quiet evening. In silence, on the roof in the twilight I watch the pure light of the stars reappearing one by one in patterned brilliance. . . .

Alone now in my bedroom—my wife's photograph here, no letter— but at least I can work. I am drawing my own face in the mirror, a stranger staring back at me. I'll bear the solitude of this battle by drawing, continuously drawing—I, too, may write about this one day—I add such a book in the corner of my drawing. But will I survive to write the book? Will I even be alive this time tomorrow? I title the picture, "The future? What?" and add today's date, 16/5/42.

CHAPTER 15

FOUR DAYS' HOLIDAY

IT IS Sunday, May the 17th—another nightmare last night, but although a nightmare—beautiful. I was pinioned yet struggling in thick darkness. Close by and surrounded by darkness was a small space of light. This spherical space shone inwardly and it seemed to have quality, both beauty and charity; although I looked into it I was kept out from it—I seemed to lie on its surface as if on the surface of a bubble. I longed to break into it. I longed to throw myself at the feet of the magnificent, seated presence that was there, yet I was held back. I struggled but I was held motionless as I watched in worship—His figure seemed to burn with pure flame—bliss lay in his presence if only I could have reached him. As his hand lifted from his lap a soft silver light fell from him. Held back by writhing, threshing things, I looked towards the shining One with awe for there was a certain terror in beholding his majesty; and yet, as light radiated from this source of infinite power, from his magnificent eyes and face, and from his seated figure, there came such peace and goodness, and a feeling of such love, that my heart was scorched with joy, joy just to behold him.

Even thinking of this nightmare gives me joy, a kind of blessing on my four days' stay at the St. Paul's Bay rest camp. The C.O. sent me over here this morning to cure myself of this Malta Dog—I don't know how to cure it so I'm going to starve for four days. It is wonderful to be back here: it is evening, the sun is almost on the hilltops opposite, silver water is dancing amongst the darkening rocks by the swimming platform, a capricious breeze blows in my face, and four Spitfires are murmuring overhead—silver wings against the evening blue. Regarding my own flying yesterday, Rome radio admits the loss of one bomber and a fighter, but they claim to have destroyed six of my eight Spitfires! We had no losses. Why then do they tell such lies?

Monday, May the 18th. I've had no food since breakfast yesterday, my body's very thin but I'm feeling much better. I'm lying on my towel, and, as I write a letter to Diana, I glance down through the water: forests of green seaweed, lapping left, lapping right, surging to and fro; further out, gay in the sunlight, white horses are hurrying past St. Paul's Island. I haven't had a letter from Diana and I can't understand it for other pilots

have each had several issues of mail—I don't want to think about that—
I've been so brutal and complaining to my young wife in my letters
during the last ten days—I want to be quiet and tender with her. Tender,
like the silence here, for the All Clear has sounded. All day the battle has
gone on—it started before first light when our night fighters destroyed
three bombers in flames. At dawn some Italian E-boats were seen off
the coast—Hurricanes were sent out to destroy them, but 109s appeared—
Spitfires were sent out to destroy the 109s—two 109s were shot down into
the sea and others damaged. Mid morning the Ju 88 Recce plane and
two escorting fighters were shot down from twenty-five thou,
all three into the water—that was the raid in which it probably
happened: Peter's been killed. A good friend, a good man, a brilliant
pilot—he destroyed fourteen enemy planes here—and now they've got
him—we will never read his stories.

Wednesday, May the 20th, I've been down here at St. Paul's fishing
village since early this morning, I've left my coat and other things up at
the Harbour Bar restaurant and for many hours I've been sitting below
one of the jetties amongst the boats. The boats rock gently, I can hear
the water smacking against their wooden sides. The sun is fairly high
above me, I suppose it's about three o'clock—I've left my watch back
there with my coat—I wanted to be timeless as I paint. For four days
I've lived as an artist, without eating, of course, and, as I've been painting
pictures, I've re-learned some old secrets—the natural feeling for time, for
instance, sensitive to the arrival and farewell of warmth, to observe once
again the flowers turning their quiet faces and the way the shadows
shorten then grow longer again.

During this four days' rest I've been trying to forget the war although
it was interesting last night to have some relative comparison of our
battle; the B.B.C. from London stated that "The bombs dropped on
Malta last month totalled a greater weight than during the 1940 blitz
on England." It is difficult to believe that tomorrow I will be back in
the thick of it again. This makes me think about our battle and about war.
Some of us may hate, but perhaps I and those of my companions who have
no emotion in the air, are even more frightening creatures: human
automatons. We concentrate upon skilful tactics to get into the best
position for an attack, while the actual moment of killing the enemy
is dominated by mathematical problems of deflection shooting to hit,
not a man but a machine. But if air warfare is impersonal for us in
Spitfires it must be even more so for the bomber crews with their puff
ball contribution on the corner of a map. This impersonality terrifies me
—more and more destructive bombs will obviously be developed in this
war, but what of the next war, and the war after that?

It is strange that in 1938 and 1939 people said that war was so horrible
that it would never happen. They had sharp and vivid in their minds the

ghastly example of what air raids could do to cities in Spain, yet we are being bombed here by weapons developed from the Spanish prototypes. The future too will take for granted its newly developed bombs, people will cringe in terror as new missiles plunge towards them out of the skies —the people who are not wiped out on the edge of their explosions will go on facing it as we are facing it.

The only hope for the future, as I see it, is if man's traditional loyalty, good in its time but out of date, be expanded by a love and respect towards all his fellows. Yet here, and I find it difficult to believe it as I look down at the gently lapping water, instead of loving I am taught to hate. To abide by what we all believe in is the real battle.

"Sir, sir." High above me on the jetty a figure in a black suit is gesticulating against the blue sky: it is the waiter from the restaurant! "It's a quarter to four, sir, don't you want any lunch?"

"It's a bit late for lunch, isn't it?"

"I'm very sorry, sir—I hunted for you most places but you couldn't be found. I saw your coat and I knew you hadn't been in to eat. I have kept two fishes for you. They'll only take a moment to cook."

"Well, bless you—I'll be up in a minute."

After four days it should be harmless to eat two fishes—I'll be flying to-morrow, I'll have to eat.

I'm walking back towards Naxxar in the late dusk—from a medical point of view this holiday's been a complete failure—the fishes and I have already parted company in beastly circumstances—I'll just have to accept this pain that doubles me up as I walk. There are screaming engines above me in the night sky—Ju 88 bombers are diving overhead towards Takali, black shapes against the fading light—bombs crack and rumble, their orange-glows quickly silhouette the stunted trees—red hose-pipe shells sail up into the darkness bursting irregularly. If I were flying, the best way to attack these bombers would be to sweep in from the east and catch their silhouettes against the evening glow.

I am in bed now, but when I came into the bar this evening, the C.O. wandered across and put a large friendly hand on my shoulder.

"Hullo, Denis, are you better?"

"Yes," I lied, for what else could I say after four days off?

Some of the others lifted their hands in greeting as Pancho came over to tell me the news. Harris is dead. Yesterday the new boy I initiated last week was shot down—he escaped by parachute. In the same fight one of our Sergeants called Mount had a lucky escape—his Spitfire was riddled with holes, his shoulders burnt by incendiary bullets and his legs peppered with shrapnel. Apparently Scotty, leading the formation, was surprised by 109s—but turning fiercely he got in a burst on a 109 which blew up, so they, too, paid a price. As the C.O. moved across to talk to Cyril reading quietly in the corner, Scotty himself came over.

"The C.O. was nearly shot down himself this morning," he told me. "He led us into another lot of Eyeties, like the lot we went into with you. We got two of their fighters—Mount got one despite his burns and Sergeant Innes got a complete sitter."

"You all seem to be doing jolly well," I interrupted, glancing at the scoreboard. The scoreboard's still a blank.

"You know, Denis," he continued, "these Italians are an odd lot—they either don't want to fight or they haven't got a clue—when you get behind them they do beautiful aerobatics, loops, rolls off the top, anything but get out of the way and fight properly. Sergeant Innes' sitter was just like that—but there I go again—I'm trying to tell you about the C.O.

"It was all the Dreaded Hugh's fault because he was the last man to fly the C.O.'s machine."

"I thought the Dreaded Hugh was in hospital."

"He was, but he came back from his dysentery lapses, just after you left last Sunday. Hugh must have done something awful to that plane, re-rigged it or re-trimmed it or something, for the C.O. could hardly control the thing. He was milling around up there when an Eyetie comes up and sits right behind him. He couldn't throw the Eyetie off. Round and round he went, finally plunging down, twisting and turning, but the Eyetie just sat there. He levelled off, expecting to be shot down, but the Eyetie comes alongside, waves his hand and fires his guns into thin air!"

"What did the C.O. make of it?"

"Dunno, but poor old Hugh got it in the neck all right—expect he wishes he was back in hospital!"

"Well, what do you make of it, Scotty?"

Scotty shrugged his shoulders.

"Scotty," I continued, "maybe you're right, maybe these Italians don't want to fight. If they disapproved of the war and yet were anxious what Hitler or Mussolini might do to their families, wouldn't they pretend to fight?"

"Well, they drop bombs on us, don't they?"

"Yes, I know they drop bombs, but it wouldn't be easy for a bomber crew to pretend—yet heavens me, they miss the target often enough—even that might be deliberate!

"Yes, Scotty, these fighter pilots must be pretending," I added, highly excited about what I was discovering. "Why else should a pilot refuse to shoot down a Spitfire? We know that fellow wasn't out of ammunition; he may even have flown alongside the C.O. to show his true feelings.

"It accounts for everything. The extravagant claims from Rome

Radio. On the last trip I made, they claimed six of our eight Spitfires—when they hadn't hit any of us. These pilots have got to make their case look good. It accounts for the C.O.'s Eyetie firing his guns into thin air—you can't claim Spitfires if you haven't fired your guns! They're pretending to fight—pretending——

"What are we going to do, Scotty? We'll have to shoot down their bombers, but their fighters—do we leave them alone?"

Sergeant Johns, his mouth in a firm disdainful line, butted into the conversation.

"B . . . s," he said, "the Italians are just a yellow-livered lot of b . . . s. They've no stomach for war. Shoot down all the b . . . s is what I say."

"I suppose you think it takes no guts to fly over here when every Spitfire is doing its best to destroy you?" I replied. "I suppose you think it takes no guts to restrain from firing your guns even in self-defence?"

"Whose side are you on anyway?" replied the Sergeant. "The Italians are a dirty lot of milksops. The Germans know how to fight; they would never indulge your pacifism."

I should have kept quiet.

"You are quite wrong, Sergeant Johns," I continued with strange calmness. "The Germans were the first people to try out an active pacifism in the face of modern war. Have you never heard of the incident in the trenches near Armentières in France on Christmas Day in 1914? The Germans started singing carols in their line and finally a German Officer of immense courage stood up, deliberately exposing himself to fire from the British trenches: but nobody did fire. He called out 'no hostilities' and suggested that both sides should meet in no-man's-land. Not only did they meet, but exchanging food and cigarettes a lot of individual Germans started making friends with a lot of individual Englishmen."

"And what happened then?" asked Sergeant Johns with a facetious grin.

"That's the tragedy of it," I continued, "I imagine that officers were ordered to go into the battlefield yelling 'No fraternisation', for both sides were certainly bludgeoned back into killing one another.

"Just imagine, Johns, what might have happened if this fraternisation had spread; if individual soldiers, not only at Armentières, but everywhere along the line had climbed out and got to know one another. Sharing a common hatred of war and inspired with new loyalty towards their individual Christian feelings, their humanitarianism, each man for his fellows, they could have spread their refusal to make war back behind the lines. Just imagine it: because a limit would have been set to what governments could demand of their citizens—the whole history of the world would have been changed, a new era of peace would have dawned, millions of men would never have died in the 1914–18 war and this war would never have happened."

There was a long pause after I had finished, but within a few brief seconds Sergeant Johns voiced the usual scornful reaction.

"So now you want us to jump out of our Spitfires and shake hands with the Huns as well?"

I should have kept quiet. I left the bar almost at once and I'm in bed now. I shudder to think of what I've been saying. Stupidly I was hurt again—I could have pulled my rank on Johns, but he is a damned good pilot and, after all, it was a personal affair. I should have kept my deeply felt convictions to myself.   When will I learn not to break out from my solitude? I must withdraw into myself. Hugh is in the third bed, fast asleep, his head at an awkward angle, his mouth half open—snoring. The C.O., undressing, doesn't seem to have overheard my indiscretions at the bar.

"Denis, are you well enough to take dawn readiness in the morning?"
"Yes."

F

CHAPTER 16

FINAL REFUGE

"HULLO Woody, Exile Leader airborne."
Three other Spitfires and I are well out over the silver and blue sea, climbing steeply into the sun:
"Hullo Woody, Denis here, any trade for us?"
Will it be the Italians this time? If they don't fire at us there may be a chance of forcing one to land, of capturing an Italian to find out what he really thinks—immense possibilities—the whole war might be shortened. Fifteen thousand feet but still no reply from Woody.

"Hullo Woody, Hullo Woody, Denis here—any trade?" I ask anxiously, banging my wireless case and repeating the message.

At last: "Yes, Denis, forty plus, twenty miles out; big jobs and little jobs, approaching from the east."

Sounds like Huns—sounds as if escort is higher than the bombers—only four of us—we'll climb up on top, dive vertically past escort, then on to bombers. I look out at the wings of my Spitfire for they are covered with huge white spots: following up my ideas on air combat I wanted to be quickly recognised so that my companions can reform to deliver a second attack on any bombers we meet. I've also had my perspex hood removed. Chiefy disapproved of the spots, but the airmen have made a splendid job of covering the whole of my aircraft—he says all the enemy fighters will fasten upon me: perhaps I'm stupid but it's worth a try.

"Hullo Woody, where are the bombers now?"

No reply, no reply to my repeated question. Blast it—either his wireless is faulty or mine is. From high in the sun over the south-easterly corner of the island there's no sign of the enemy. Without my perspex hood I have a particularly clear view of the coastline, serrated by narrow bites of sea, twenty-five thousand feet below. In Kalafrana Bay, the largest bay, down there I can see the *Breconshire*, the overturned ammunition ship from the last convoy, widely encircled by promontories of brown earth: she looks like a long red nail with a plume of rust curling away from her in the blue water. Over there—a sudden bomb burst on Halfar—Woody's voice blares in my ear-phones:

"The bombers are going out west, low on the water, get them chaps."

I swing violently downwards over the southernmost lump of the island, but the vital information has come through too damned late. We're dropping almost vertically at full throttle, red dusted Halfar is swallowed under my Spitfire's nose, and now, bouncing jerkily with my controls almost solid with pressure, the cliffs and the sea are racing up to meet my windscreen. An 88—low on the water—could easily misjudge our pull-out and plunge straight into the sea—careful then. As the 88 leaps towards us I glimpse back into the glaring sun: we're in perfect position to attack.

That silver, brilliantly shining sun? Something there? Screwing up my eyes, searching the blinding light—blurrs of grey, incongruous lumps of black, then, quite clearly for an instant, straight black wings.

"109s behind, Exiles," I frame the words calmly and quietly, "Break Right".

If I spoke carefully, I'm now heaving at my controls with all my strength. Sudden island detail close in front of my nose, then sky as I climb. The 109s scatter like spray. Twisting in my seat; my companions can't have heard my order—I'm alone. Enemy fighters everywhere. Two race low overhead; four more on my right. As three more 109s dive head-on under my nose I watch the fourth turning towards me; in a few seconds he will pass below to my left. There's plenty of time to shoot him down. This should be easy.

Controls a little to the left, give him more deflection than that, a little more to the left—that's fine. He's flying beautifully now, straight towards the red centre spot of my gunsight. I can feel the hump of the firing button beneath my thumb—wait a little longer: Clatterclatter-clatterclatter, machine-guns, Bom, bom, bom, bom, bom, my cannons making their slower beat as I adjust my fingers. He's sweeping closer and closer, larger and larger. Flashes on his wings and fuselage. Gigantic in size he disappears under my wing. I heave my Spitfire into a steep turn. On his tail now!

Where is he? Where's he got to? With my Spitfire in a violently nose-down attitude I'm leaning forward in my straps, peering through my windscreen: on the left the tall narrow rock formation called Filfla stands alone and sunlit, its flat top yellow with grass, some narrow ledges on its vertical sides and white surf breaking round the foot of it. The sea is deep blue and my 109 was black. It's obviously there, somewhere in front of me. Damned if I can see it. A sudden call in my earphones: "Something's gone in near Filfla."

It must be my 109 that has crashed—the splash must be right underneath me.

As I stare downwards I hear a quiet voice:
"Turn right."
The voice is not in my earphones. It is louder, firmer:
"Turn right."
"TURN RIGHT!"
A roared command: my hands and feet jump to obey: my Spitfire

pitches sideways: against the pressure I look back over my shoulder: an exploding cannon shell just where I was, two, three, four, five more in a straight line across the blue.

More 109s on my right, more above them . . . I'm cut off from the island . . . 109s coming down . . . tracers . . .

. . . at last I've got away from them, the cliff tops flash below me, God knows how long I've been twisting and turning—may have got two more—couldn't follow them down—practically out of ammo? Twisting and turning over Safi valley I watch two 109s, black against the yellow fields, now against the flat patch of Halfar aerodrome, flash behind the Takali hills—two Spitfires are after them—but four more 109s, up-sun, after the Spits—I yell a warning. Over there a 109 by himself—I'll get him—search the sky, search the sky; it's all clear as I climb nearer and nearer—yes, I'll get this fellow—it's a trap: five more 109s in the sun . . . coming down? I crouch lower in the cockpit as I dive headlong behind a hill-top, hoping not to be noticed. Wing tip close to the walls, round the hill—out over open country—thank God, sky clear—but keep twisting and turning—twisting and turning, I can hardly believe it but the sky really is empty—safe for a moment—the empty sky is a wonderful royal blue. Clatterclatterclatterclaaatttter . . . over on a wing tip . . . where is he? Where the hell is the 109? Cllaatttercllaattterclaaatttter . . . I can't see him, Oh God, I can't see him. Keep turning hard Cllaatttercllaatttercllaaatttter . . . it's army gunners firing from the ground—you bloody fools . . .

Unlike the Hurricane that was shot down, I managed to sweep clear of the army gunners, and I landed soon after. I apologised to Chiefy for all the extra trouble I'd caused him and got him to paint out the spots at once: he smiled back at me with such a patient, kindly, understanding smile. I'm still shaken after that trip; when I was fighting the 109s over the sea it seemed like hours. I am back at Naxxar now—it's difficult to believe that only yesterday, with the war dismissed from my mind, I was sitting peacefully on the steps of the harbour, painting boats. Oh how desperately I need some real friend to talk to; but Peter's dead.

Could I talk to Chiefy? A deep tie of friendship seems to have sprung up from our exchanges at the dispersal point; he seems to respect me in a strange way although I'm continually making an ass of myself. I need his almost fatherly affection for I have little else—I dare not risk it by revealing my real inner thoughts.

I can't talk to the C.O. either. I was reminded of that this afternoon when he came to take over the Squadron.

"What the devil have you done to that Spitfire?" he asked.

I looked at the Spitfire: I could see nothing wrong with it: after the fight all the spots had been meticulously painted out, there wasn't a trace of where they had been. I looked at the C.O. in bewilderment.

"You . . ." He bit off his words for I am his senior Flight Commander and there were airmen present. I could see nothing wrong with the damned aeroplane, but the C.O. turned to Chiefy and I overheard his expressionless order: "Have the perspex hood put back at once."

So that was the trouble! Flying without a hood! I considered that a first rate idea, I still do: with the 109s in the sun my quick vision may have saved all our lives this morning. I walked away from the dispersal point, past "G" shelter towards the mess. The C.O. was damned lucky that I brought his Spitfire back at all.

Neither can I talk to the Doc. Drinking in the mess, he was holding forth in declamatory terms about us pilots: "The index of anxiety neurosis amongst pilots is getting phenomenally high on the island," he said. "The trouble is that there are too many of them and not enough aeroplanes."

"None of you," he continued, looking in my direction, "get enough flying".

"You're all yellow," he added, with an obvious sneer in his voice.

His attitude may, of course, have been some kind of psychological treatment for us, you never know with Docs. Perhaps I could talk to a padre, but no padre has been anywhere near us since we arrived. I could talk to Diana if she were here—but she's not. I've poured out my feelings in letters to her, but I have no reply. While I was in the mess I searched again through all the mail boxes just in case my first letter had arrived and got muddled up with somebody-else's mail, but it wasn't there.

Down at the mess I did have a chat with old Greg, the Catering Officer. Not a real chat, nothing but the surface glitter, the same old stuff as if to say, "are we downhearted? No!" I must have been quite funny for I had him doubled up with laughter. The same old shell that the world calls "putting a happy face on things", but who the hell knows what's going on underneath the shells with which we face one another?

Greg told me there was a ration lorry going down to the supply dump at Marsa, so I hitch-hiked for the ride. We were approaching Grand Harbour when the sirens went off. "I hate that b . . . noise when I'm down here," said the airman driver, his horrified eyes protruding from his round face. Although we both laughed at each other's expressions, I didn't like the sound of it either, particularly as the streets were new to me.

In the street next to the supply dump the ground-floor windows of the gutted houses were boarded up, blue sky stared through the fractured upstairs windows, while twisted wrought-iron balconies hung down from the stonework—furthermore, the street was packed with herds of goats. With a cry of delight at such a subject for drawing I leapt down from the lorry and pulled out my sketch book. Oh the sheer joy of drawing. The people pushing their way through the herds didn't stay long: at the first sound of enemy engines the men rushed down the street kicking the goats out of the way, while the women, snatching up their children, waddled after them. I watched the irregular white pattern of shell bursts suspended against the blue, with the 88s diving steeply towards us. The goats stayed so I stayed. During the bombing the goats surged restlessly, poor helpless creatures; standing with them in the straw and dung of the street, with fleas gathering in my khaki socks, everything seemed unimportant compared with the drawing of the goats. "If I get killed," I said to myself, "it'll happen while I'm doing my proper job as an artist." My head rang with explosions but nothing came dangerously near.

Finally the red drizzle of bomb dust drifted away, the noise of aircraft faded into the distance, the people started coming back. The first was a woman with a very thick body, her full breasts hanging down inside her crumpled dress as far as her apron where a frayed length of string was tied round the middle of her.

"Good afternoon," I said, smiling as she passed.

She looked at me, scowled and grunted. She had the face of a brute with thick protruding lips, wild eyes and coarse hair. She was an animal of a different species and, although she wore clothes, she looked as if she too might leave her droppings behind her in the road. I came to the conclusion that I liked goats best.

The lorry had been loaded all too quickly so reluctantly I climbed aboard. The All Clear sounded as we whirled through the streets of Hamrun and by the time we reached Birkikara our route was crowded with people. Sitting next to the airman driver with my round blue Air Force hat on the back of my head, I smiled to myself as I watched hundreds of people forced slowly back each side of us like the prow wave of a ship—happy people with their heads thrust forward gobbling at each other, just like my friends the goats. As I stepped down from the lorry here at Naxxar I decided that a crowd of people would be my next subject.

So here I am in my bedroom smiling down at Diana's photograph. Its been wonderful drawing once again, for, standing with the goats, all my troubles seemed to slide away; now, however, Naxxar Palace thrusts me back into the old dilemma. Fight and sleep, fight and sleep. We have, for example, no Administration of any kind and therefore there's no Adj. here to chat to. There's no Squadron Intelligence Officer who would normally be another friendly fellow to have about. The confusion of my thoughts mills round and round in my head. I need some friend to tell me I'm not going mad—someone even to tell me I'm doing my job well as a fighter pilot.

I can't help thinking how different it would have been in England tonight: the Squadron I.O. would have been excited with quiet efficiency. Take that first 109 for instance.

"Well, old boy, did you observe strikes?" he would have asked.

"Yes and no," I would have replied, "I saw something, maybe strikes, might have been sunlight glinting on him. It was all so quick, practically head on with no time at all after I started firing. He was so huge I don't see how I could have missed him."

"Well, is there anything else that would support your claim?"

"Yes. He went steeply under my left wing and disappeared. A few seconds afterwards someone called up on the R/T and said: 'Something's gone in near Filfla.' Whoever it was didn't claim it or he wouldn't have called out. Something went in and so far as I know I was the only Spitfire over Filfla at the time."

"Well, old boy," our I.O. would have said, "I'll hunt up your somebody who saw it and we'll see what we can do for you."

He'd probably have seen me later and said: "Got that 109 for you," or perhaps: "Bad luck, old boy, no go, we can't get confirmation." I don't think I would have minded so much about the lack of recognition for he would have tried.

But not here in Malta, oh no. We are Malta pilots. We have no Squadron Adj., no Squadron I.O., no special Doc., no Engineering Officer and none of the other closely associated types who help to make the wheels go round and who contribute much more than I ever believed possible to the spirit of normal Air Force life. We are alone.

But I must stop this—I must snap myself out of this despondency. Even if I am tired out, riddled by the Dog and shaken by this morning's trip, we are all in a bad way and this battle has got to be endured. It has got to be endured. I will take the very strength of my own solitude and, until I am killed, I will paint and I will draw. I will draw, draw, draw. But please God let one other thing happen soon—let there be a letter from my wife. I can be oblivious of the battle while I'm drawing, but I cannot forget my wife.

I have been drawing desperately while the battle has continued and changed its shape. Last Friday night after drawing the goats there were unusual engines in the night sky, and not only enemy planes: ten Wellingtons arrived from Egypt: the first batch of our new bomber force, for Hugh Pugh considers that our Spitfires have reached daylight supremacy. As they landed on the flare-path during the bombing that was going on, two of them crashed into newly formed craters. I don't think Hugh Pugh would approve of my enthusiasm for the wreckage of his two valuable planes, but the reawakened artist in me was delighted when I arrived here at Luqa for readiness yesterday morning. For a long time

I was on readiness, leading the Spitfires, but at three o'clock in the afternoon, when the C.O. took over from me, I sped across the aerodrome with my sketch book: I was only just in time for two men had started to dismantle the tail plane of the first bomber.

The fuselage of the wreck with its tall rudder lay among the flat surface of the aerodrome, but from the centre of its body, where the fabric-covered geodetic construction had ruptured, the front half of the plane plunged steeply into the crater. The whole hundred-foot span of its wings clasped the rocks in a gesture of pathetic helplessness, the steel propellers were curled up like springs, the wireless aerial, which had twanged apart, hung down like a single strand of curly hair, and where the front gun-turret had broken off, a black mouth gaped at me. I felt the sorrow of our wind-whispered bomber lying so still and helpless under the glaring sun.

It seems to me that the more closely wrecked planes resemble slugs and insects and other humble animate creatures, the more dearly do I feel for them. It was like that with the second bomber which I drew later, just before dusk. As I was drawing I heard the sound of heavy engines, although no warning had been given: the sky was suddenly filled with more strange aircraft. I was astonished. Formations of R.A.F. Bristol Blenheims, Beaufighters, and torpedo-carrying Beauforts flew in from the sea; they circled majestically above our aerodrome and, one after another, they rumbled in for their long landings. It was the second wave of our new bomber force, a fantastic sight, the first time I have seen our own bombers flying here in broad daylight. In an unreasonable way I resented their intrusion into our private battle with the Hun.

Perversity of human nature, for today I feel very motherly and protective about these bombers, dispersed into the fields and valleys round the aerodrome: I am on readiness, watching for the take-off signal, for surely the Germans will make another attempt to wipe them out.

I have been drawing and painting this morning. I have been painting one of the monuments to the last bomber force we had here—one of the wreck pits on the side of the haunted valley of Safi—a stupendous subject, although my painting was a failure—a deep pit cut into the golden rock and filled to overflowing with the blue-black wreckage of Wellingtons, Marylands, Swordfish, Hudsons and many other aircraft, all rustling together quietly like dried bones. I wonder how long our new bomber force will last? There was a raid while I was working—bombs on the other side of the aerodrome, although I timidly crouched behind a rock for it's usually Safi that gets it. I watched a 109 shot down about a mile away, but very much closer, just a few hundred yards along the perimeter track, an Italian Macchi 202 plunged into the ground at fantastic speed—a huge bubble of fire shot back into the sky. The pilot baled out. For a moment I thought we were going to capture him for his 'chute was creamy yellow against the blue sky for an instant before it burst. He was spattered all over the grass—we'll never know what that poor Italian thought about the war.

Since taking over readiness from the C.O. and awaiting my turn to fly, I have been drawing the airmen here. I have been talking to them and they're a magnificent lot. Some have faced the strain of being here three or four years, in some cases six or seven years abroad. Their reliefs are long overdue, but because of the siege they cannot be replaced. Most have faced every kind of disaster, yet they smile and they laugh. They make me feel ashamed. Eight out of the ten married men here on the dispersal point tell me that their homes are breaking up, most of them broken up already—their wives are carrying on with other men, mostly foreign troops stationed in England. To my offer of help they replied with sad resignation: "It's no good now, sir; it's no good any more." These airmen accept their smashed marriages as the inevitable refuse of separation and war. I envy their quality of endurance in this battle, but must a man lose everything so that no other disaster can befall him? Must we lose everything we love and everything that promises fair in life—I am twenty-two years old, I have spent a few short weeks with my young wife—is this, then, our future?

A car is speeding across the aerodrome towards us. As it draws up, Group-Captain Woodhall, our Senior Controller, ducks out of the door. Woody is visiting us! With a smile I leave my Spitfire to meet this small wiry middle-aged man wearing shorts that are much too big for him. His khaki shirt bears an impressive array of rank while below his wings two full rows of medals testify to his wide experience. The sunlight catches his bleached moustache and from under the gold-encrusted peak to his hat his merry eyes twinkle up into mine.

"Hullo sir."

"Hullo Denis," he replies.

As we shake hands he holds the whole of my extended forearm, squeezing it gently.

"Anxious to get up into the air?" he asks.

"Yes, sir," I reply, for Woody has an infectious enthusiasm for the battle, "but why are we held so much on the ground?"

Woody looks like a sparrow, holding his head on one side and staring down at the dusty ground as he listens to my question.

"At the moment," he replies, "the Hun is only putting his little toe into our sky and we don't need many of you boys to tweak it. When he puts his head in again we'll send you all up to punch his nose."

"Now will you get all the boys around," he asks restlessly.

As Cyril, Pancho, Baby Face and several of the new boys come running towards us, I feel that Woody's visit is more than just a friendly one; he has, I think, a very deliberate reason for visiting us today. I can

hear my heart thumping with apprehension as I wait for his news. What
the devil are they going to do to us now?

"Well, we've made a decision about you fellows," Woody begins.

What decision, I ask myself with anxiety, for a lot of changes seem to
be taking place.

"You all know," he continues smiling mischievously, "that the normal
overseas tour of duty is two or three years, and that's what you all
expected when you arrived here. The intensity of the Malta fighting is
now officially recognised: it's been decided to give you all a rest in three
months time. You're not going to be sent to the Middle East, you'll
be sent to England. You've all done a fine job and we'd give you a rest
right now if we could, but, of course, you realise that since we're besieged
here the manner of your replacement will depend on seats in the available
transit planes. We are however, going to start sending pilots home
straight away. Pilots who have been here six months already will be
leaving tonight or as soon as we can arrange seats. After that, three
months will be considered as a full Malta tour for fighter pilots."

"What about the ground crews, sir?"

"They'll be going on the next convoy."

I am astonished at Woody's news. My heart beats hard and strong with
joy. Joy for all the pilots here, especially the old hands who have flown
and sweated and suffered much longer than we have. Joy tinged with
sorrow for all those who will never return, sorrow for all those who will
never welcome them home; but predominantly joy at this sudden hope of
survival. I immediately think of Diana: how surprised she will be when
I walk in the front door. Three months, Woody said. I immediately
start working out how long I have been here already and how much
longer I will have to stay to do this wonderful thing. I've been here
five weeks. Only five weeks. It seems impossible, for they feel like a lifetime. I have only passed through one third of my duty period, I have
two whole months more; I've got to stay alive, but what chance have I
got? I'll never do it. I'll never see Diana again. Never, never again.

"Good news, isn't it, Denis?" I'm aware that Woody is looking up at me.

"Yes, sir, jolly good," I reply with an attempt at a smile as we walk
towards the car.

"You'll be pleased to get back to your wife?" he asks.

As I hold open the car door I realise that it would indeed be wonderful
—but there's no chance; I'm surprised however that Woody even knew
I had a wife.

Woody pauses and, fumbling in his pocket, looks up smiling.

"By the way, Denis, there's a letter come for you."

The letter is not from Diana. At Naxxar I cannot still the anxiety of
my heart. I don't know whether it's because I'm a bit shaken from bomb

blast that bowled me over in the sharp raid we had after Woody left, or whether it's what the airmen have been telling me of their smashed marriages, but I'm on fire with jealous anxiety for my wife. As the airmen described their homes to me I imagined their wives, perhaps tired, perhaps bored. I imagined men taking their wives out, and from what the airmen tell me, indeed from my own observation of adult life in war, a man taking out a married woman always leads to one thing in the end. Although I try to tell myself that I'm stupid to feel such anxiety, this letter I'm holding in my hand is from a man who has been taking Diana out, describing what they have been doing together. It was posted in England last week—where then are Diana's letters to me?

I suddenly respond to the chatter of the pilots in the bar: Woody's and Hugh Pugh's scheme for sending pilots home to England is indeed starting tonight. With mixed feelings I learn that two of our pilots are leaving in a few hours time.

One is Scotty. Seeking him out to congratulate him on this splendid news, I give him Diana's address and beg him to get in touch with her for me. Scotty, although he flew in with us from the U.S.S. *Wasp* is going home. After Max's death Scotty has no doubt been living in an agony of solitude; what inward tortures he has been enduring no one can tell—nevertheless there comes a time when a fighter pilot over-runs the period of his maximum efficiency and starts to disintegrate through sheer exhaustion. If he is pushed beyond this point he is usually shot down and killed. I am glad Scotty has survived for he had always been one of the most gallant members of our team.

The other man is a Flight Sergeant from "B" Flight. He is being sent home in disgrace for cowardice. Despite it being unfashionable to sympathise with cowardice I feel for him in a strange inner way: he must have suffered horribly because of his fear of flying, yet some day he must turn round to face it squarely or his life is ruined for ever. May God go with them both.

Laughter all around me. The C.O. gives me a great clout on the back. "Ha, ha," he says with a great laugh, "I've had another letter from home while poor old Denis here has had nothing!

"I have concrete evidence," he continues, sparring away from me as if he wanted to start a playful boxing match, and lowering his voice into a mock growl, "that the lovely Diana has been unfaithful!"

Anxious though I am, I can draw and paint. I have settled comfort-ably on a huge rock thrown up by a recent explosion; I have opened my beer bottle filled with water and unfolded my paint-box; I've started painting and I've discovered that I'm in a free brave mood with everything coming right in my picture: I'm drawing confidently and rhythmically in broad happy strokes. I am an artist, yes, I am an artist. Whatever madness and brutality the war throws in my face, I can paint. Despite the continuous sharp-edged pains of the accursed Malta Dog in my stomach, in fact, in spite of everything, I can live in ecstasy with the joy of rich and tender colour. I am painting with love and intense sorrow for the tragedy of these Valetta ruins. Painting as I have never painted before.

In shadow, just in front of me, rises a sweeping archway lined with prussian-blue tiles chipped white by bomb splinters; part of its curve has fallen away making the arch bleed the pebbled detail of brown ochre rubble. Through it I can see the remains of a palace: mountains of rectangular rocks piled in disorder into the sky, dazzling against the blue, pressing heavily on the honeycombs of collapsed cellars. To the right of the arch, beyond an open square, is an undamaged palace, beautifully proportioned with tall windows, weathered red in colour, a pale venetian red of incredible subtlety. Its end is facing me, while the length of it extends back into space down a long street. The street reveals ruin after ruin stretching away into the farthest distance.

A man is seated on the kerbstone a few yards away, leaning forward with his head bent over into his hands. He wears dark blue trousers, a pale waistcoat and he sits there, just in front of me, exactly where I would have placed him. Only he, of course, can experience the full, vivid pathos of his city's destruction, but I seem to feel his emotion transmitted across the blown dust between us.

One part of me feels with him, while a second part is obsessed with the technicalities of my trade. I am trying to keep this picture bold and simple in keeping with the scars of ruthlessness. I lift my paint brush, dropping in tender variations of colour on the dazzling ruins: I have to be careful in suggesting these colours to keep the area both light and brilliant.

A hand is placed on my shoulder.

"Where is your permission to paint?"

Looking up I find three Maltese policemen staring down at me. I hesitate in bewilderment.

"I've been given permission by the Group Captain in charge of my aerodrome."

"You have it with you?" asks the tall policeman.

"No, it was verbal permission."

"Then you'll have to come along with us."

"But surely," I ask, utterly unable to believe in what is happening, "can't I finish the picture first?"

The policeman stares with callous indifference at my work. "No."

"But I've got to finish it," I reply—I know full well that I may get shot down and killed before I have another chance—"I've got to finish it, I've got to . . ." I manage to blurt out, "or am I under arrest?"

"Not under arrest, but we've got to make immediate inquiries."
Trying to conceal my distress I try to think, for I know these men
have got to carry out their job.

"All right," I suggest, "here is my name and my aerodrome. If you
ring the Group Captain he will vouch for me. I won't go away, I'll
stay here working on the picture and I'll come straight round to the police-
station as soon as I've finished."

"That's no good." The tall policeman gestures towards a nearby
civilian at the front of the crowd that has gathered: "This gentleman has
reported your activities to us. You'll have to come at once."

I look at the civilian concerned, for he is staring at the ground and
rocking to and fro on his feet, suggestive of amusement. From under
lifted eyebrows his eyes look sharply up into mine: he IS laughing; the
man is actually laughing; laughing he turns on his heel, laughing he walks
away through the crowd. A wave of anger overwhelms me: I turn to
the policeman in protest, but . . .

"Are you coming or do we have to take you?"
Surging with anger and swallowed up in bitterness—for have I not gone
up into the sky and risked my life shooting down 88s so that bombs
would not fall on these homes?—I find it difficult to control myself,
difficult to bend down and fold up my paint box. In my own small
innocent way, can't I be left alone to paint my sympathy for a world
gone crazy? A great bell of madness clangs and clangs in my brain, clangs
and clangs. The great bell grows monstrous about me, heaving and heavy,
bearing me down. Tears blurring my eyes as I am led away—pink
blobs on either side of me, hostile inquisitive faces as the crowd parts
to let us through.

I am now back at Naxxar with my mind reeling: my sketch books have
been ripped to pieces so I fling my useless painting equipment on to my
bed. Of all my paintings I have only paper stubs left between the card-
board covers of my sketch-book. I have only a few pen sketches left in
my diary and two water-colours left in the drawer to show for all my
work on the island. I look at my wife's photograph for some kind of
consolation—please God let there be a letter from her. Tears still blur
my eyes. I've got to control myself. Got to pull myself together.

"Denis," the C.O. calls across to me, "there's a cable for you down at
Luqa; the Dreaded Hugh is bringing it with him when he comes off
readiness."

Hope, hope at last; with bombs falling upon us, we take our places
for the evening meal—the cable is undoubtedly from Diana, an answer to
all the cables I have sent in recent weeks begging for news; the minutes
drag; at last Hugh arrives, waving the orange envelope. I move forward
to claim it but the C.O. grabs it instead—he tosses it to Pancho—Pancho

to Cyril—Cyril to Johns; I'm being baited so I set on my chair with my hands folded. This then is the moment: I am holding it firmly; I am ripping open the top of the envelope. The words dance and blur— couldn't she even reply to me herself?—no love here, a cold message, brief and factual, signed abruptly with her father's surname: "What the devil are you worrying about man? Pull yourself together," is what they seem to say.

"It's not even from my wife," I blurt out as I rush from the room. Black despair flings me down on my bed. I listen to the friendly shriek of bombs: let them come, let the walls engulf me downwards for I can stand no more. In vain I hear the moan of departing bombers, the faint stutter of more distant guns. Silence. I watch my face in the mirror, pebble eyes staring back at me, a reversed face I have known all my life. This is the end. My service revolver is heavy. Its metal is cold as I load the bullet: such a small passport to oblivion. No hurry about it—through the mouth or through the temple?

CHAPTER 17

A NEW HOME

I AM at peace. In pyjamas, with a rug wrapped about me, I am sitting on the balcony outside my bedroom looking out over the moonlit garden and listening to the occasional 88s diving at Takali with screaming engines, to the deep-throated explosions, to the echoes fading amongst the hills, to the mysterious silence that re-envelopes the island. It is twenty-four hours since I lifted my service revolver; during today, Wednesday, May the 27th, the bombing has gone on, the pain of the Dog wrenching my stomach has gone on and I have fought with 109s in the sky. When orders came through for the Squadron to stand down for the night the C.O. arrived with an unusual invitation: merrymaking in the night clubs of Valetta. Having so often been accused of taking life too seriously, I decided to go.

The three of us, the C.O., Pancho and myself, looked out through the windows as we drove through moonlit Valetta: heaps of black rubble, shells of buildings shining with silvery-blue light against the sky, baroque façades of palaces, eerie and deserted. We found a sentry near the partly broken Palace of the Old Masters and he promised to look after the car. The first club was shut. We tried another. Its heavy door was solidly unyielding: the merrymakers were probably in the cellars for an enemy bomber throbbed its ummer-ummer-ummer above us in the night. We walked towards the Mayfair Hotel hoping it would be open for a few preliminary drinks—there was a swish-rush of air—we crouched down beside some wreckage—a brilliant flash—the bombs crashed, with prolonged avalanche, in the next street. Finally we entered a small club-room of canned jazz.

Instead of blue moonlit gentleness, lamps and orange candleflames danced their fumes to the blackened ceiling; here were smells of burnt paraffin, cheap wine, plump legs and sweat. I immediately started a drawing of a woman seated among the tapering bottles that gleamed with highlights on the bar counter: her dress was the colour of red wine, her skirts were lifted high on her lap, making an oval frame from which the whole length of her stockinged legs swayed out into the room. As I started my drawing she was leaning back on her straight slender arms, tossing her head with laughter, but I had to change it, because a tall

Flight Lieutenant, wandering across, stood beside her; her old face stared into his young one, while he, looking down, patted her knees.

"If you want a good subject," chuckled a civilian leaning forward from the next table, "wait until she dances: she doesn't wear anything under that dress."

Soon after, in a flurry of red skirts, the woman bore down upon us, settling on the C.O.'s lap like a broody hen. He had hardly overcome his astonishment before she was off again, linking arms with a delighted Wing Commander who had just come in. We learned that she was a scalp hunter, boasting to have slept with three Flight Lieutenants, four Squadron Leaders, two Wing Commanders and a Group Captain during the last week.

When the poor light from the fluttering candles had made my eyes ache, when I had exhausted myself by drawing, when I felt like a limp rag on the rest of the party, I came home. I enjoyed the solitude of the drive along the moonlit roads with the lazy murmuring of the enemy bombers patrolling overhead, and now I am here, alone on the balcony. There is a delicious smell of the earth replenishing itself in the garden below. I, too, am trying to replenish myself, trying to understand the facts of my own nature, how it can be related to Malta and to war.

Last night utter despair made my finger curl round the trigger, but even as I stared into my revolver's muzzle wondering about the best way to do it, I realised that other imaginative pictures existed in my mind: lowering my revolver I started to think:

I was imagining how the shot would sound from a distance, how the C.O. and all the pilots would come running in to find my lifeless body with my brains blown out. "That will make them realise how much I have suffered" some childish part of my nature was telling me. Whatever events of hate, killing, strain, illness, separation and hopeless loneliness had led to my despair, I suddenly knew I was acutely sorry for my miserable self; that I was craving some understanding of some kind from somebody; that if I could not have it in life then I would have it directed towards me in death. With stark clarity I understood that despair is essentially selfish. The fact that a thoughtless whirlpool of selfish emotion had brought me to the brink of suicide overwhelmed me with horror. I suddenly realised that the inner essence, going on after death, would have been held accountable for throwing my life away; that I would have appeared before the inner judge of all things as a small boy who had broken a very precious gift, broken it in a fit of temper, a fit of the sulks, smashed it because he was not living in the kind of world he wanted to live in.

I have resented the world for the last five or six weeks and, because of my resentment, I have been banged about by it. I suppose everyone, sooner or later, has quite deliberately to relate himself to his environment.

I can either pit myself against this world at war—but such action has led to despair—or I can conform to its character—but I reject this also, for by hating, by doing things I do not believe in, I would be giving up ideals that I know to be good. What then is the answer? Is there a third course open to man in this predicament?

Sitting here I feel that I should not expect so much from the world. Obviously a belief in God, a belief in peace and love by which to try and lead one's life are not enough—for sanity one must understand the world too. How simple the answer seems—just not to expect so much of the world. And I have been terribly selfish. How strangely wonderful it is to learn the bitter truth about one's tent of selfishness, to be humiliated by one's weaknesses, and yet to feel that each one of us is sought out by a power, a purity, and an overwhelmingly great love that is far beyond our highest conceptions; to know that finally, when all human weaknesses are purged away, spiritual union with God is the ultimate destiny of all men.

A week ago an English lady from Sliema, who is expecting a child and who has been trying to get away from the island, at last took her seat in a transport plane during the night bombing at Luqa. Her flight to Egypt had considerable significance for us, for she had told the C.O. that once she was safely in Egypt we could take over her house as a new mess. A fuel pipe in one of the engines of her plane must have been fractured by a bomb splinter, for the plane hadn't flown more than thirty miles out to sea before it caught fire—a rosy torch in the darkness—but it managed to stagger back and land safely. A few nights ago the C.O. arranged another seat for her second attempt. She has arrived safely. We have moved from Naxxar and I am alone in the sitting-room of her house; the other pilots are out on the flat roof watching the enemy planes—from the roar of engines there seem to be several waves of bombers. What a din! I can imagine what her life has been like, for an anti-aircraft gun, sited only a few hundred yards away, is adding its periodical explosions to the crash of falling bombs, the walls shake and my eyes seem to dance in my head. Settling back into the comfortable depths of her armchair, it is with warm happiness that I look around the room—this is luxury. The walls are a soft egg-shell blue, a gentle light filters through the window opposite, the carpet which practically fills the stone floor is rose madder in colour, spattered at the moment with lumps of white plaster that are shaking off the ceiling. I hope the other armchairs, the settee against the left hand wall, and the triangular divan that fills the far left hand corner are not going to get engrimed with dirt like the Naxxar furniture—it is unlikely the Maltese women servants who worked for the Sliema lady are continuing to work for us.

It is the feminine touch that makes this house so pleasant to live in: there are flowers arranged in a glazed earthenware pot on the walnut writing-desk to the right of the window, while the fireplace on the right-hand wall, lavishly equipped with a polished brass fender, is crowded with lavender-coloured blooms picked from the sunken walled garden.

I have my diary on my knee and I stare down at the brief entry I have just made for this morning, Thursday, June the 4th: "At dawn searched for the crew of a lost Wellington bomber; banks of mist over the cliffs; the sun rose from the sea—all the moving water shone into green; we searched for an hour and a half: no trace of them."

There's a similar entry for yesterday, Wednesday, June the 3rd: "Squadron searched for Spitfire survivors. Twelve Spitfires, flying to us from the aircraft carrier *Eagle*, were intercepted by 109s from Pantallaria: four shot down: the only trace of our lost pilots—an empty yellow dinghy on the waves—heavy price for eight Spitfires that did reach us. Vital reinforcements—rumours that our long-promised convoy is about to sail."

Earlier diary entries for Tuesday and Monday last show how our battle progresses. The usual successes and occasional losses—it's always the new boys that go—two of them recently: one through inexperience, but the other, who held great promise as a fighter pilot, was stupid—he wanted to be the great individualist—he would break away from the formation to go hunting alone—although warned—that was the end of him.

I look up from my armchair for the air raid seems to be over—the pilots are coming in again. In the centre of the rose-madder carpet stand the Dreaded Hugh and the handsome Sergeant Johns, his hair meticulously brushed. Both are about to go out to dinner with the daughter of a senior army officer that they've recently met. Johns is claiming that he can get any woman he wishes for, but I can't help smiling at him.

"How do you do it, Bill—line up Brigadier's daughters and things?"

"Well," says Johns, "during last night's moonlight bathe with the girl I just fell on my feet." "Yes," he continues, relishing the memory, "her body's all right—but she's not got much of a face."

"What would you do if you met someone prettier?"

"Just leave the Brig's daughter to old Hugh here. Well, cheerio chaps, we're off, we'll bring you back a hair of the old dog!"

I listen to the clip-clop of a horse and the garry bells passing beneath the window and I look across at the walnut desk with flowers on it. Cyril's sitting in the far corner of the room, oblivious of the banter. It's all very harmless, this banter—how stupid I've been to worry about it. I suppose the ancient Greek cities with their magnificent architecture, with their marble columns and caryiatids white in the sunlight, were filled with people laughing and cursing and joking. I've been stupid to have imagined otherwise.

There is a classical feeling about Sliema, indeed my diary entry for last Saturday, May the 30th, records my first impression as we arrived here: "Our new mess is on a high promontory; waves surging against the rocks; looks like Greece." And for that same evening I wrote: "Baron Scicluna invited us all to a cocktail party; his Dragonoya Palace is built out into the sea on a neighbouring headland."

At the Baron's party, between the heads of his many guests, I noticed a girl in a white dress; I watched her proud little head that hardly moved as she talked; I watched her slim figure with her young breasts beneath the white material and her beautifully moulded arms and hands—she looked Greek. I got out my sketch book and, edging a little closer, started to draw. I suppose I'm a romantic idealist, a crazy dreamer, expecting her to be some kind of goddess—it was stupid of me but, so overwhelmed was I by sadness at her trite conversation that I left the party and walked back alone by the sea.

It was just the same after I had left, for as I walked I met an English civilian with his wife and their young daughter aged six or seven. I talked with him for several minutes. The child had a streaming cold with mucus running all over her upper lip, the wife flirted in glances with soldiers passing to and fro along the road, while the man cursed the island, cursed the war and cursed the Germans. Beyond the man's head, on the opposite shores of the narrow bay, the walls of this new home of ours, and of other flat-roofed houses high above the rocky boulders, were exquisite shades of grey-gold, dark against the cool evening sky—gold that reflected steeply down into the lapping blue water. Continuing my walk I seemed to be possessed by the spirit of beauty that hovered about the bay. I started thinking of the ancient animistic religions in Greece and how people once worshipped the spirits that lurked in a grove of oak trees or dwelt invisibly in parched valleys of rocks. I thought of the girl in white and I longed to meet someone who also felt the charm of the evening.

Sliema is a beautiful place, but last Friday evening, our last evening at Naxxar, was a noble farewell to the old life. I was writing to Diana, a hot-tempered letter demanding news, but I was so ashamed that I tore it up. How difficult it is to live up to one's ideals in everyday life. Suddenly I was aware of the sky. Leaving my writing things in the palace I wandered out on to the familiar hillside.

The sun, sinking in splendour behind the church, turned the square buildings and all the roof-top balustrades into a dark silhouette against golden cloud. Looking eastwards I watched the shadows creep over the island landscape; over the terraced fields that led downwards layer by layer into the wide central valley; I watched white cities brilliant in the distance engulfed by shadow and lost against the purple hills. As the island darkened some horizontal bands of cloud, still lit by the sun, were laid across the sky, a pink carpet for the pale moon: Then they were deserted by the light becoming dark ribbons. A cold wind began to blow. The bright bowl of light that lingered in the west was perceptibly fading, but in the darkness luminous colours began to shine. In the first field below me the cut vegetation was a rich brown, the pale walls were a soft yellow grey, the goats that clambered through the openings of crumbled stone were vivid with browns and reds. The stunted trees, normally so dry and arid by daylight, were a deep olive green. From among the trees a procession of people emerged: probably labouring people returning from their work in the fields, although some of them may have been strolling over from a neighbouring town for the sheer joy of walking in the evening air. As they approached and filed past me, their predominantly dusty clothes were full of colour, soft blues, madder pinks, saffrons, all of overwhelming subtlety against their dark-tanned faces and arms. They came silently, most of them treading the path with bare feet. First came a woman with a bundle on her head, walking erect, then two people together, a middle-aged man in the palest of blue trousers with a brown-black waistcoat and cap, accompanied by a woman wrapped in a heavy black cloak and muttering her prayers. There were some long gaps in the erratic procession. From time to time a few young couples wandered past more slowly; the men were handsome and their smartly dressed girl companions were beautiful to look at. There were occasional children and all the while the sky darkened and the moon grew more brightly silver. One of the children approached me:

"Johnny, give me a penny."

"Go away."

I did not mean to be unkind but I wanted to watch without having hands tugging at my sleeves. All too soon I stood on the hillside alone. The moon, faintly encircled by a halo of rusty light, was mounting steadily higher, the proud equal of the fading light in the west; the sky was much darker, no longer a royal blue but a quiet grey, while the moving clouds, which had hitherto been black, now started to shine with silver. Anxious lest all the previous miracles of colour had faded, I looked down at the dark ground but a new kind of miracle was taking place; the walls and fields were luminous with moonlit colours. The moon had become the undisputed queen of the night—the halo which encircled her silver coin had increased to a brilliant shining bronze.

I had started walking slowly past a cornfield of waving phosphorous yellow, towards the summit of the hill when a figure, emerging from the shadows, approached along the path. He was perhaps a peasant returning from his work much later than the others; quite alone, we drew nearer one another. We must both have been aware of the wonder of this particular evening, for, as we closed and faced each other, bereft of communication by the barrier of language, we each lifted our right arms and placed our hands firmly on each other's shoulders. We stood like that for a minute of silence, perhaps longer, an eternal moment before continuing our separate ways. As I walked on tears were brimming into my eyes.

Later, as I was returning, the sirens started to wail their opposing melodies of frightfulness. The moon was shining down through a layer of haze so that the light, that cast black shadows under the walls, was pale red, like diluted blood as it fell upon the fields. With the enemy bombers throbbing overhead I noticed that against the dark olive trees there was a girl in a white dress: she was walking slowly this side of the darkest shadows with the moonlight shining full upon her young figure. I felt a peculiar need of someone feminine to share all the beauty with. Not having heard from Diana I stared across the field at the strange young girl, but, remembering Diana, I walked on alone listening to the crash of the bombs and to the orchestra of crickets in the surrounding grass.

Friday, June the 5th. I think I've adjusted myself to life here; I'm still assaulted by terror when I have to fly and fight, I still long for Diana's letters to start arriving, but I have settled down. I bless the Sliema lady for letting us have her beautiful house. I couldn't believe that a simple carpet on the floor could mean so much. Last night another seal was set on my new life for it was my turn to have a hot bath—the first chance since leaving the aircraft carrier last April! I was apprehensive that the bombs which were falling might knock the wall down to leave me suspended and exposé in mid-air, but I sang for joy as I scrubbed and splashed in a foam of soap. Afterwards I settled in a deck chair on the flat roof at the back of the house; I watched a tender veil of grey being drawn over the sky, while lazy-looking clouds coming in from the north grew larger into great blocks of cumulus, taller and taller until their tips merged with the veil above them.

This morning, before dawn, we climbed into the bus to be taken to the aerodrome. It was inky dark and the airmen driver, with his usual recklessness accelerated down the hill towards Valetta: at the bend at the bottom the bus skidding violently, plunged into a tree; none of us were really hurt. Scrambling to my feet I looked out: for a brief moment in the blackness the hilltop was silhouetted against the pale flank of a huge cloud, a moonlit cloud passing slowly behind the houses— a reflection gleamed in the road—it had been raining for the first time since April!

The driver scratched his head, restarted the engine and let in the clutch with care. Looking back as we topped the hill on the outskirts of Valetta I saw a jagged stream of lightning slither silently down the sky, disappearing behind another monstrous cloud that was following us. The bus plunged on in the darkness. Moving to the front seat, with the warm, damp, earth-smelling air blustering merrily into my face, I watched the blurred road slide under the bonnet. I stared intently, searching for any especially dark patches that might mean new bomb holes or that the earth and rubble fillings had been washed out of the old ones by the rain. We swerved past some of these holes, dropped into others, lurched through narrow funnels between stacks of wreckage and finally with a clatter of pistons climbed the last hill and stopped on the plateau of the aerodrome.

Then the deluge began. "G" shelter which had been a ghostly black shape barely twenty yards away was obliterated by the rain. Rain plummetted into the ground turning the mud into torrents. Spray drifted through the windows, filling the air; in an effort to keep our parachutes dry we took them off the seats, stacked them in the gangway, then sat on then. The downpour continued so I waded to "G" shelter, climbed down the waterfall steps to the lighted cavern to report that conditions were quite hopeless for flying. With permission we splashed our way over to the mess, but we had to laugh—the carpet was soggy and the newspapers had been turned to pulp—the walls of the Mess had been eased outwards by repeated bomb blast, the roof no longer fitted—water was cascading in.

Later, after breakfast, the storm having subsided, I was standing beside my Spitfire watching the fantastic panoramas of daylight cloud when an astonishing thing happened: Woody, calling me on the field telephone in a new tent that has been erected at our dispersal point, said that as no enemy aircraft were stirring from Sicily I could take up three new-boy pilots for a practise flight! A practise flight—I had never heard of such a thing! We were soon in the air, sweeping amongst avenues of vapour, diving through tunnels that closed over our heads, glimpsing down at the yellow hills laid out between rolling white cloud tops, and through other gaps at the grey sea. I did normal turns and steeper turns, diving and climbing turns, abrupt changes of direction, but the new boys had no idea of the standard of flying required. Even restricting myself to gentle manœuvres it seemed quite beyond their power to stay in position. I had been cursing my number two who was persistently six hundred yards behind me, when Woody called:

"Hullo Denis—got some trade for you: eight 109s four miles south-east of Kalafrana, coming north.'

We were at ten thousand feet over the harbour, above a faint layer of cloud that looked as if someone had breathed out deeply in front of my windscreen, the breath having smeared horizontally between two towering storm pinnacles. But I could not manœuvre, I had to fly slowly to persuade my flock to join formation, I knew that the enemy fighters would not do gentle circles if we were surprised.

"Little jobs approaching you now."

"Keep up Yellow Four," I called desperately as I watched the corner of a steep edifice of creamy vapour swinging nearer and nearer towards us. The 109s might be behind it, we might surprise them, they might surprise us.

"109s diving out to sea, on the deck, victor zero three zero," said Woody's voice.

Anti-climax: but it suddenly struck me that perhaps the German formation were new boys too; we dived in pursuit, plunging in and out of cloud, through shafts of sunlight and volumes of cool shadow until we reached the wave tops half-way to Sicily. No sign of the enemy but we were confronted by a magnificent raging storm that lifted its peak to tens of thousands of feet above us. It laid a curtain of rain low into the water beyond our wing-tips. A superb storm! We were patrolling on the flank of this monster, which seemed to be scornful of our puny aeroplanes, when I realised with alarm that it was swallowing our island. I sent the three new boys into land then swept in quickly on to the runway behind them. We were hardly out of our cockpits and into shelter when great black clouds rolling overhead darkened the sky. As the rain roared on to the tarpaulin I watched the retreating gleam of light beyond the far side of the aerodrome: it was quickly snuffed out by the wall of falling water. I watched a lake spread round the wheels of my Spitfire, and three airmen, who had been sheltering under the Spitfire's wings, race towards us for cover: they came in panting with heavy blocks of red mud clinging to their boots. The smell of the earth and the reviving life was wonderful. The tarpaulin above us sagged ominously, full blown with water. The air grew darker still. Above the roar of the rain the siren started to wail: a muffled screaming and moaning. A sheet of lightning lit the sky, disappearing in a glaring white bolt behind the silhouetted look-out tower, at the same instant a crash of thunder split our heads as loud as any bomb; split and left our heads ringing.

As the thunder and masses of cloud rolled away towards the south the storm abated to a moody downpour. Within a few minutes the sky above us was revealed, washed clean, a dazzling white prelude to oncoming blue. The rain spattered erratically then stopped. The airmen, stepping out into the sunlight, with dark patches of dampness drying slowly on their khaki uniforms, cursed the rain and cursed the mud. I pointed out how the sky had been cleansed, how the drab dust had been washed from the ruins of Luqa village making them glitter, how the earth in the surrounding fields was a matt crimson, and the broken wheat a pearl yellow against lucid grey walls. The airmen went happily back to work, carrying silver cans to refuel the Spitfires: they told me they'd never noticed colour before.

It's happened, it's happened! Saturday, June the 6th, a date I'll remember. It happened just a few minutes ago! My section's at fifteen minutes availability—it was by sheer chance that I wandered down to the mess! Not only a cable from Diana but a whole batch of letters as well! I can't describe the happiness that overwhelms me—I seem to be bursting with strength. The golden aerodrome's flooded with glory, the delayed-action bombs that are going off are sending their perpendicular black clouds, bubbling with gaiety, high into the blue. There goes one near the look-out tower—a perfect smoke ring!

I am sitting on a rock fifty yards short of the Spitfires and I've read each of the letters through several times already. I have checked the postmarks and find that Diana has written regularly ever since the night I left England. I can't understand why I haven't received these letters before—perhaps some Army or R.A.F. clerk has been letting them accumulate in his office—criminal thoughtlessness—but I forgive him—no bitterness now that I'm swallowed up in joy. . . .

I have written, not only to Diana today, but pages and pages to almost everyone I know—strange letters probably for I was banged about by pressure waves from the exploding bombs: my head ached with noise; after each unheralded crash it took about thirty seconds for my pounding heart to resettle. At lunch time I was airborne despite a bit of trouble with my wing-tip, but, by tea I had completed six letters of fantastic length—all posted now—going off by tonight's mail plane. I've been dancing: not crazy leaps along the empty beach—too much barbed wire—but with sobriety and restraint in this valley here. There's a concrete dance floor, an orchestra, lots of other people and apparently dancing goes on every Saturday night—I never knew this place existed till this evening when I came out exploring.

When I arrived here the sun was already low. I came and sat down at this table: shaded by the gnarled old tree behind me, I have watched the couples, waltzing, mostly civilians but with a few young soldiers in battle-dress. I noticed an army Captain sitting nearby, looking so miserable that I invited him over for a drink. I longed to give him some of my joy but I knew I mustn't speak about myself. I tried to get him to talk: he made a few remarks, highly uncomplimentary, about the local beer and the local women, then we sat in uncomfortable silence. When the air-raid warnings screamed about half an hour ago he left at once. In sad relief at his departure, I leaned back in this chair and watched formations of enemy fighters crossing the turquoise sky—then I grew bored.

Dancing was the only answer and this is what I've been doing. The English girls looked such a sulky lot with their pouting lips that I've chosen a Maltese girl. After waltzing merrily, we've settled back at my table. Of course, I'm drawing her. Bianca is a splendid model keeping wonderfully still, and she's smiling back at me with her great brown eyes. She's about eighteen with dark sun-bleached hair piled high on her forehead.

She's probably wondering what my life is like for I'm the first pilot she's met—I'm certainly wondering about her: her smile, so mischievous and gay, is unusually strange, defying all my efforts to capture it in a pen drawing. I think I know what it is—those great brown eyes are watching me from under eyelids that have paid the price of our Malta battle; she's young but her eyelids are heavily wrinkled and burdened with strain. My fountain pen with its hard lines is wretchedly inadequate—I need oil paints to modulate this drawing by more tender colouring—I could show both her youth and her premature age in the same portrait. I've made an awful mess of this picture, but it's not the pen's fault—I'm not skilled enough.

I want desperately to be able to continue my life as an artist. Everything is so beautiful here that I'm tempted to cry out: the sun has dropped behind the flat-roofed houses and such a tenderly coloured shadow has engulfed this na.row valley with its orchestra and moving dancers. Renoir pales beside this reality. I want to paint. I would be utterly content to live in the humblest home in Malta, in squalor and filth if necessary, if only I had a real chance to paint, to paint all the time and all my life.

In gathering darkness we are walking back up the hill for Bianca lives just beyond the mess. The dusk bombing has started. As the guns roar out their salvos the black shapes of the houses either side of us flicker on and off into dazzling yellow cubes.

Much later now, in my bedroom, in fact the results of today's fighting have already come through: twenty enemy planes have been destroyed or damaged during daylight, while during the dusk raid three of the twenty-one bombers that came over were shot down into the sea; the troubles of the others were by no means over because the "Y" Service intercepted a despairing enemy broadcast from Catania in Sicily: "No more bombers are to land here to-night—four have crashed on the aerodrome already." A wonderful day and once again I am reading through Diana's letters. Her last one was only written a few days ago. I share her astonishment that government ministers are making "Party" broadcasts over the B.B.C.—England must be as stirred up as everyone here by the latest war news.

The news that a *thousand* R.A.F. night bombers have twice flown out to bomb Germany has triggered off the most violent optimism. Although I cannot but think of the terrible suffering that has now started to be unleashed on the women and children of Germany, the news is indeed like a pair of field glasses lifted suddenly to our eyes: the end of the war, which has been too remote to think about, let alone talk about, has jumped into vivid focus ahead of us. Everyone is filled with a sense of responsibility for what will happen after final victory. In the last three days I, too, have heard views about post-war socialist and conservative governments, about the need for equality of opportunity, about education as the key to the future, in fact in the tent yesterday Pancho got so carried away that he gave us a thirty minute impromptu lecture about education in the Argentine. People talk about morals and religion and of the need for a new leader in spiritual matters, a leader with both enlightenment and authority, but perhaps the most speculative subject concerns what must be done with Germany after the war. Some pilots have suggested exterminating the Germans so that their militarism can never rise again, others believe that splitting Germany up into small states will solve the problem, while one of the Wing Commander Controllers, lying on his tummy beside Pancho, stated that the Allies should occupy Germany for three generations until a rising youth, untainted by the Nazi evil, can emerge in a fit state to govern themselves.

I have stood on edge of such discussions, listening. I am astonished that men who have been undivided for seven terrible weeks in the thick of the battle here, can argue with so much heat. With all the present discussion both here in the mess and down at Luqa it's strange to remember that seven weeks ago, when we first came to Malta, the war was continuous withdrawal, continuous defeat; we were thinking in terms of a black tunnel of war, an endless tunnel without light of any kind. We were fighting for our very existence. Having at last related myself to such a battle the whole complexion of the war has suddenly changed. All over the world the enemy advance has been stemmed. In the Far East the Japanese flood tide has withdrawn from Ceylon and seems to be contained in Burma and the Pacific. In Russia both sides appear exhausted by their terrible struggles, while even closer to us, just a few hundred miles away from here, in the battle that is waging at Knightsbridge in Lybia we seem at last to be matching Rommel's strength by our own strength. The change and the new optimism has been so sudden—hopes and thoughts of returning to my wife to live for the first time as an artist have made such a golden impact on my mind that I feel poised between two worlds. Hope for the future is unreal, yet gloriously real. This is undoubtedly the turning point of the war. There is one black fact: peace is not yet here—we must go on fighting. This siege of Malta is a relic of the first phase of the war, a phase of enemy advance, of pockets of Allied resistance being left isolated and alone far behind the front line— so were our other contemporary sieges of Corregidor and Sevastopol. We have been exchanging wireless messages with Sevastopol and its fall is imminent; Corregidor has alas fallen; Malta will most certainly fall if we do not succeed with our convoy.

CHAPTER 18

CONVOY

SATURDAY, June the 13th, exactly a week since I received Diana's letters and danced at the café. Although the C.O. and the rest of the pilots are themselves dancing at the Sliema Club, I am alone in the mess, for I need all my strength, unblunted by alcohol, to pull me through the ordeal of the next few days. Leaning back in my armchair and looking to the right of the window I notice that the Maltese women have arranged new flowers in the earthenware pot: like new blooms on a grave. The war goes on; now the convoy battle is upon us. The moment draws closer. In the darkness that has settled quietly over our Mediterranean world, our Reconnaissance planes and Wellington bombers, patrolling close to the Italian Naval bases, wait for any sign of movement from the enemy fleet: that fleet must get up steam and sail shortly to achieve an effective interception with our slowly approaching merchantmen. Enemy fighters and bombers must also be prepared, for, in the last forty-eight hours, not a single daylight air raid has disturbed the silence here. I don't want to die; I long to return to my wife; I am no doubt boring my unmarried companions by my continuous talk about her; the C.O. tells me I am "too much married" as if it were some kind of vice; I want so desperately to see her again yet I feel caught up in some inexorable pattern that must be seen through to the end. I remember Bob during the Sweeps last year. I remembering him standing apart from his companions in the dispersal hut, explaining his jinx, how things had gone wrong on his last three flights; I remember his determination to face it and how he died in flames over Le Touquet. Although I do not believe in jinx as a third and evil force between God and individual men, I am aware of pattern, and things have gone wrong in each of my last three flights.

Last Saturday, just after receiving Diana's letters, there was a raid coming in. Not only had I a long way to taxi, but I had to taxi fast to reach the runway and take off before the coolant temperature of my engine went beyond the danger mark. Taxi-ing fast was not easy, with my wing-tips perilously close to a cliff face on one side of the narrow track, and a stone wall on the other—the long nose blocking my vision did not help—but I was thoroughly enjoying the skill required. I knew, of course, that Maltese labourers are removed from the aerodrome when there's a raid, but I did not expect their bus driver to take a short cut. Suddenly the bus came round the corner at me—I risked tipping the Spitfire on to its nose by applying fierce brake—but the bus, without making any attempt to stop, swerved towards the gap between my wing and the wall: there wasn't room: the driver's cab struck my wing tip with a crash of metal: the nose of my aircraft, with its turning propeller, swung towards the passengers crowding the bus windows—an anxious moment —but managing to stop the propeller I enjoyed the inevitable impact. The cannon protruding forward from my starboard wing ended up inside the passenger's compartment: the expressions on the quickly withdrawn faces were magnificent. The Maltese streaming out of the bus, ran off down the road—with the driver running after them. Time was short, the raid was approaching; Chiefy was quite right in not wanting me to fly the damaged plane: the crumpled wing tip did have an adverse effect on the controls as I climbed steeply into the sky.

After the action I gave no more thought to this particular incident but on Monday last, when I flew again, the pattern began to close in upon me.

On Sunday night Luqa was heavily bombed; although delayed-action bombs were exploding on Monday morning, I was soon airborne leading Baby Face and two new boys.

"Hullo Denis," Woody called. "Little jobs, angels twenty-five, ten miles north of Grand Harbour, coming south."

Both new boys, making their first trip, were flying erratically, my number two's formation flying was quite hopeless.

"Hullo Denis. Little jobs over Luqa; angels twenty-seven; we'll fire some marker shots."

Through the windscreen, beyond the elongated flat nose flanked by exhaust stubs, I saw the white marker puffs appear in succession across the blue. Turning the formation, clambering upwards towards the sun, my attention was divided between eight 109s high up on my left and the new boy who had bungled the turn.

"109s coming down, look out . . ." somebody called—a black Messerschmitt flashed past from a different direction. As I swerved towards him I noticed two more 109s immediately above us; after checking the new boy I was preparing to give chase but glanced into the sun first: there were six more 109s in the act of turning down upon us—it was, of course, a trap and we were almost embroiled in it. At that precise moment the new boy panicked: he dived steeply downwards in lonely silhouette. It was just what the Huns wanted. By leading my remaining two Spitfires swiftly to cover him, we were wide open—the Huns seized the opportunity. We were lucky—in the brawl that followed we managed to destroy one of the enemy without loss.

When it was all over I stared down at the familiar pattern of runway,

"G" shelter and perimeter track rotating slowly below me—I realised I would have to give the new boy a pretty stiff talking to after I had landed, but the peace of gliding downwards was so gracefully delicious that I relaxed—the aerodrome sailed up to meet me. Just above the ground I levelled off, making a beautiful three-point touch down—BANG— hard left rudder wouldn't hold it—the Spitfire, out of control, swung violently off the runway, over the rough grass, circling towards some open bomb craters. Missing the craters it came to rest in a cloud of dust, left wing high in the air: shrapnel had exploded the starboard tyre. Climbing out I discovered red flags: my aircraft and I were squatting on a scattered nest of delayed-action bombs! Chiefy and his airmen realised the danger for they came hurrying out: holding a replacement wheel at the ready, we had just lifted the right wing when—thunderclap in our ears—we fell flat, aeroplane on top of us—I have never seen men work so fast to replace a wheel as they did then—it wasn't until we had pushed the Spitfire back to its pen that we discovered that the freak blast from one of the bombs had killed a soldier and someone wearing a blue hat in the opposite direction.

With my attempt at a third flight last Wednesday, the pattern of freak accidents closed more tightly. I was lying in the hot sun, studying from my history books the gay influence that Pharoah Akhnaton had had on Egyptian art, when Scramble: not us, the C.O.'s section of four Spitfires were first off—I glanced up to watch them. A few minutes later the air men were pointing up at a formation of Italian bombers, very high in the sky, silvery against the blue. They seemed to be heading straight over the top of us, but, running for the slit trenches, we estimated that the slight discrepancy of angle might make all the difference. The air rush of bombs ended in the first explosive crack—this giving me the direction, I peered over the sandbags—the first stick was bursting across the end of the runway streaming towards us in bubbling columns of black smoke, passing, however, to our left—another clump was erupting behind the look-out tower, huge black columns leaping up from the hills and valleys —Scramble—our turn!

At the end of the runway I opened up the throttle for take-off—half way down the runway, with the engine spluttering and banging, I knew I was not going to get the machine into the air—closing the throttle and swerving in and out of the rocks thrown up by the bombs, I turned my Spitfire back along the perimeter track. Agrily determined to get airborne, pumping the throttle to clear what I hoped might only be a choked carburettor, I arrived once again at the take-off point. The plane accelerated; despite bangs and crashes from the engine I pulled it up about twenty feet—with sudden alarm I knew we were not going to gain enough height to clear the hilltop. I cut the throttle, slammed down flaps and sideslipped back to the ground. As bomb-holes, stray rocks and the walls rushed to meet me, again I was lucky, for, with full brake, full rudder, swerving off the runway, I pulled up the plane in a cloud of dust beside the astonished Chiefy. Instantly he found an alternative Spitfire—with sweetly firing engine I opened up for yet another take-off attempt: BANG—a grinding of metal behind me—the tail wheel had fallen off—refusing to stop, risking damage to the elevators, which for all I knew were being wrenched to pieces along the ground, I slammed the stick hard forward to get the tail into the air—the din finally ceased as I swept over the low hills in pursuit of my three other machines.

We carried out our duty without much opposition; the rescue boat that we covered picked up Sergeant Innes, one of the C.O.'s section, who had been shot down into the sea. He'd had a miraculous escape: in combat with the Italian fighter escort a cannon shell had exploded under his seat—the seat had fallen forward, pinning him helplessly against the instrument panel—with full throttle the Spitfire had plunged vertically from twenty-five thousand feet—with the speed of its dive it had finally broken to pieces—Innes had been thrown out, his parachute torn open—for the remaining few feet he had been lowered quite gently into the sea.

After I had landed with a scraping and screeching of metal, poor Chiefy came and stared at me. Shaking his head sadly about my plane, he urged his men to get going with repairs. He had also found the trouble with my first Spitfire: the magneto points had been so widely opened that most of us suspected sabotage. My old friend Chiefy was doubtful. Perhaps sabotage was responsible for what happened today, Saturday, June the 13th: one of our Beaufighters was circling the aerodrome when, quite unaccountably, it plunged earthwards. In this sudden disaster, not only the pilot and observer were killed but many old friends—Chiefy and a crowd of his airmen had no chance to run clear—they were killed instantly.

Thus I sit here, stretched out in the arm-chair; the pattern still unfolds as we who are left await our turn to die. With my hands hanging loosely over the ends of the chair I listen to the ticking of my wrist-watch; the convoy battle draws closer. I feel that music would be wonderful to ease the foreboding that overwhelms me: none of us can go on surviving this kind of thing for ever. Leaning over to the wireless I switch it on.

I have found some music, hardly what I expected, but some European station is playing Verdi's "Requiem". The sound of it washes over me like great waves, my breathing slows and my awareness of my body diminishes; closing my eyes I can actually see the huge waves with foaming crests thundering towards me—the music seems transmuted into dream. I watch the greenness of the waves crashing about me, then rushing past. The water is rising above me. Violent movement is calmed for I am below the surface of the ocean watching the gently rocking greenness shafted by sunlight—an endless succession of waves overhead. The greenness becomes more quiet, darker and deeper; sinking downwards motion is stilled, colour solidifies to grey. A blacker and blacker grey grows rigid about me. It is rock. I am embedded in rock. I am firmly held; tenderly held; fossil-like I drift untroubled and timeless.

Sudden relief in the darkness: the ruggedly hewn space of a cavern has opened out. Without lights of any kind I thought its rectangular greyness was empty, but there is, stretched out on a tall slab that rises from the floor to dominate this tomb, a huge figure, powerfully massive in chest and limb, its strong head tipped back on the slab in death. Fastened in the rock I cannot move, but watching that immobile strength I feel, somewhere deep inside me, that it lives.

Suddenly a voice, ringing with command, echoing the cavern with power—and far below, buried in hidden catacombs, life stirs in release— men and women race upward in joy through the night of the rock to the surface of day, cell after close-packed cell are freed, streaming upwards in quickened ecstasy of living.

In a twinkling of an eye my turn must have come, for I was suddenly poised on a green hilltop watching the last of the hosts of people floating silently out over a wide valley.

Our flight seems to swing outwards from the world, and in fear, as the earth shrinks away in to the darkness, we are nearing the fountain-head of power and love. It is the procession of God in all his sublime majesty moving purposefully through creation; it is an assembly of beings without number, in a form that is neither spherical nor pyramidical nor in any dimension but glory; a rising and descending movement of praise and adoration. . . .

It is the evening of Sunday, June the 14th; not many minutes ago on our roof-top at Sliema, our A.O.C., Air Vice-Marshal Hugh Pugh Lloyd, briefing us about our part in the convoy battle, told us that two convoys, from east and west, are approaching our island simultaneously.

From the east, the convoy from Alexandria, code name "Alex", is under heavy air attack from Crete and Cyrenaica. It is far beyond the range of our fighter aircraft and its own defensive air umbrella has mis-carried: Rommel has broken through our desert army and our aero-dromes on the North African coast are being over-run. The convoy is being defended by the only ships we have to the east of here—just a few cruisers and destroyers—yet the Italian fleet of vast numerical superiority, including battleships, is steaming to intercept it.

From the west, the convoy from the United Kingdom, code name "U.K.", steaming towards us from Gibraltar, has already lost several merchant ships to enemy bombers from Sicily and Sardinia—lost them despite being protected by a battleship and other units of the British Fleet. Yet the battleship and heavy units must withdraw tonight—the Admiralty, because of losses in the Far East, dare not risk them any further. The convoy, lightly escorted by a cruiser and some destroyers, is to slip through the narrow channel, between the coast of Tunis and the western tip of Sicily, during darkness within a few hours time—our twin-engined night-fighter planes will be out there to help them. But the worst attacks are expected to develop at daylight tomorrow. The convoy with its diminished escort will have ten hours steaming under the noses of the enemy bomber force of four or five hundred planes. At seventy miles out the convoy will come under the full air umbrella of Spitfires from Takali and Halfar, but the distance from one hundred and ten miles to seventy, beyond the effective patrol range of Spitfires, is critical. This critical distance is to be covered by us. Long-range tanks have been fitted to our machines, for only we at Luqa have sufficient length of runway to get into the air with the extra weight of petrol.

As the Air Vice-Marshal went on to explain that only four of our Spitfires can be over the convoy at any one time, one section on its way out, a section over the convoy, and a section on its way back, I stared at him—four of us against a possible four or five hundred. He further explained that if the convoy is attacked as we are leaving we are to stay and fight; when our petrol runs out we are to bale out by parachute in the hope of being picked up by one of the ships. With horror of what is expected of us, I stared past his stocky figure at the houses turning gold on the far side of the bay; I could hear the people chattering and laughing and the girls giggling in the roadway below.

Monday, June the 15th—dawn on the aerodrome—the first two sections of four Spitfires each, led respectively by the C.O. and the Dreaded Hugh, have flown out towards U.K. Convoy. I lead the next section. On "G"-shelter roof I watch the Wing Commander aerodrome Controller as he briefs me for my flight. He has already told me bad news about "Alex" and that although the heaviest possible strike-force of torpedo-carrying Wellingtons have been out during darkness, the Italian fleet is still steaming to intercept the convoy. What he has told me about "U.K." fills my mind, for this is where our duty lies. All the merchant ships have been sunk except three; two of these are still in position, but the third having been badly hit is creeping along behind; the convoy is a long way behind schedule—we will have to fly out at least a hundred and forty miles—but its exact position is uncertain: the last message received from it was two hours ago. At that time it was not only being shelled by two Italian cruisers of heavier calibre than the escort, but it was being bombed by Ju 88s and 87s, bomb-carrying 109s, Cants and C.R. 42s. I stare at the Wing Commander—his last words remove all doubt: "There's no news of your first eight Spitfires—we're afraid they've been shot down." Desperately I try to look at him calmly—

I must listen to his last instructions: "Steer 287 degrees Magnetic—take off in five minutes."

As the jolting bus takes me back to my Spitfire I stare at the familiar rhythm of the wood grain under the window; as I step down on to the hard ground I feel the minute stones through the soles of my shoes. No, I can't tell my waiting pilots that we're expendable, that we're going to our deaths—this is my final responsibility to bear alone.

"287 Magnetic's the course and the convoy's about a hundred and forty miles away. By the way," I add, smiling, " we'll probably see a couple of Eyetie cruisers."

In the intimacy of this cockpit, helmeted, with my goggles on my forehead and oxygen mask covering the lower half of my face, I'm apparently a killer as I steer this modern fighting machine along the dusty track towards the 'drome—yet tears are pouring out from under my eyelids: I have got to die. Never have the yellow sunlit fields appeared more beautiful: there's a group of Maltese children, a perfect little group for a painting, waving to me from the corner of the labourer's field on my right. With my last throb of joy for them—I wave back.

I feel but a husk of a person—a charred shell—empty—burnt out. I can no longer pretend—yet I've got to keep up the appearance of an enthusiastic fighter pilot. It is Tuesday night—the convoy battle is over. I suppose we've done our duty: not a single merchant ship was lost to enemy air action after Spitfires arrived over U.K. Convoy at dawn yesterday. There were repeated attacks by waves of enemy bombers as the relics of the convoy crept nearer and nearer to our island, and now two ships that everybody's efforts have dragged through the mouth of hell, are being unloaded. I've been patrolling over them, over the oil stains from the escort ship that blew up on a mine last night, over the disabled destroyer that limped so slowly and so nakedly towards the coast, occasionally turning my section over the harbour smoke-screen below which the unloading has been going on. Although when flying I've been watching the skies with protective anxiety lest enemy bombers struck the ships from an unsuspected direction; although other people have been in action today destroying enemy bombers—no attack coincided with my patrols. I've seen nothing. It was much the same yesterday —my efforts coincided with moments when the enemy was refuelling his planes.

Yesterday, as I took off, I was numbed by the news that our first two sections had been shot down; I was resigned to the inevitable—yet the Wing Commander was wrong: most of our planes did return—in fact throughout the whole of yesterday's battle our Squadron only lost three Spitfires—it's ironical to look down at the farewell note I scribbled in my diary for my wife—strange even to think about yesterday.

G

. . . Steering 287 I passed close to the yellow beach of Linosa Island—the empty sea ahead—a vast expanse of blue with the smoke of battle drifting in brown-black layers. Two ships, one steaming behind the other and picked out white by the sun, suddenly appeared from the smoke below us . . . threw up salvos of shells: the Italian cruisers! Flew on till E.T.A. but no sign of our ships—flew on another five minutes—then seven minutes more: empty sea. . . . I grew increasingly worried. Sweeping through layers of smoke, repeatedly called Convoy Control Ship . . . no answer: it must have sunk. Deciding to trace smoke to its source, I turned north. Enemy island of Pantallaria with its conical mountain loomed towards us, startlingly clear at times—at others, dark and sinister in the smoke. Passed over two destroyers almost stationary—friend or foe?—no means of telling—four more nearer the island heading west—west!—our convoy should have been heading east: they must have been enemy. Turning south again, found a cruiser or battleship burning furiously—smoke gushing up into sky. No sign of convoy. Found oil stains on water—some curled and ended abruptly—ships gone down? Submarines depth charged?—followed others southwards. Our convoy was miles south of its expected position—returned after an hour in battle area.

. . . Went to "G" shelter to report. Green and Le May on the roof watching twin-engined Beauforts circling 'drome—all trying desperately to land: after going to the rescue of Alex Convoy, after lobbing torpedoes into Italian Battle Fleet, they were all in a shot-up condition—three had crashed. One wreck lay opposite us, pulled clear of the runway on its belly. Watched another coming in with rudder controls shot away—wildly off the runway, sweeping towards the bellied wreck, it was revving its port engine in a desperate attempt to avoid disaster—seemed poised there—with a great crash it tore through the stationary machine, flinging debris and puppet-like bodies high in the air, crabbing onwards over the grass, buckling, its fuselage snapping in two, and a tongue of fire appearing under one engine. Flames leapt skywards as airmen ran to help—one black figure, then another got out of crumpled cockpit on to wing. . . . As I gave my report—watched other machines crash—seemed as if monsters men had created had broken loose to reap a bloody revenge.

. . . Then back to the tent. Stayed in the tent for hours waiting for my second trip out—muffled heat with telephones ringing. Another section came back—only three of them. Baby Face had shot down an 87 in flames and damaged another, Ingram claimed a probable 87, Smith claimed a probable 87 and a 109 damaged—the fourth man, Rowlandson, was down in the sea. Convoy fifty miles S.S.E. Pantallaria.

. . . Then we heard of Beaufort formation's achievement: with their torpedoes they hit a battleship, two cruisers and a destroyer—their gunners shot down a Cant 1007, a Macchi and an 88.

. . . Went on like that—hour after hour—waiting in the tent—sweltering hot. The C.O. lay flat on the dried grass with his head close to the side—he rolled up a flap of the tent to get a breath of air across his face. We were all exhausted—an effort to rouse ourselves to cope with serviceability. Smith, who'd been moved to a different section to make up numbers, went out again—but never came back. Then MacC, one of the best of our pilots—also missing. Finally got out my helmet and parachute and walked out to my plane for my second trip—the convoy I was told was coming up between Linosa and Lampedusa Islands . . . but sudden reprieve: the convoy was at last being plotted on the ops-room board: Spits from Halfar and Takali were taking over.

. . . Last night—a great crowd of us in the lounge at Sliema. Baby Face, so happily modest about his successes, in the centre of an adoring bunch of South Africans—left him to his victor's laurels. Listened to some other pilots: they were delighting in a tale of horror of how they shot down an Italian seaplane they found by itself, of how they went on attacking it as it lay on its side in the sea, went on attacking until it sank. "The old Eyeties must have been scared stiff when we went on shooting," they boasted. Everyone's blood was up—I seemed to be a sorrowful onlooker. Then we heard that U.K. Convoy close to our island was being repeatedly attacked by waves of 87s—we imagined a slaughter of German machines—resentment in the mess that having brought it so far, Takali was reaping the reward of easy victories. I was too tired to care—wanted to get to bed—knew we were on at dawn.

And today, Tuesday, the day after the battle—patrols over the two merchant ships being unloaded and some dismal, dismal news: the convoy from Alexandria has turned back. Despite all our bombers' efforts Alex Convoy has turned back. It's fantastic—our bombers, and other bombers from Egypt, have repeatedly hit the enemy so hard that the Italian Battle Fleet is in full flight back to its harbour at Taranto—the way is clear for Alex Convoy to reach us—yet the convoy is heading back towards Egypt. Surely someone's blundered. It is said that the convoy has run out of anti-aircraft ammunition—but it was practically within our fighter range—we could have brought it safely in—all day long the whole of our Malta fighter force has been available to protect it.

Our battle is therefore a failure. Of the two merchant ships that have reached us, one is damaged with its Number Four Hold full of water. Malta has been reprieved for only a few short weeks. God knows how long we can last. Rations hardly exist, yet now we must anticipate cuts. Someone advises throwing all the weighing machines into the sea.

A few minutes ago Smith, whom we thought was dead, walked into the lounge here. He's been telling us that yesterday, over the convoy, he shot down an 88 but his own engine was set on fire. After baling out he was picked up by a destroyer. He's been describing how the deck of his destroyer was already crowded with merchant ship survivors, how they stood as Ju 87s and 88s dived upon them, and how, just as they were about to enter Grand Harbour, a Polish destroyer beside them blew up on a mine. More survivors came aboard, most of them cut by flying metal, their teeth chattering with cold. One Pole, whose stomach had been split open, having jumped into the sea without clothes, being stung all over by jellyfish, looked up at Smith with a single question: "How many planes has the R.A.F. shot down?"

All this makes me realise how much a fighter pilot's life is abstracted from the horrors of war: courageous MacC, for instance, no horror in his passing—someone saw what he thought was a bird, but no—it had Spitfire's wings as it glided towards the water—then a splash far below. When I consider what the Navy and the Merchant Navy have faced I am utterly ashamed of feeling so utterly tired and burnt out. Would it be different if I'd had any successes in the last two days? If I had met enemy planes over the convoy and shot some down I might have felt entitled to lead all these keen men so full of energy. I am Flight Commander in name only. I have never possessed the "offensive spirit"; in combat I have always erred on the side of caution, something for nothing has always been my policy except when desperate occasions demanded risks. I have only one thing to be happy about—I have never lost a single pilot whom I have actually been leading in the air—but nobody cares about that. I've destroyed seven enemy planes, one of them shared, of course, with Ingram—but inevitably it's an "unofficial" score, so it's not much good—it's not a solid recognised achievement that would command the respect of my pilots. And now I'm burnt out. I seem cut off from all my excited companions, yet there's only one thing to be done: I must build on the ashes of myself some kind of intense enthusiasm by which I can pretend to lead and inspire them.

Wednesday, June the 17th, by our planes. Petrol is now so short that we're only allowed to run the bus once a day—this means that we all come down here before dawn and stay for eighteen hours continuous readiness. Much worse for the airmen; their reliefs don't seem to have arrived: with pitifully small rations they're on duty day after day, and often night after night, on this sun-blistered aerodrome, without much chance of a day off or rest. What's going to be the outcome of losing almost ninety per cent of the convoys? We've very little petrol, very little food, no reliefs and practically no ammunition. So the war goes on. What really worries me is the way my body's in open revolt. For weeks past I've fought the increasing Dog pain, and, in the last few days, its utter lifelessness; but this morning I've been vomiting without success in the ruins of a stone house behind my Spitfire, vomiting into my oxygen mask while flying over the harbour, and repeatedly leaving this tent after coming down on the ground again. I suppose the C.O. must have told the Doc, because a few hours ago I was taken over to Umtarfa Hospital for an examination. Docs, and hospitals, with all their genuinely wounded patients make me feel a fraud—thank God I've got back here to Luqa on the job again.

We're sitting in the tent; it offers some shade against the hot sun. Wellington bombers and Beauforts are continually taking off and circling somewhere above us, some may be on air test, others may be going up on strikes. I've written to Diana. I can hear another Wellington's engines running up before take-off. Now the Wellington bomber throbs low overhead. I'm reading Eric Newton's *European Painting and Sculpture.* Sudden silence, a cough of the engines, then silence—it's going to crash. "Ring for the ambulance." "Come on, Clarke, on your motor-bike."

We are first on the scene but, thank God, the huge bomber hasn't caught fire—it has ploughed its way through the trees and lies against the broken walls on the hillside at the end of Safi valley. Of the six people in it, three are lying out on the rocky grass slope, two others are walking about aimlessly, while the pilot, his hand streaked with blood, staggers towards me: "Have I been hit in the back?" he asks. Turning him round I lift his torn shirt to see a gaping hole where the seat has crumpled into him. Forbidding him to light the cigarette with which he is fumbling, I ask if he had time to turn off the fuel and ignition, for there may still be a danger of fire. "Don't think so." After wriggling through the buckled angles of metal into this compressed cockpit, I have turned off the ignition switches, but the fuel levers are too badly bent—can't move them. Straightening up in the cockpit, I look out over the hot engine, across the flat areas of bent wing, and through the gap of sliced trees: beyond the quiet figures on the grass and the waiting ambulance, I can see the whole length of Safi valley with the wind-whispered wrecks standing up on stilts. Alas, I must climb out and get back to my Spitfire, but I hesitate: there's something so familiar in the silence of this haunted valley, a silence disturbed only by the drip, drip, drip of petrol. The dying warmth of this newly sprawled wreck would make a splendid foreground for a drawing. No time to draw, must hurry to readiness.

Friday, June the 19th. Although Woody took me off to the hospital again today it was a great joy to be able to spend the time between medical examinations just as I liked. A hot sirocco wind, filling the air with steam, and laden with perfume from the flowering trees, blew me down the steep hill from Umtarfa Hospital and up the other side into M'dina. I discovered a museum. Going inside I met a certain Professor Scortino, lately of the British School of Painting in Rome. He was superintending his students in the endless task of renovating masterpieces of painting, pictures that had been wrecked and shattered in the Valetta bombing.

The Professor was most kind to me. He showed me the mosaics, for the museum is built on an ancient Roman villa. Explaining that the finest pavement is protected by a layer of rubble lest the Germans blow down the building, he uncovered part of it to show me its quality. I looked down at the colourful monument from the past then stood back, staring down the Museum hallway with its tall marble pillars. I stared at all those men repairing the pictures, their palettes covered with thick wriggling oil-colours, seated there, working busily behind their easels. As a pilot debarred from their world I stared at them. The simple fact of men making things, creating beauty, putting things together instead of being engaged in destruction, evoked such pain of sanity that I had to leave.

As if there was no escape from the good, true and beautiful things, I happened to glance, as I was walking back through the M'dina streets, through an open wooden door into what I thought was a carpenter's shop: the sunlight fell upon the green apron of a seated figure—a gaunt man with a yellow moustache and tightly pursed lips was working busily at a Corinthian pillar capital. The least I could do was to help Joseph Farrugia the gilder, so I swept his studio for him and brewed his pot of tea. After sharing tea, he taught me how to lift the delicately thin gold leaf with a soft brush, how to lay it in place on the capital without folding or creasing it, and how to smooth it out and polish it.

These simple visits have, I think, revived some of my energy for I have been trying to draw since arriving back here at Sliema. But now the air-raid sirens are screaming. Forty more Ju 87s have arrived in Sicily and the Germans have not yet sunk our ships in Grand Harbour—I expect this'll be a big raid. I wander out on to the flat roof. No sound in the sky. Nothing disturbs the star-strewn blackness above the sea—perhaps the Germans are transferring the 87s to Libya? The news from the desert is very bad: Rommel is pushing our armies further and further back towards Egypt, Gazala has been evacuated and there are fantastic rumours that Tobruk has been surrounded.

Sunday, June the 21st. Continued bad news from Libya—our armies are in full retreat—Rommel's not only encircled Tobruk, he's making a full-scale assault.

Our own siege reflects these events—it is unusually silent as we wait in the heat by our Spitfires. In the distance Beauforts and Beaufighters are being refuelled. Malta is not idle. Even if we fighter pilots and anti-aircraft gunners, once described by Hugh Pugh as Achilles' Shield, have no immediate raids to deal with, the bomber boys and crews of torpedo-carrying aircraft have been out fulfilling their ancient rôle—striking at Rommel's supply ships—Achilles has regained his sword.

As for me sitting here high on the sandbags behind my aircraft, I am fed-up with my stupid body. I am trying to draw, trying to obliterate its continuous sensation of sickness and pain, while any minute I may have to force it into the cockpit there. The Docs, who sent for me again yesterday, don't know what's the matter with me—and I am worried: there is an ugly rumour that our Squadron's going to be sent to Egypt. Although I so desperately want to see Diana again, if another parting is destined—then so be it—one cannot deny help to our desert armies— but, and I can't help asking myself this—in my present lifeless condition am I going to be an asset or a liability to the Squadron?

Nine Beauforts have just taken off—how clumsily they stagger round the sky with their cargo of courageous humans—how clumsily they bear the weight of the long black torpedoes slung beneath them. The twin-engined Beaufighters of their escort flash silently in pursuit—more graceful machines. Watching them I know that however lifeless I feel I've got to stick it out—there's no escape from war till the enemy delivers death. To break out of my lifelessness, I'll draw—and look: the torpedo formation is turning and setting course—how sweetly delicate the grey and white camouflage on the top of their wings, pale against the blue sky. I must forget the quiet colours and the gentle things of life. I'll plunge myself in war, enmesh myself with machinery, mentally impale myself on torpedo, bomb and bullet. Paint the empty sky a cruel blue, grade it to the whiteness of death out there over the sea. I'll turn the quivering heat into anger, the dust into blood, and the rocks into huge white corpuscles torn from the earth.

11.30 p.m. News of disaster—Tobruk has fallen. Tens of thousands of our men have been captured together with vast stocks of petrol and war material—Rommel can laugh at Malta's efforts to sink his supply ships— freshly supplied he can drive straight on to Cairo—nothing but our defeated armies to stop him. Official now—the Squadron flies to Egypt tomorrow—indeed I've been superintending the fitting of long-range tanks. I stare down at the route that the Squadron is to fly—such an impersonal route on the map. After crossing the sea it will have to follow, in broad daylight, what is now the hostile coastline of Libya where enemy fighters are operating. It will approach the contracting battle-front from behind enemy lines, but whether it can reach the Allied front at all depends on how far back Rommel has pushed our armies.

But I am not going—I could not believe it when Woody, ringing through on the field telephone this afternoon, told me that I had done my two hundred operational hours, that I was "tour expired", that I was being sent home to England—not only that, but sent home to England tonight! To England tonight! I still can't believe it. I thought he was playing a cruel joke on me. I still couldn't believe it when he came over to the mess this evening and stood me a drink at the bar. It

200 MALTA SPITFIRE PILOT

wasn't until Air Vice-Marshal Lloyd himself wished me a good trip that hope flared into golden certainty. I am going home to England! Even now I am waiting in "G" shelter cavern—bombs are crashing on the aerodrome above. I am staring with joy at the Aircraft Arrivals board shaking and shuddering on the rock wall: two P.R.U. Spitfires, a Beaufort, eight Wellingtons, two Blenheims, two Hudsons and a Lodestar are due to land here and depart again during darkness. I will be flying in one of the Hudsons!

Although I am joyous, wildly joyous, I am at the same time imagining the silent battle that must be waging in the hearts of each of my old companions: the C.O., Hugh, Pancho, Cyril, Baby Face and many others will also leave this aerodrome in a few hours' time, flying eastwards to an unknown destination. I already know their courage, I know them as men, but how I wish I knew so very much more about them, their individual experiences, even the inspiring things they've each done here, both on the ground and alone in the air. Inevitably I have been looking out at the war through only one man's window. I have seen my companions with immature eyes. Already I am beginning to see them more clearly. I will never forget them.

The raid is now over. I have climbed the shelter steps. Although my Hudson will soon be arriving, hot jagged shrapnel must first be swept clear of the runway over there—the stick of delayed-action bombs that has also fallen along it must either be dug out or covered over. I gaze across at my old dispersal point for the last time—there are flickering fires with huge shadows dancing across the red aerodrome: two of our Spitfires appear to have been hit. There are other fires, magnesium white, behind the look-out tower. The moon is half full and the stars are quite perfect.

Five and a half hours ago, with the blackout curtains drawn across the windows and no lights of any kind allowed in the narrow cabin, we took off from Malta. Imprisoned in darkness we have sped out past Pantallaria and south of Sardinia, but now the curtains have been drawn back: we are high in the air over the western Mediterranean, the vibrating wings of our twin-engined plane poised over a pre-dawn sea. We spot an enemy ship and wireless for bombers. In exactly two hours' time we will land at Gibraltar. From my seat in the tail I look down the length of the drumming fuselage, pale green, starkly functional with curved metal ribs. I wonder about the three other passengers: a naval officer, seated on some mail bags at the far end, smoking a cigarette as he talks to one of the crew; an army lieutenant asleep on the right; while on the left of the cabin, sprawled on a low bed that we've fixed up for him, a wounded soldier returning to England with only one leg. What are their thoughts and dreams?

I think of Diana as we fly out of darkness . . . for beyond the windows dawn is brightening into day. I am imagining the joy of our meeting . . . for I can see the light pursuing us across the sky. Diana doesn't know I'm coming home. . . . Now the sun itself is rising out of the sea behind the tail plane—through the rusty haze, the mountains of Algiers look golden as they pass slowly along the port windows.

AUTHOR'S NOTE

THE diary I kept through the Malta battle was very detailed; entries followed on from page to page; drawings were fitted into available spaces. The diary dates visible in some drawings are not necessarily those on which they were done. Although care has been taken to present the facts in a coherent order it is possible that some slight errors of dating may occur in the text.

I would like to thank Mr. E. V. Rieu, the editor of the Penguin Classics, for his permission to use certain passages from his translation of *The Odyssey*, and Mr. Jan Cordner for the patient and skilful way in which he has photographed my drawings.